SERVANTS OF GLOBALIZATION

SERVANTS OF GLOBALIZATION

Migration and Domestic Work

Second Edition

Rhacel Salazar Parreñas

Stanford University Press
Stanford, California

Stanford University Press
Stanford, California

Printed in the United States of America on acid-free, archival-quality paper

Library of Congress Cataloging-in-Publication Data
Parreñas, Rhacel Salazar, author.
    Servants of globalization : migration and domestic work / Rhacel Salazar Parreñas. — Second edition.
        pages cm
    Includes bibliographical references and index.
    ISBN 978-0-8047-9151-9 (cloth : alk. paper) —
    ISBN 978-0-8047-9614-9 (pbk. : alk. paper)
    1. Women household employees. 2. Foreign workers, Filipino.
3. Filipinos—Employment—Foreign countries. 4. Women—Employment—Foreign countries. 5. Philippines—Emigration and immigration—Government policy. 6. Globalization—Social aspects. I. Title.
    HD6072.P27 2015
    331.4'12791—dc23

                                                    2015008137

ISBN 978-0-8047-9618-7 (electronic)

Typeset by Thompson Type in 10.5/15 Adobe Garamond Pro

For my nephew Lakas Shimizu, 2005–2013

CONTENTS

PREFACE

THE FIRST EDITION OF SERVANTS OF GLOBA-
lization, published in 2001, looked at the outflow of women
from the Philippines in the 1990s and tracked their entrance into domestic
service in scores of destinations across the globe. It looked closely at the lives
of migrant Filipina domestic workers in Rome and Los Angeles, the two most
prominent destinations for Filipino migrants in Italy and the United States,
countries that historically have had the largest population of Filipinos in Western Europe and North America.[1] Nearly twenty years later, Filipino domestic
workers continue to immigrate to both countries, but they also work in larger
numbers in Canada (Pratt, 2012), Israel (Liebelt, 2011), Taiwan (Lan, 2006),
and Hong Kong (Constable, 2007), among others.

This second edition of *Servants of Globalization* updates the original study,
expanding on the initial set of data that I gathered in 1995 and 1996 (forty-
six interviews with Filipina domestic workers in Rome and twenty-six in Los
Angeles) with twenty-five in-depth interviews conducted with Filipino domestic workers in Rome in 2011 and 2012, a survey conducted of 100 Filipino
domestic workers in Los Angeles in 2013, two focus group discussions with
thirty Filipino domestic workers in Los Angeles in 2012, and three follow-up

interviews with domestic workers I had initially interviewed in the mid-1990s. To provide context for the global migration of domestic workers from the Philippines, I also draw from interviews I conducted with Filipina domestic workers in Denmark (seventeen) and the United Arab Emirates (forty-seven).

Many of the theoretical claims I make in *Servants of Globalization* regarding the international division of reproductive labor, partial citizenship, and contradictory class mobility still bear much weight in our understanding of migrant domestic work. The notion of the "international division of reproductive labor," which refers to the phenomenon of women passing their caring labor as paid or unpaid work to other women in a global context, seems to have struck a chord in the general public. It was not only featured in *The Chain of Love*,[2] a film produced by VPRO-TV in the Netherlands, but also documented in a front-page article in the *Wall Street Journal*[3] and later by a working paper titled "Global Care Chains," by the UN International Research and Training Institute for the Advancement of Women.[4] In Chapter Two of this new edition, I revisit my original discussion and address the continuing utility of the concept for examining unequal divisions of labor among women in globalization.

The idea of partial citizenship is one I revisit in Chapter One. This concept refers to the liminal legal status that migrant domestic workers occupy when they are not full members of host countries, but at the same time not fully protected by their home countries. In its discussion of partial citizenship, the first edition of *Servants of Globalization* solely focused on domestic workers who could freely choose their employers without being penalized by the state, as this had been their situation in Italy and the United States. What I did not include in my earlier discussion of partial citizenship is the lack of freedom that domestic workers experience in most other destinations in the diaspora. The majority of Filipino migrant domestic workers across the globe—in Canada, Asia, and the Middle East—are not free; they are bound legally to work solely for their sponsoring employer. For instance, domestic workers in Singapore and the United Arab Emirates have to be released by their employers before they can seek a new sponsor. The restricted labor of migrant domestic workers, specifically those bound to work for their employer without the flexibility to change jobs, now needs to be in the forefront of our discussion of migrant domestic work. However, with the exception of Pei-Chia Lan's discussion of "legal servitude" (Lan, 2007) in Taiwan and the earlier works of Bakan and Stasiulis (1997a) on Canada, this remains largely ignored in the literature. Accordingly, I account for the condition of this lack of freedom when revisiting the concept of partial citizenship.

Discussions initiated in the earlier edition of *Servants of Globalization* continue to resonate, partly because much has remained the same for migrant domestic workers in Rome and Los Angeles. Most Filipina domestic workers are still highly educated, having completed some years of college prior to migration. This gives continuing credence to my discussion of contradictory class mobility. As I describe in Chapter Five, this process refers to the simultaneous experience of upward mobility and downward mobility in migration as earning more abroad usually comes at the cost of a decline in occupational status. Transnational families also remain the norm, as I discuss in Chapters Three and Four, but with one significant difference being the increase in children reunifying with their mothers, particularly in Italy. I accordingly update my discussion to account for the greater presence of youth, specifically teenagers, in Rome.

Drastic changes have also taken place in the Filipino migrant communities of Rome and Los Angeles. For one, in Italy migrant Filipinos are now eligible for permanent residency. Another change is the greater number of male domestic workers in both Los Angeles and Rome. Finally, we see a larger number of older domestic workers in their fifties and beyond. Their presence raises the question of retirement options for domestic workers. Accordingly, this new edition of *Servants of Globalization* includes two additional chapters that look specifically at the situation of male domestic workers and what happens when men find themselves occupationally segregated into domestic work (Chapter Six), and examine how elderly migrant domestic workers fare in old age (Chapter Seven). In my focus on men and the elderly, I illustrate the continuing challenges that Filipino migrants confront in Rome and Los Angeles. These include the racial segregation of Filipinos into domestic work in Europe and the heightened precariousness of labor among low-wage workers in the context of a shrinking welfare state.

R.S.P.

Singapore

August 2014

SERVANTS OF GLOBALIZATION

CHAPTER ONE

THE GLOBAL MIGRATION OF FILIPINO DOMESTIC WORKERS

TWENTY-NINE-YEAR OLD NENE SORIANO is one of approximately 4,000 Filipino au pairs in Denmark.[1] As an au pair, Nene works only thirty hours a week, during which she mostly performs light cleaning and occasionally helps in the kitchen and with afternoon child care. Her workload is a vast improvement over her previous job in Singapore, where she had been a domestic worker for five and a half years, working every day from 6 am to 10 pm. Her duties included general cleaning, cooking, washing all the household laundry by hand, cleaning the car, and child care. By relocating from Singapore to Denmark, Nene saw not only a reduction in her workload but also a jump in her salary from US$270 to US$580 per month.

Nene and I met in the Roman Catholic Church of St. Anne's in Copenhagen during the summer of 2012.[2] Nene hoped Denmark would be a launching pad to the European Union and eventually Italy, where she wanted to secure long-term employment as a domestic worker.[3] Italy is an attractive final destination for someone like Nene not only for the promise of long-term residency but also for its amnesty programs that regularize the status of undocumented domestic workers (Codini, 2010). Italy granted amnesty to undocumented migrants in 1987, 1990, 1995, 2002, and 2009 (Parreñas, 2008b; Codini, 2010). Yet, without established networks, Italy is not an easy destination to reach.

Not wedded to the idea of being a domestic worker, Nene was also open to finding a husband to secure long-term residency. Her preference for white men encouraged her to actively participate in online dating sites, where she looked for a potential husband from Germany, Denmark, Norway, Sweden, or the United Kingdom. Nene even maintained communication with a pen pal serving time in a federal penitentiary in Tulsa, Oklahoma. Nene had also asked me to introduce her to a potential partner among my friends in the United States. Though I was unsuccessful in finding her a match, I later learned that she did not need my help after all. Quite attractive, Nene eventually married a Norwegian man nearly twenty years her senior in the fall of 2013, after meeting him through an online dating site. Nene now lives with him in Norway, where she is a stay-at-home mom.

Nene's story provides a glimpse of Filipino domestic workers' wide range of migration. Her goal of becoming a long-term resident outside the Philippines also points to the continued construction of Italy and the United States as coveted destinations in the diaspora, as they are but two of four locations—along with Canada and Spain—that have historically provided domestic workers with a gateway to permanent residency. Lastly, her story shows that domestic work takes multiple forms, ranging in her case from au pair to child care worker to all-around cleaner; is a long-term career for migrant women; and, for some like Nene, is tied to marriage and desires, fantasies that exceed political-economic approaches to understanding labor markets and migration processes.

A culture of emigration is pervasive in the Philippines. Migrants include land- and sea-based workers. Women primarily work on land, and the majority of them are domestic workers like nannies, housecleaners, and caregivers for the elderly. Domestic work, according to the UN International Labour Organization (ILO), refers to "work performed in or for a household or households."[4] Filipina women are the domestic workers par excellence of globalization. As they did in the 1990s, they work across the globe, including in East Asia, West Asia, North America, and Western Europe. In 2010, the top destinations for domestic workers and caregivers from the Philippines included Canada, Cyprus, Hong Kong, Kuwait, Israel, Italy, Saudi Arabia, Singapore, and the United Arab Emirates.[5] With no migration recruitment program, the United States has never been an official destination for Filipino migrant laborers seeking domestic work, but it has been reached by those migrating with a tourist or immigrant visa.

The number of newly deployed Filipino migrant domestic workers has steadily increased through time, from approximately 60,000 in 2008 to 80,000 in 2009 and 100,000 in 2010.[6] According to the Philippine Overseas Employment Administration (POEA), women make up a disproportionate bulk of these workers: In 2008, 57,354 women left to do domestic work in contrast to only 2,835 men;[7] 78,389 as compared to 2,395 in 2009;[8] and 103,630 versus 2,245 in 2010.[9] It is difficult to determine the exact number of Filipino migrants doing domestic work around the world.[10] These official figures do not include rehires as well as those who leave the country as undocumented workers and those who secure employment outside official channels, for instance someone who departs as a tourist and secures employment once in the destination country. As these Philippine government figures are based solely on migrants annually deployed as temporary contract workers by the POEA, they also do not include the mostly female au pairs whose outmigration is processed by the Commission on Filipinos Overseas, the Philippine government branch responsible for the departure of those seeking permanent residency abroad (for example, spouses of foreigners and those leaving the country with an immigrant visa), as well as those who are relocating abroad but without the intention of securing migrant employment (for example, students).[11]

While the Philippine government does not provide an estimated count of migrant domestic workers, neither does the ILO, which, in its study of domestic workers, reports that data limitations make it "not possible to give a reliable estimate of the share of migrants among domestic workers."[12] Yet it is probably safe to say that at least 50 percent, or 1.4 million, of the estimated 2.8 million female temporary migrant workers from the Philippines are domestic workers.[13]

PATHS OF MIGRATION

The outmigration of Filipina domestic workers is not a historical accident but emerged from the state's promotion of migrant labor exportation. In the early 1970s, President Ferdinand Marcos institutionalized the export of labor as an economic strategy when he implemented the "manpower exchange programme" (Basch et al., 1994). Government ministers and President Marcos himself canvased for the importation of Filipino workers into East Asia, West Asia, Europe, and North America. The establishment of POEA in 1982 only solidified the country's economic strategy of exporting labor, which the government promotes not only by assisting departing migrants but also by pursuing "marketing missions" and securing memoranda of understanding on the hiring of migrant workers with an array of labor-receiving countries. The annual number of migrants has expectedly increased since the 1970s. Whereas fewer than 50,000 per annum departed in the early to mid-1970s, this number has since escalated, jumping from 266,243 in 1981 to more than 700,000 in 1994 and more than a million per annum since 2009 (Martin, 1993; POEA, 2013).

Migrant Filipina domestic workers are located in more than 160 destinations, raising the question of how one chooses a particular destination. In the diaspora, that is usually based on what one can afford, with the cost largely decided by potential wage earnings in a particular place. In the mid-1990s, recruitment agencies charged approximately US$600 in fees to prospective domestic workers in Hong Kong, where the standard labor contract indicated a monthly salary of approximately US$410 (Constable, 1997). Today, the fees have jumped to US$3,000. In contrast, Singapore remains a more affordable destination than Hong Kong, costing migrants only an initial fee of US$115 to $230 and a three- to five-month salary deduction (approximately US$350 per month). Even lower-cost destinations than Singapore are the Gulf Cooperative Council nations, including the United Arab Emirates, Kuwait, and Saudi Arabia, which cost prospective migrants only US$115. This figure covers the costs of their passport, medical clearance, and other documents required for migration. But although the Gulf nations cost less, domestic workers' wages are lower there.[14]

A more expensive destination for domestic workers is Israel, which costs up to US$5,000 in placement fees (Liebelt, 2008: 108). There, domestic workers can earn anywhere from US$500 to US$800 per month (Liebelt, 2011). In

Canada, domestic workers earn more. For this reason, the cost of migration is significantly higher for those coming directly from the Philippines, reaching up to US$16,000 (Paul, 2011: 1855). Similarly, the fees that travel agencies charge to go to Italy are enormous, having steadily increased over time along with Italy's reputation as a humane destination that offers high wages and minimal risk of deportation.

The migration costs shouldered by the family of one woman I interviewed, Michelle, illustrate this steady increase. Although her older sister initially paid US$3,250 to migrate to Italy in 1986, it cost Michelle US$4,250 to follow her in 1989. In 1994 a third sister had to pay the exorbitant amount of US$12,000. Women who migrated to Rome in the early 1990s usually paid anywhere from US$6,400 to US$8,000 to enter Italy. By 2011, fewer individuals were using "travel agency" services. Migrants more often entered cost free as the direct hires of Italian employers. However, I did meet one woman who paid US$12,000 to enter Italy clandestinely; she used a Paraguayan passport, which exempted her from having to obtain a visa. Also requiring economic resources, the United States has long been an elusive destination for prospective migrant domestic workers. If not entering via family reunification, they enter with a tourist visa that requires proof of property, investments, and savings in the Philippines.

Cost is not the only factor that determines where migrants go. Educational qualifications matter as well, as those without a high-school degree are restricted from employment in most destinations in Asia (Singapore, Taiwan, and Hong Kong, for example), and those without at least two years of tertiary education cannot be domestic workers in Canada. Aspirations also determine migration paths. Migrant domestic workers who desire permanent residency will set migration to Europe or the Americas as their long-term goal. Others may view migration as a strategy for accumulating enough capital to operate a business in the Philippines. These migrants would be comfortable setting their sites on lower-cost destinations. Individuals I met in Dubai, for instance, would rather invest the money they earn in a business than pay to migrate somewhere else. Religion can also determine a location, with Muslims preferring to migrate to the Gulf region (Silvey, 2000).

As established in migration studies, social networks and "migrant institutions" determine one's migration pattern (Goss and Lindquist, 1995; Castles and Miller, 1998).[15] Migrants will relocate to follow friends, family, and neighbors.

This had been the case for many women I met in Singapore,[16] the United States, and Italy, indicating their reliance on social networks. In contrast, migrants in the United Arab Emirates usually relied on a "migrant institution" and only went there because it was the first destination offered to them by the recruitment agency in the Philippines. For those relying on a "migrant institution," a destination is determined not necessarily by the prospective migrant's networks but by the institutionalized relationships that the recruitment agency has forged with partnering agencies in specific destinations across the globe.

Across the diaspora, the migration patterns of most Filipina domestic workers do not fit the classic assimilation narrative, as their children do not necessarily follow them and integrate into the society (Portes and Rumbaut, 1996). This is because domestic workers are disqualified from permanent residency in most destinations, including Israel, Singapore, Saudi Arabia, and the United Arab Emirates. This exclusion results in varying paths of migration for Filipina domestic workers, with many working in different countries prior to retiring in the Philippines or before settling in one of the few countries that grant them permanent residency (for example, Italy, Canada, the United States, and Spain). Although some migrate directly for a prolonged stay in only one destination, they do not necessarily settle there permanently. For instance, their children do not migrate but instead stay behind in the Philippines; moreover, many plan to retire in the Philippines and not the migrant host society. This had been the case with Rose, who did domestic work for ten years in Dubai, as well as Aida, who worked in Singapore for twenty-four years.

Three of the most salient paths migrant domestic workers take include direct migration, serial migration, and step migration. Direct migration applies to the majority of my interviewees in Rome and Los Angeles, as most migrated directly from the Philippines to each of these destinations. In contrast, serial migrants (Siu, 2007) relocate to new destinations between labor contracts. These migrants are often searching for a "new experience" and a "good employer," prolonging their stay when they find one and moving on when they do not. Serial migrants have managed to extend their career in migrant domestic work by moving across the diaspora; for example, one might work for four years in Kuwait, then three years in Dubai. Lastly, some are what Anju Mary Paul (2011) would describe as "stepwise international migrants," referring to those who participate in a multistage process of international labor migration.

In this scenario, a typical migration path would begin in a low-cost destination such as the United Arab Emirates, then proceed to a medium-cost one like Taiwan or Hong Kong, and then eventually move upward to coveted and high-cost locations such as Canada and Italy.

What differentiates serial migration from stepwise migration is the lack of upward mobility in the former; a serial migrant moves across borders within low-cost destinations like Jordan, Kuwait, and Singapore. Conditions from one destination to another do not necessarily improve in serial migration, suggesting that this type of movement exceeds rational calculation. Conditions that would extrinsically improve the quality of life for domestic workers include wage rates, family reunification policies, citizenship eligibility, or labor benefits such as health coverage and access to a day off. Considering the various paths of migration in the diaspora, who chooses one path of migration over another, and why? What factors determine the migration trajectory of domestic workers? And what can specific mobility paths tell us about the organization and segmentation of the Filipina domestic worker diaspora?

STEP MIGRANTS

Sociologist Anju Mary Paul (2011) describes a four-tier hierarchy of destinations for Filipino domestic workers. At the bottom are the low-cost destinations of countries in West Asia, including Saudi Arabia, the United Arab Emirates, and Bahrain; at the third tier are the Southeast Asian destinations of Singapore, Malaysia, and Brunei; in the second tier are the East Asian destinations of Taiwan and Hong Kong; and finally the top and most coveted in the diaspora are the United States, Canada, Spain, and Italy. Paul (2011) argues that Filipino domestic workers engage in "stepwise migration," meaning the process of embarking on a hierarchical progression across countries in the diaspora as they make their way toward their preferred destination. The concept of "stepwise migration" adds an element of intention to the long-established concept of "step migration," described by the International Organization of Migration as "the mobility from an original residence to first one and then another destination, e.g. in a 'stepwise' or sequential fashion" (International Organization of Migration, 2008: 51).

In this schema, Paul asserts that migrants follow a pattern of step migration that goes from the bottom toward the top of the hierarchy of destinations. She places countries in a tier according to their affordability; average wage—the higher the tier, the higher the wage; labor conditions—the lowest tiers offering the least labor protection; and, lastly, citizenship—the highest-tier countries being distinguished by the possibility of permanent residency.[17] As Paul's research establishes for Canada, Hong Kong, and Singapore, many in the diaspora chose the path of stepwise migration. My research, however, indicates a greater number of direct or serial migrants.

Migrant domestic workers may aspire to earn higher wages and accordingly move up the hierarchy of destinations, but what they want does not necessarily reflect what they do. Various factors may preclude them from moving up, such as a lack of either financial or social capital. My original research in Italy and the United States yielded just a handful of "stepwise migrants." Although my recent survey of domestic workers in Los Angeles indicated that thirteen of 100 migrants had worked elsewhere, they did not use the social and economic capital they acquired in the process of step migration to get there. Instead, they entered the United States via happenstance, fleeing an abusive employer on vacation in the country or being petitioned by a family member, usually a sibling, to join them in the United States. Likewise, in Italy, the four migrants who had worked elsewhere in the diaspora had gotten there by jumping ship (as a seafarer) or legally following a family member, either as a family dependent or a direct hire. In the United Arab Emirates, only two of forty-seven interviewees intended to migrate elsewhere as "stepwise migrants"; they specifically wanted to relocate to Canada for the promise of permanent residency.

The majority of domestic workers I have met had neither the desire nor the aspiration to relocate to a higher-tier destination. This is perhaps because of the location's inaccessibility. For instance, most did not plan to move to Canada, as they had not achieved the minimal educational level—seventy-two units of postsecondary training—required to participate in the Live-In Caregivers Programme. Highly educated migrants were more likely to aspire to work in Canada, as the opportunity for permanent residency gives them the promise of transitioning out of domestic work.

Filipino migrant domestic workers in Dubai are fully aware of the wide span of destinations in the diaspora and have somewhat of a sense of the opportunities available in various destinations (such as permanent residency, wages, and better working conditions). Despite their knowledge, not all aspire to relocate to what would seem to be the most desirable destinations (Canada and Italy). Even if they are eligible to enter Canada or have the resources to go to Hong Kong, many are risk averse, preferring to stay where they have become accustomed to living but also wanting to minimize the expense of their migration. Relocating would not only add to their migration cost but also might not yield the stable employment they are looking for. Among my interviewees in Dubai, the majority did not wish to relocate to a higher-tier destination. For instance, second-tier countries are less preferable given the higher cost of entry, the risk of deportation imposed by policies like the "two-week rule" in Hong Kong, and the undesirable restriction of employment options in Israel and Taiwan to elder care work.[18]

Significantly, labor conditions do not necessarily improve as one moves up the hierarchy of destinations. Returning to Nene's case, she described her situation in Singapore as more humane than it had been in the higher-tier destination of Denmark, despite her higher salary and fewer work hours. In Singapore, she had a "good employer," while in Denmark she told me she was "like a slave" because she did not have complete control over her physical movements. As she told me, she could consume food from the refrigerator only with her employer's permission and use the toiletries her employer selected, and she could not move around her home—that is, her employer's home—freely. Her employer would even kick her out of the house, regardless of weather conditions, whenever she wanted to be alone. For Nene, freedom is defined by her ability to control her corporal movements, which she could not do in Denmark. In contrast, Nene felt much freer in Singapore, despite her lower pay, longer work hours, and the absence of a day off during her first two years of employment. According to Nene, she had freedom in Singapore because her employers neither screamed at her nor dictated how and when to cook or clean.[19]

Nene's situation and the differences between her labor experience in Singapore and that in Denmark point to the significance of employer–employee relations in determining the conditions of labor migration. Domestic workers aim to secure and hold on to "good employers" as much as they want the highest extrinsic rewards (for example, salary, citizenship, labor conditions).

Those who secure "good employers" usually hold on to them, suggesting that intrinsic rewards, which are centrally defined by the relations of mutual respect they cultivate with employers, may sometimes supersede the extrinsic standards Paul uses to measure the desirability of destinations in the diaspora. In this scenario, a domestic worker with a "good employer" in a low-tier destination like the United Arab Emirates may decide to stay long term. This is the case, for example, with Rose, who now earns US$1,000 as a domestic worker for a retired British couple in Dubai. Jocelyn is another example; she sacrifices a day off and stays with an Emirate employer who lets her leave the house only to do grocery shopping every morning because they "treat [her] well" and pay her US$680 per month. For instance, not once have her employers screamed at her or limited her access to the Internet and a mobile phone. Finding a "good employer" is the primary factor shaping their migration path and has encouraged their long-term employment in Dubai.

Despite the near absence of stepwise migrants among my interviewees in Italy and the United States, I recognize migrants' aspirations to reach destinations where they would have greater labor-market flexibility, more humane labor standards, pathways to permanent residency, and the ability to participate in society. In the Philippine diaspora, migrants consciously measure and compare the costs and benefits of settling in various destination countries. They try to learn about opportunities to resettle in other destinations, as demonstrated by the vast knowledge domestic workers in the United Arab Emirates have of the labor systems and standards in a variety of destinations in the diaspora. Interestingly, domestic workers in Italy and the United States tend to know less about the conditions elsewhere, suggesting they are indeed more likely to be direct migrants.

DIRECT MIGRANTS

Direct migrants are those who migrated to one destination in the diaspora and continuously renew their contract with one employer there, those who seek other employers but in the same host country, and those who have likely reached their target location in the diaspora. Migrants stay in one place for many reasons, including the presence of a robust network of family and friends, the cultivation of good working relations with employers, and their social and cultural integration in a locale. For example, as I have already noted, migrants may select a particular destination for religious reasons. Indonesians, for instance, choose to work in Saudi Arabia because the practices there agree with their religious beliefs and allow them to uphold a pious lifestyle (Silvey, 2000).

Most of the domestic workers I have met in Los Angeles and Rome are best described as direct migrants. They did not need to settle somewhere else first to amass either the human, social, or economic capital they would need to enter these more desirable destinations. Instead, they often already had a robust social network of family and friends there, as well as the economic resources to cover the high fees recruitment agencies charge to go to Italy, or the financial capital they must demonstrate to obtain a tourist visa to enter the United States. Indeed, sixteen of the twenty-six domestic workers I interviewed in 1996 entered the United States with a tourist visa.[20]

Whereas most women I interviewed in Los Angeles entered the United States legally with a tourist visa, most of the women in Rome entered Italy by crossing the border clandestinely. Many initially entered a country in Eastern Europe, then traveled to Italy with the prearranged assistance of a "coyote." Of forty-six female interviewees in Italy, thirty entered illegally with the assistance of recruitment agencies, or "travel agencies," as they are referred to in the community. Other research participants entered with a valid visa: eleven with a tourist visa, two as direct hires, and three with a family visa.

Among the twenty-five domestic workers I interviewed in Italy in 2011 and 2012, most were direct migrants who followed a family member who had sponsored their migration or found them a sponsoring employer. Only four had worked elsewhere: one in Taiwan, one in Dubai, another in Saudi Arabia, and one as a seafarer. Two of the four had followed their spouses to Italy. Of those who participated in the survey I conducted in Los Angeles, only thirteen had worked somewhere other than in the Philippines. It is unlikely that the direct migrants I met in Los Angeles and Rome would consider relocating elsewhere; they are more likely to choose a path of assimilation and integration instead of serial or step migration to another destination.

Despite their restricted geography, most direct migrants are aware of the wide scope of domestic-worker migration. Many are part of multinational kinship networks that link them to far-flung destinations in the diaspora. As they increasingly rely on migrant institutions (Goss and Lindquist, 1995) and not their social networks to determine their path of migration, friends and family may end up in different locations. Vanessa, a single woman who followed two sisters to Rome in 1990, is the seventh of eleven siblings who opted to work abroad, as two of her sisters and a brother live in Kentucky while an older brother works as a seafarer. The youngest among her siblings, Ruth works in Rome while one sister resides in Switzerland and another in Saudi Arabia. All three send remittances to their parents in the Philippines. Gloria, a nurse who failed her board exam, is a domestic worker in Rome, while her older sister works as a nurse in the United States. Randy, a vendor who sells Filipino food outside the Philippine Embassy in Rome, shares the responsibility of supporting his parents in the Philippines along with siblings in the United Arab Emirates, United Kingdom, and the United States. Libertad, a domestic worker in Los Angeles, at some point had children working in the Philippines, Greece, and Saudi Arabia. Together with her children in Greece and Saudi Arabia, Libertad sent money to her children in the Philippines. Direct migrants might not physically circulate in the diaspora, but they function within its terrain because many participate in the circulation of money, information, and emotions across multiple nations.

SERIAL MIGRANTS

Anthropologist Nicole Constable (1999), capturing the ambivalence of settlement for migrant domestic workers in Hong Kong, describes how they long to return home to the Philippines only to yearn for their life in Hong Kong once they return. Working in Hong Kong involves a process of learning "to make themselves at home, away from home" (224). Constable found that Filipina domestic workers continuously renew their labor contracts to work in Hong Kong for most of their adult life. Serial migrants share these same sensibilities of home. Yet, unlike the domestic workers Constable observed in Hong Kong, they look to other countries when prolonging their stint abroad.

Of the forty-seven domestic workers I had interviewed in Dubai in June and July 2013, almost half of them had worked elsewhere prior to the United Arab Emirates, and most did not see themselves returning home "for good" anytime soon. Some intended to renew their contract at the end of their current two-year agreement, whereas others hoped to stay in Dubai but under the sponsorship of a different employer. Some planned to return to the Philippines for a three- to six-month hiatus, after which they would apply to work elsewhere in the diaspora. The serial migratory paths of domestic workers in Dubai were often limited to low-cost destinations. Prior to the United Arab Emirates, they had worked in a plethora of other countries in West Asia, including Bahrain, Kuwait, Lebanon, Iraq, Jordan, Saudi Arabia, and Qatar. A handful had worked in the slightly more costly destinations of Singapore, Malaysia, Hong Kong, Taiwan, and Israel, relying on the "fly now, pay later" system of recruitment agencies. Describing the "fly now, pay later" system, Pei-Chia Lan (2007) notes that domestic workers in Taiwan pay for the costs of migration via a salary-deduction system, under which all of their wages during their first year of employment would go toward covering the recruitment agency fees. Other destinations, including lower-cost ones, also have such a system in place. In Singapore, for instance, Filipino migrant domestic workers do not usually receive a salary during their first three to five months of employment, being restricted instead to an allowance of US$40 per month during this time; employers give the rest of their salary directly to the recruitment agency to pay their migration cost. Likewise, in Hong Kong, domestic workers can pay the US$3,000 fee via a monthly salary deduction during their first year of employment, which gives access to prospective migrants with limited resources.

Although salary-deduction systems make more expensive destinations accessible, serial migrants still avoid them to minimize the risks of migration. Serial migrants tend to have a low level of economic capital. For this reason, they limit their range of prospective destinations to those with minimal fees to avoid being saddled with debt, despite the lower pay they will receive. They also avoid destinations with risky employment systems, including Hong Kong and Taiwan. When I asked why she did not go to a higher-paying destination like Hong Kong, Mary, who had been a domestic worker for nearly twenty years in Singapore and had recently migrated to the United Arab Emirates, responded, "I would never go to Hong Kong. It is because there I would face the Terminator." When I asked her to explain what she meant by the "Terminator," as I doubted that she was referring to Arnold Schwarzenegger's famed film character, Mary explained how domestic workers in Hong Kong are made particularly vulnerable by the "two-week rule."

Under this policy, a domestic worker terminated by his or her employer, regardless of reason, will be deported if he or she does not secure a new sponsoring employer within two weeks of termination (Constable, 2014). Deported employees could include those who had amassed significant debt to cover the US$3,000 recruitment fee. Another serial migrant, Elaine, likewise avoided Hong Kong, opting to go to Dubai after seven years in Lebanon. Explaining why she will not consider going to Hong Kong, she stated pointedly, "Termination. If you get terminated, then it is over for you. I have a friend who got terminated after three months. She was forced to go back to the Philippines. She still had not paid off the [US$3,000] she borrowed to go there. She pawned her house and the land of her in-law. She had no payment because she was terminated. . . . It costs a lot to go to Hong Kong. . . . Then if you get terminated, you have no fight. You have to go home."

In contrast to the threat of termination in Hong Kong, domestic workers also avoided Taiwan due to the six-year residency cap it once imposed on unskilled migrant workers, which was extended to twelve years in 2012. They also avoided Taiwan due to the greater demand for elder care work—a twenty-four-hour job that many do not want. Lastly, serial migrants are unlikely to migrate to the high-cost destinations of Canada, Italy, and the United States either because they do not meet the educational requirements to enter Canada or because of the networks and resources they would need to enter Italy or the United States.

Serial migrants do not move in an upward trajectory from a less desirable location to a more desirable one. Their migration plans rarely involve a strategic plan to reach a target destination. The serial migrants I encountered in Dubai had relocated there after being displaced by wars in Iraq and Lebanon, having to end their last contract due to a family emergency, or hoping to secure better employment after completing a two-year contract in another country. The United Arab Emirates had not necessarily been their destination of choice, but it was one determined by the recruitment agency that processed their deployment.

Without a high level of education, many of the serial migrants I met in Dubai saw their job prospects limited to domestic work. Their primary goal had been to secure a "good employer," which they were more likely to find by extending their labor market to encompass multiple nations. However, securing a good employer is made more challenging by the job-placement system for migrant workers; as it is now, employers learn a lot about the domestic workers they hire, as recruitment agencies provide them with information including job history, health record, and skills. Domestic workers, however, do not learn much about their employer until they arrive at their household. This system, in turn, encourages domestic workers to change jobs more frequently, which some are willing to do across multiple nations for minimal financial cost until they secure that "good employer."

HUMAN TRAFFICKING

The category of human trafficking had not yet legally existed in the United States, or Italy, during the time of my original field research. Yet the experiences of some of the domestic workers I had initially interviewed in 1995 and 1996 would arguably fit our common understanding of trafficking victims. The UN Protocol to Prevent, Suppress and Punish Trafficking in Persons, especially Women and Children (otherwise known as the Palermo Protocol) defines "trafficking in persons" as:

The recruitment, transportation, transfer, harbouring, or receipt of persons, by means of the threat of use of force or other forms of coercion, of abduction, of fraud, of deception, of the abuse of power or of a position of vulnerability or of the giving or receiving of payments or benefits to achieve the consent of a person having control over another person, for the purpose of exploitation. Exploitation shall include, at a minimum, the exploitation of the prostitution of others or other forms of sexual exploitation, forced labour or services, slavery or practices similar to slavery, servitude or the removal or organs.[21]

According to this definition, trafficking involves three essential elements: There must be transportation of a person; that transportation must involve force, fraud, or coercion; and it must be for the purpose of exploiting him or her. Adapting the principles of the Palermo Protocol, in October of 2000 the United States signed the Trafficking Victims Protection Act into law, criminalizing the forced or deceptive movement of individuals into exploitative labor conditions.

Filipina domestic workers who accompany migrant Filipino professionals or business owners and their families to the United States are arguably vulnerable to human trafficking. Often of a lower class status than middle-class domestic workers who enter the United States with tourist visas, the domestic workers of professional Filipinos tend to have limited networks and lack the resources and autonomy needed to change jobs. As a result, they are usually more vulnerable to exploitative work conditions and forced labor. Additionally, employers can easily deceive them by saying that they will sponsor them for a green card when they have no intention of doing so. The migrant has no way to hold employers accountable to this promise. One woman I spoke to who was deceived and subjected to forced labor is Marilou Ilagan, a domestic worker in the United States since 1972:

> *MI:* I came in through a Filipino family . . . . The woman was pregnant, and so they also wanted someone to take care of their baby.
> *RP:* How long were you with them?
> *MI:* Seventeen years.
> *RP:* They were that good to you?
> *MI:* They were OK, but I couldn't just leave them. I did not know anyone here. I had no friends. I had no outlet. I could not just go out if I wanted to because I had nowhere to go. So, I had no day off. I had no place to go to since they took me along with them. So, I did not go out. I did not know anyone.
> *RP:* They did not take you out with them?
> *MI:* Yes, they took me out here and there. When they go out as a family, they would take me with them once in a while. But just by myself, I did not go out. I was with them for seventeen years. After seventeen years, after I finally was able to legalize my stay, I left.
> *RP:* How did you get papers?
> *MI:* They helped me. This was in 1989 with the amnesty.
> *RP:* How much did you earn?
> *MI:* Very little. Unbelievably low, very, very, very low.
> *RP:* Five hundred dollars a month?
> *MI:* Not quite.
> *RP:* Less?
> *MI:* Four hundred dollars a month.
> *RP:* This was until 1990?
> *MI:* Yes.

RP: Wow.

MI: That was it. I made a $100 a week. No, they only paid me $300 a month for my services. That is why when I was able to leave them I was happy.

RP: More like ecstatic?

MI: Yes. [Laughs.] . . . That is why when I was finally able to leave them, I felt like my life was beginning. You know what I mean—my life changed. I felt free. And can you imagine the first job I got after that paid me $400 a week? Can you imagine that? And my salary with them was only $300 a month.

Although Marilou could have sought employer sponsorship elsewhere, the isolation enforced by her Filipino employers ensured her dependence, guaranteed her continued service, and accordingly denied her the option of seeking higher-paying jobs. It was only after her employers' children were older, almost in college, and her services were no longer needed that they helped her obtain legal status. From the interviews I conducted in the mid-1990s, this pattern of isolation emerged among three of the four other women who entered the United States with professional Filipino migrants. For example, one who worked in New York was expected to stay at home at all times; in the two years she worked for them, her employers never gave her a coat or winter boots. Notably, none of the domestic workers I met in Italy in the mid-1990s faced the same vulnerability. Their lesser vulnerability in Italy is perhaps because the legal residency of domestic workers in this country does not bind them to work for only one sponsoring employer, as is the case for their counterparts elsewhere, including Canada, Denmark, Singapore, and, among other destinations, Qatar. In most destinations, migrant domestic workers are bound to their employer in servitude, as they can work for only one sponsoring family. By being bound to the will of another person, domestic workers are rendered vulnerable to human trafficking. Yet servitude is not a uniform condition but varies in degree according to the conditions of citizenship across nations, including employer flexibility, permanent residency eligibility, and, among others, family reunification eligibility. Notably, the servitude of migrant domestic workers points not only to their vulnerability to human trafficking but also to their limited citizenship rights, specifically their partial citizenship vis-à-vis the receiving nation-states of migration.

THE PARTIAL CITIZENSHIP OF MIGRANT
DOMESTIC WORKERS

Rendered partial citizens in the process of migration, Filipina domestic workers are neither fully integrated in receiving nations nor completely protected by the Philippines. In other words, they are denied full citizenship at both ends of the migration spectrum. However, not all destinations are equally exclusionary. More desirable destination countries like Italy, Canada, and the United States offer higher wage rates for domestic workers, as well as the option of permanent residency. In Italy, migrant domestic workers can gain permanent residency, and obtain a *carta di soggiorno*, after six years of legal residency. This notably had not been the case in the 1990s, when Filipino domestic workers had been restricted to a *permesso di soggiorno*, which is a temporary residence permit that they had to renew with the sponsorship of an employer. In Canada, domestic workers can enter under the Live-in Caregivers Programme and become eligible for landed immigrant status after working continuously for one sponsoring family as a live-in domestic worker for two years.[22] In the United States, domestic workers can most easily have access to permanent residency via marriage. In the past, domestic workers qualified for permanent residency in the United States if sponsored by their employers under the Labor Certification Program. In this situation, a migrant worker becomes an "out of status" migrant until her or his petition is approved, which according to a representative of the nonprofit organization Damayan in New York City took an average of ten years for migrant domestic workers. During this time, the migrant worker is not eligible to sponsor her or his dependents. Approximately 40,000 domestic workers received immigrant visas via this program between 1988 and 1996 (Kuptsch and Pang, 2006: 94).

In contrast, domestic workers in almost all other destinations cannot easily transition to permanent residency. They are instead limited to a renewable two-year residence permit that binds them to work for their sponsoring employer. This is the case in East Asia and West Asia, with the exception of Taiwan, which grants domestic workers a twelve-year residency permit, and Israel, which allows a domestic worker to reside in the country until the death of his or her employer (Liebelt, 2011). Table 1.1 provides a comparison of labor migration standards for domestic workers in key destinations, indicating that conditions of partial citizenship vary according to ineligibility for long-term

TABLE 1.1.

Labor migration standards for domestic workers.

Destination	Mandatory Live-In Employment	Flexibility to Change Employers	Average Salary (USD)	Residency Cap	Labor Protection	Pathway to Permanent Residency	Right to Family Reunification	State Policy on Pregnancy
Singapore	Yes	No[1]	$365	None	No	None	No	Deportation
United Arab Emirates	Yes	No[2]	$215	None	No	None	No	Incarceration (if unmarried) and deportation
Hong Kong	Yes	Yes[3]	$500–550	None	Yes	None	No	State benefits
Israel	Yes	Yes	$500–800	63 months[4]	Yes	None	No	Deportation
Taiwan	Yes	No	$700	12 years	Yes	None	No	Deportation
Canada	No[5]	Yes[6]	$1000+	4 years	Yes	Yes	No	State benefits
United States[7]	Yes	No	$1000+	None	Yes	None	No	State benefits
Italy	No	Yes	$1000+	None	Yes	Yes	Yes	State benefits

[1] Two-month wage penalty. Requires employer permission to change sponsors before and after the end of a contract.

[2] Only between contracts. Otherwise requires employer permission.

[3] Must identify new sponsor within two weeks to avoid deportation.

[4] If a domestic worker stays employed with the same sponsoring employer, the employer can petition for an extension past the limit of sixty-three months.

[5] This has been the case since 2014.

[6] Limited by requirement that domestic worker remains employed by one sponsor for two continuous years within a span of four years to qualify for permanent residency.

[7] Temporary visa program for domestic workers sponsored by ex-pat employers, foreign investors, and diplomats.

residency, the absence of employer flexibility, denial of the right to family reunification, limited reproductive rights, and, among others, their status as bound laborers whose legal residency is contingent on their continued live-in employment with a citizen sponsor.

Italy and the United States are considered more desirable than other destinations not only for their higher wages and the possibility of permanent residency but also for their higher standards of employment. In Italy and the United States, domestic workers have more residence flexibility than in other destinations, where the legal residency of migrant domestic workers is usually contingent on their live-in employment. The latter is the case, for example, in Singapore, Taiwan, Hong Kong, the United Arab Emirates, Saudi Arabia, and even Canada after 2014 (Lan, 2006; Constable, 2007; Pratt, 2012). Notably, this is also the case for migrant domestic workers employed in the United States with a temporary migrant visa.[23] Also distinguishing Italy and the United States are the higher wages of migrant domestic workers relative to other destinations, averaging more than US$100 a day for elder caregivers in Los Angeles and reaching US$13 an hour for domestic workers in Rome.

In contrast to Italy and the United States, other destinations offer less favorable conditions for migrant domestic workers. In most other places, conditions of partial citizenship are starkly more exclusionary. First, average wages are significantly lower, limiting the mobility of domestic workers, deterring their ability to accumulate savings, and maintaining the cycle of their dependency on migration. In Singapore, domestic workers can expect to earn no more than an initial monthly salary of US$365; in Hong Kong, their starting salaries are slightly higher at US$520; and in Gulf Cooperative Council countries salaries reach a monthly average of only US$215.

What also differentiates Italy and the United States from other destinations is the recognition of domestic work as labor (Rinolfi, 2007; Covert, 2013). In Italy, domestic workers have the right to various benefits, including employer-paid social security, an extra month's pay per year, and a weekly day off, among others. The United States offers weaker legal protection for domestic workers than does Italy, disqualifying domestic workers from the right to collective bargaining and excluding them from the right to overtime pay (Glenn, 2012). However, in the United States domestic workers are protected by the Fair Labor Standards Act, which gives them the right to a minimum wage. In contrast, many other locations do not recognize domestic work as labor, resulting in fairly low standards of employment including the absence of a minimum wage, exclusion from overtime pay, and no days off. Those include the top destination countries of the United Arab Emirates, where domestic worker immigration was handled by the Ministry of Interior instead of the Ministry of Labor until January 1, 2015; Singapore, where domestic workers received the right to a weekly day off on January 1, 2013, but remain exempt from the Employment Act (Singapore Ministry of Manpower, 2013); Taiwan, where domestic workers are not covered by the Labor Standards Law (Taiwan National Immigration Agency, 2012) and the newly enacted Domestic Workers Protection Act gives domestic workers only the right to negotiate for their employment conditions but does not grant minimum labor standards; and Israel, where domestic workers have the right to a weekly day off, although a 2009 Supreme Court ruling excluded them from the Work and Rest Hour Law (Kav LaOved, 2010). In Asia, only Hong Kong and Malaysia grant labor protection to migrant domestic workers, guaranteeing them a minimum wage and a weekly rest day (Asia Pacific Forum on Women, Law and Development, 2010).

Another distinction between Italy and to a lesser degree the United States from most other destinations in the diaspora is the flexibility workers have to change employers. In other destinations, migrant domestic workers are not only occupationally segregated but also bound laborers with restricted employer flexibility. In Hong Kong, domestic workers are limited by the "two-week rule," which requires they secure another sponsoring employer within two weeks to avoid deportation (Constable, 2007). In Gulf Cooperative Council countries, domestic workers can change employers only with the permission of their current employers, making it quite difficult to leave abusive employers (Sabban, 2012).[24] This is also the case in Singapore, where domestic workers suffer a one- to two-month salary reduction when they change employers. In Taiwan, migrants can work for only one employer, which they cannot change, unless their employer declares bankruptcy, dies, relocates to a foreign country, or cannot pay their wages (Taiwan National Immigration Agency, 2012).[25] Likewise, domestic workers in Israel cannot easily change employers (Liebelt, 2011).

Notably, domestic workers cannot participate as freely in the labor market in the United States as they can in Italy. For instance, domestic workers participating in the U.S. Foreign Labor Certification Program lose their sponsorship once they change employers. In the United States, temporary migrant workers, specifically B-1, A-3, and G-5 visa holders, also do not have labor-market flexibility (Glenn, 2012). B-1 visa holders are "servants" of former ex-pats who return to the United States with domestic staff who had worked for them for at least one year outside the country. As nonimmigrant visa holders, they cannot transition to permanent residency, must remain an employee of their sponsor, and do not have the flexibility to change employers. A-3 visa holders (household staff of diplomats) and G-5 visa holders (servants of officials and employees of international organizations such as the World Bank) are in a similar situation.[26]

As another condition of partial citizenship, some countries impose a residency cap on migrant domestic workers. In Israel, domestic workers lose their residency status on the death of their employer (Liebelt, 2011). In Taiwan, domestic workers can stay in the country for no more than twelve years (Taiwan National Immigration Agency, 2012). In most other destinations (Singapore and Hong Kong, for example), domestic workers can continuously renew their residence visas but without the option of permanent residency. They would have to return to the Philippines only once they are mandated to retire (sixty years old in Singapore, for example). Notably, domestic workers in Italy and the United States, with the exception of nonimmigrant visa holders, do not have a residency cap and can transition to permanent residency.[27]

Most destination countries deny domestic workers a family life, also contributing to their condition of partial citizenship. For example, only Italy grants migrant domestic workers the right to family reunification. However, if they do not yet have a *carta di soggiorno*, meaning permanent residency, or the required housing, they can sponsor a family member only with the approval of their sponsoring employer (Parreñas, 2008b). In Canada, domestic workers did not historically qualify for family reunification until after they obtain landed status. In most other destinations, family members cannot join domestic workers. This would include nonimmigrant visa holders in the United States and historically those whose status was still pending under the Foreign Labor Certification Program. The limited citizenship rights of migrant domestic workers are also reflected in their limited reproductive rights. Singapore, for instance, automatically deports pregnant domestic workers and likewise bars foreign domestic workers from marrying Singaporean nationals.

Lastly, the "postnational membership" (Soysal, 1994) accorded to undocumented domestic workers in Italy and the United States, meaning their ability to walk the streets freely without the threat of deportation and to have access to a robust informal economy as well as health care, draws prospective migrants to these destinations. In other host countries, domestic workers' partial citizenship is aggravated by the lack of opportunities in the informal labor market. Not all destinations offer domestic workers a robust economy for undocumented workers. In other words, they cannot opt out of domestic work and seek other forms of labor as undocumented workers in the informal economy. This is the case in Singapore, Hong Kong, Saudi Arabia, and arguably the United Arab Emirates—where absconding from a sponsoring employer, as it is illegal, leaves undocumented domestics in too precarious a situation. Other countries, however, do grant undocumented migrants postnational membership. For instance, in Malaysia and Taiwan, undocumented workers have the opportunity to work in the informal labor market (Lan, 2007; Chin, 2013); according to sociologist Pei-Chia Lan (2007), illegal workers who escape their sponsoring employers are in a better position to negotiate for fair working conditions than legal workers under contract to their citizen sponsor. The situation in Israel is quite similar (Liebelt, 2011), as domestic workers there could also escape into a robust undocumented migrant economy.

Although partial citizenship exists to varying degrees, it does set a tone of exclusion from the host society. Partial citizenship reminds us of the limited rights migrant domestic workers have, even in the most inclusive of nations. This is illustrated in Canada, where eligibility for landed status had been contingent on two years of live-in residency until 2014. During this time, they are ineligible for family reunification. As noted earlier, this was also the case for migrants sponsored via the Foreign Labor Certification Program in the United States. As sociologists Stephen Castles and Alastair Davidson (2000) argue, destination countries impose a process of "differential exclusion" on migrants and accept them only within strict functional and temporal limits; they welcome unskilled migrants, including domestic workers, as laborers but not as persons, and as temporary sojourners, not long-term residents. Without question, destination countries do not accord migrant domestic workers the same rights as their own citizens.

Partial citizenship is admittedly less severe in Italy and the United States, but more pertinent to those whom we can consider unfree laborers, such as domestic workers whose legal residency ties them to a sponsoring employer as a live-in worker. Still, the condition of partial citizenship is significant as it helps us understand the idealization of Italy and the United States in the diaspora and explains why they are coveted destinations. Moreover, it is the negotiation of partial citizenship that prompts individuals to find "good employers" as direct, stepwise, or serial migrants. "Good employers" and the cultivation of relations with them ease the restrictions that conditions of partial citizenship enforce.

The reality of partial citizenship in economic globalization puts the Philippines in a tenuous position.[28] On the one hand, the denationalization of economies compels the Philippines to respond to the demand for low-wage laborers by extending their range of exports to include able-bodied workers. On the other hand, the renationalization of politics renders the Philippines incapable of protecting its exported citizens. Though international human rights codes may protect migrant workers (Soysal, 1994), the fate of Filipina domestic workers remains largely dependent on the conditions of membership set by receiving nations, which as we see impose policies that render the workers vulnerable to servitude. This is not to say that sending nations like the Philippines do not advocate for the safety and well-being of migrant workers or discourage their pursuit of vulnerable occupations such as domestic work. On December 16, 2006, the Philippine Overseas Employment Administration Governing Board voted to implement a US$400 minimum salary for all migrant domestic workers, a doubling of the prevailing wage rate in destinations in Southeast Asia and West Asia (POEA, 2007). A government representative informally told me that this had been done in hopes of reducing the demand for domestic workers from the Philippines, rendering them "too expensive" for undesirable markets.

One could argue that the Philippines' lack of juridical power in various receiving nations makes this minimum wage nothing but symbolic. Indeed, the average salaries of migrant Filipina domestic workers in several destinations remain below the minimum wage. In the United Arab Emirates, the terms of employment for migrant domestic workers rarely abide by the written contract, which guarantees them a salary of US$400 and a weekly rest day; they usually follow the oral agreement domestic workers make with their employers prior to migration. Still, most migrant domestic workers in places like the United Arab Emirates are conscious of the minimum wage and use it as a standard when renewing their contracts or to justify their need to change employers. The Philippines' power to determine migrant workers' labor conditions is extending not just because of the demand for their labor but with the increasing influence of human rights discourse, spurred by the antitrafficking movement and charges of enslavement of migrant domestic workers in West Asia (ILO, 2012). Events in Saudi Arabia illustrate the extension of this influence.

In protest of the minimum-wage hike contractually demanded by the Philippine government and the consequent rejection of Saudi Arabia's petition to reduce the minimum wage to US$200, on July 2, 2011, the Labor Ministry of Saudi Arabia initially banned Filipino domestic workers from entering the country (Agence France-Presse, 2011). Yet, just four months later, on October 1, 2012, it lifted the ban and agreed to the US$400 minimum wage demanded by the Philippine government (Ruiz, 2012). This case suggests a more complicated relationship between sending and receiving countries and indicates that employment standards are not solely determined by market demands. Yet, without question, employment standards for migrant domestic workers in Saudi Arabia continue to stay low, and protectionist policies remain difficult to implement.

THE DISLOCATIONS OF MIGRATION

Discussions of Filipino migrant domestic workers should not ignore the wide scope of their global migration. Still, most studies on their experiences are contained to one destination, focusing solely on Hong Kong (Constable, 2007), Taiwan (Lan, 2006), Malaysia (Chin, 1998), Israel (Liebelt, 2011) or Canada (Pratt, 2012). Yet, the similar experiences of migrants across various destinations, including their shared exclusion of partial citizenship across the diaspora, make the need for a global perspective particularly pertinent. In Rome and Los Angeles, for instance, most migrant workers maintain transnational families; as such, their labor migration entails the negotiation of the pain of family separation. A substantial number of them are also mothers who directly care for other children and not their own. In both cities, most Filipino domestic workers have completed a few years of postsecondary education, leading to their shared experience of contradictory class mobility or inconsistent social status in the labor market; these remain as salient now as they were in the mid-1990s.

My analysis of the experiences of migrant domestic workers does not concentrate solely on domestic work as an occupational issue. Instead, it examines various aspects of their migratory experience, including their family life, gender relations, labor-market incorporation, and the precariousness of retirement for workers outside the formal labor market. I specifically focus on what I refer to as *dislocations*, meaning the positions that marginalized members of society occupy as a result of external forces. My analysis of dislocations looks at how they are constituted and the means by which migrant Filipino domestic workers resist or negotiate their effects in everyday life.

It surprised me to find similar dislocations for migrant Filipina domestic workers across destinations with remarkably different government policies, labor-market conditions, attitudes toward different ethnicities, and societal makeup—or what Portes and Rumbaut refer to as "contexts of reception" (1996: 86). Italy and the United States, for example, have quite different contexts of reception for Filipino migrant workers. Italy is notably a country of emigration, whereas the United States is a country of immigration. The former channels Filipinos solely into domestic work, whereas the latter accommodates Filipinos across diverse labor-market sectors. Accordingly, one migrant community is comprised mostly of the working class, whereas another includes members across a wide range of class backgrounds. Additionally, Italy only recently granted Filipino domestic workers the right to permanent residency, while the United States has long included them into the social polity. Lastly, among their many differences, one has to consider the gender composition of the community; in Italy, approximately two-thirds of all entering migrants from the Philippines are women, whereas in the United States there is a more proportionate balance between men and women.

One of the underlying questions this study asks is why migrant Filipino domestic workers in cities with different contexts of reception share similar dislocations of migration. The answer lies mostly in their shared role as low-wage laborers in global capitalism, or, to put it in other terms, as servants of globalization. By identifying the shared dislocations of migrant Filipina domestic workers, this study underscores the similarities engendered by globalization among low-wage migrant domestic workers in the economic centers of global capitalism (Portes, 1997).

This book thus analyzes how particular subject positions and dislocations are constituted for Filipino domestic workers in migration. I frame this analysis around two related questions: What are the particular dislocations that define the experience of migrant Filipino domestic workers, and how do they deal with these conditions?

In the first edition of *Servants of Globalization*, I described how partial citizenship resulted in an imagined diasporic community of migrant domestic workers, one that materialized through the circulation of magazines, like *Diwaliwan* and *Tinig Filipino*, across the diaspora. Although these are no longer in print, migrant domestic workers continue to communicate and build allegiance with one another through other means, including social media. Many migrants thus are aware of the conditions of partial citizenship they will face but are not deterred by them. Instead, they manage their limited citizenship rights and the partial citizenship in a variety of ways. Their strategies are not uniform; some become serial migrants, whereas others pursue stepwise migration. Notably, partial citizenship also potentially deters prospective migrants from leaving the Philippines or encourages some to return home and live life as an "ex-abroad." Still, many aspire to reach the coveted destinations of Canada, Italy, and the United States. As we will see in the subsequent chapters that detail the dislocations of family separation, distance mothering, contradictory class mobility, the crisis of masculinity among male domestic workers, and the precariousness of retirement, domestic workers in these countries, particularly Italy and the United States, still confront a number of challenges similar to their counterparts in other destinations, albeit not necessarily to the same degree of difficulty.

CHAPTER TWO

THE INTERNATIONAL DIVISION OF REPRODUCTIVE LABOR

IN RESPONSE TO THE QUESTION "WHY DID you migrate?," interviewees often interspersed their economic reasons with examples of the gender inequalities that also spurred their migration. They spoke, for instance, of fleeing domestic violence, labor-market segmentation, and the unequal division of labor in the family. These responses do not fit traditional discussions of the causes of either male or female migration, which usually avoid gender issues and are based solely on economics. Yet, the stories I heard make it difficult for us to ignore the fact that gender is a constitutive element of the larger structural forces behind migration. In light of this reality, how do we structurally account for gender in our discussions of the causes of migration? How do we systematically include gender in our analysis of the political economy of migration?

Here I examine the causes of migration, calling attention to the unequal gender relations that prompt domestic workers to leave home. To account

for the gendered political economy of migration and the resulting dislocations, I go beyond discussions of economic globalization that consider only
productive labor to include *reproductive* labor—the labor needed to sustain
the productive labor force. Such work includes household chores; the care of
elders, adults, and youth; the socialization of children; and the maintenance
of social ties in the family (Brenner and Laslett, 1991; Glenn, 1992). Relegated to women, particularly women of color, reproductive labor has long
been a commodity that class-privileged women purchase. As Evelyn Nakano
Glenn (1992) has observed, white class-privileged women in the United States
have historically freed themselves of reproductive labor by purchasing the
low-wage services of women of color. In doing so, they maintain a "racial
division of reproductive labor" (Glenn 1992), which establishes a two-tier
hierarchy among women.

The globalization of the market economy has extended the politics of reproductive labor to an international level. Thus, my analysis extends Glenn's
(1992) important formulation to consider issues of globalization and the feminization of migration. I argue that Filipino women's migration and entrance
into domestic work constitute an *international division of reproductive labor*.
This, which I also call the international transfer of caretaking, refers to the
three-tier transfer of reproductive labor among women in sending and receiving countries of migration. Whereas class-privileged women purchase the low-
wage household services of migrant Filipina domestic workers, these women
simultaneously purchase the even lower-wage household services of poorer
women left behind in the Philippines. In light of this transnational transfer
of gender constraints, the independent migration of Filipina domestic workers
could be read as a process of negotiation for different groups of women in a
transnational economy. In both sending and receiving countries, most women
have not achieved a gender-egalitarian division of household work; instead,
they have used their race and/or class privilege to transfer their reproductive
labor with responsibilities to less privileged women.

The international transfer of caretaking links two important but separate
discourses on the status of women—Glenn's discussion of the "racial division
of reproductive labor" and Sassen's earlier discussion of the "international division of labor"—and demonstrates that these foundational formulations need to
be expanded to take into account transnational issues of reproduction (Glenn,

1992; Sassen, 1984, 1986). To develop my argument, I first analyze the gender constraints that confront migrant Filipina domestic workers in both the sending nation of the Philippines and the receiving nations of the United States and Italy. I then illustrate how these gender constraints lead to the international division of reproductive labor. This division links women in a transnational hierarchy across race and class; as noted by Glenn (1992), women with means pay poor immigrant women of color to help reproduce their family, and I add that these women in turn transfer their care to women left behind in the Philippines. By presenting this division of labor, I establish that global capitalism, patriarchy, and racial inequalities are structural forces that jointly determine the subject-positions of migrant Filipina domestic workers in globalization.[1] This chapter focuses not on the dislocations of migration but instead situates our discussion of domestic work in the macrostructural context of the global economy. By introducing the concept of the international division of reproductive labor, it foregrounds how gender constraints determine migration. At the same time, it shows how the global economy is formed not only by the trade in material goods and productive labor but also by the purchase of services and reproductive labor

The concept of the international division of reproductive labor has gained significant outside traction. Take, for example, its documentation in a film called *The Chain of Love* (2000), directed by Marije Meerman and produced by VPRO-TV in The Netherlands. I originally introduced the concept of the international division of reproductive labor in my dissertation (Parreñas, 1998), which Arlie Hochschild (2000) later renamed "the care chain." Although that iteration has brought greater attention to the concept, it has also unfortunately eliminated the political-economic foundation of my original analysis by narrowing the framework to the distribution of care and redirecting the focus away from reproductive inequalities. Thus, I make a case against the misappropriation of the concept as a "care inequality" and call for the continued examination of the reproductive inequalities that the migration of domestic workers elicits among women and households across a global terrain. A return to reproductive labor inequalities in our discussion of the "care chain" allows us to better account for the constitution of transnational, regional, and local inequalities in the commodification and racialization of the household division of labor in globalization.

GENDER: A HIDDEN CAUSE OF MIGRATION

Filipino men and women share the economic displacements that spur labor migration in global restructuring. Neither group is immune from the economic disparities that distinguish the quality of life for the middle class in developing countries like the Philippines and industrialized countries like the United States and Italy. In the Philippines, only 20 percent of the population belongs to the middle class (Kimura, 2003), which has not constituted a comfortable and secure lifestyle in the last thirty years (Israel-Sobritchea, 1990; Kimura, 2003). Not surprisingly, in response to my question, "Why did you migrate?," most interviewees shared stories about the economic insecurities they had faced as members of the middle class in the Philippines. Among them was Michelle, a single woman who followed her sister to Rome in 1989, who told me, "My sister was the first one here. The truth is that our family had a lot of debts in the Philippines. Our land was just about to be confiscated by the bank. My sister couldn't afford to pay for the debt on her own. So what she did was she took me over here. When I got here, we helped each other out, and we were able to pay for the debt on time."

Michelle's story of economic precariousness resonated among most of my interviewees. This is not surprising if we consider the decline of the middle class in the Philippines that began in the mid-1980s when the International Monetary Fund (IMF) devalued the peso after the GDP plummeted due to the political and social upheaval sparked by the assassination of Senator Benigno Aquino Jr. in August 1983 (Kimura, 2003). It is not surprising then that "by the 1980s, even a schoolteacher could not afford to buy more than two chickens a month and could only purchase low quality rice" (Basch et al., 1994: 232). However, despite the economic displacements that men and women shared in the Philippines, it is important that we account for gender and identify the different meanings of "economic" migration for them. Gender, as I illustrate, is a hidden cause of migration.

"I migrated to support my family"—a frequently stated reason domestic workers provided for their migration—means something different to women than it does to men. In the Philippines, women confront the traditional gender ideology of the patriarchal nuclear family: Men are expected to sustain the family, and women to reproduce family life. The traditional gender division of labor haunts women in the Philippines, as a recent report released by the Human Development Network (2010) noted, "The tasks of taking care of children, the sick, and the elderly, preparing meals, and general housecleaning are still predominantly carried out by female household members. In addition, the traditional view that women's primary role is that of homemaking while that of men is 'breadwinning' continues to have a strong influence in many households" (31). Consequently, gender distinguishes the meaning of independent labor migration for men and women. For women, labor migration in itself questions gender prescriptions in society. As ideological constructs of feminine identity are molded from mothering and caring roles in the domestic arena, the independent migration of women constitutes a direct liberation from them (Israel-Sobritchea, 1990).

In Rome and Los Angeles, most respondents migrate to help sustain the family, an obligation that stems from the strong bond of family allegiance and filial piety in the Philippines (Chant and McIlwaine, 1995; Paz Cruz and Paganoni, 1989). Yet the meaning of migration as a strategy of family maintenance is very different for men and women. By migrating to sustain the household, women reconstitute the traditional gender division of labor in the family as they take on the role of income provider. Because independent migration frees working women of household constraints, migration is not only a family strategy but also a covert strategy to relieve women of their unequal division of labor with men in the family. As Filipina feminist scholar Carolyn Israel-Sobritchea observes, "Despite the growth of female labor force participation, there has not been a commensurate decrease in their child care and household responsibilities" (1990: 35). Women in the Philippines, according to the economist Jeanne Illo, do more housework and child care than men do: "A study conducted in the early 1990s suggests that the time allotted by mothers for child care jumps from 9 percent to 21 percent in rural areas and from 12 percent to 15 percent in urban areas with additional young children in the family. . . . In contrast, fathers in rural or urban areas spend no more than 6 percent of their time with their young children" (Illo, 2010: 6, citing a study conducted by a team of economists at the University of the Philippines in 1994).

Migrating to negotiate the unequal division of labor in the family applies not only to mothers and wives but also to single and childless women. In the traditional Filipino household, daughters—more so than sons—are expected to care for their parents in old age. As the only daughter in her family, Lorna

Fernandez felt a great sense of responsibility for her family but simultaneously felt suffocated by the duties they expected her to perform:

I am the only girl and the oldest in my family. I have all brothers. There were many reasons why I came [to Rome]. I had a good job. [She finished in the top ten of the national board exam for midwifery.] I was employed in a private office for seven years. I was making decent money. But I wanted to leave because, even if you have a decent salary in our country, it does not allow you to save any money. And then, I kept on thinking that my parents are not going to see their situation improve very much. . . . So one of the reasons I came here was for my family. . . . I came here also for the change. I was very tired. I was sick of the routine I was in. Every month, I received my salary and divided it up to my parents, brothers, and then hardly any would be left for me. . . . The first thirty-seven years of my life was given to my family, and I feel this is just when I am starting out for myself.

Although the family is considered a central site of support and assistance, some single women simultaneously wanted to reconstitute how to fulfill their responsibilities, which they often complained exceeded those of their male siblings.

The different positions of men and women in the Philippine labor market also distinguish the reasons for their economic migration. Although the lack of opportunities in the Philippine economy affects both men and women, the sex segmentation in the Philippine labor market further aggravates women's already limited opportunities. In the Philippines, the ideology of women as caretakers constrains their productive labor activities in many ways, including their segregation in jobs resembling "wife-and-mother roles" such as household work on plantations and professional work in nursing and teaching (Eviota, 1992; Chant and McIlwaine, 1995; Human Development Network, 2010). Women are concentrated in sales and service, and among professionals in the lower-paying rungs of nursing and teaching (Human Development Network, 2010). In the Philippines, women earn less, have a higher unemployment rate, and are financially constrained by their occupational segregation in "feminine" jobs (Human Development Network, 2010).

Despite these constraints, women do participate in the labor force. In 1992, the female share of total employment in the Philippines reached 37.7 percent (Chant, 1997). In 2012, women saw an increase in their rate of labor-market participation to 49.7 percent, a figure that remains substantially lower than that of men, who participate in the labor market at a rate of 78.3 percent (National Statistical Coordination Board, 2013). Like migrant women from the Dominican Republic, most migrant Filipina domestic workers have premigration paid work experience (Grasmuck and Pessar, 1991). Because they have more means than others do to migrate, educated women in the Philippines may turn to employment opportunities outside the Philippines to negotiate their low wages. Many research participants in Rome and Los Angeles had been employed in "female professions" (as teachers and administrative assistants, for example) and sought the higher wages that they could earn outside the Philippines, even if only as domestic workers.

Women's intense responses to the question of why they migrated corroborate the assertion that independent female migration is a way to negotiate gender constraints. In Rome, fourteen of the twenty female respondents who were legally married when they had migrated wanted to leave an abusive or unfaithful husband or had irresponsible partners and could no longer afford to raise dependents as single mothers. For example, some migrated because they could no longer tolerate their husband's infidelity. As Trinidad Borromeo explained, "You know why I came here? I had to leave the Philippines. If I didn't, I would have ended up killing someone. I had caught my husband with another woman." Clarita Sungkay likewise dealt with infidelity and violence:

My husband used to beat me up and have affairs. Then he left me for another woman. . . . I went to Kuwait after my husband and I separated. See, I tried to commit suicide two times. The first time I swallowed poison, and the second time I slashed my wrists many times. At the hospital, my mother was able to talk to me, and she told me that if I can't take the actions of my husband, I should just go abroad. I was still very young, and I already had my children.

Then there is Ruby Mercado, who had to escape an abusive husband:

I came to Italy in 1983 to look for a job and also a change of environment. . . . You have to understand that my problems were very heavy before I left the Philippines. My husband was abusive. I couldn't even think about my children. The only thing I could think about was the opportunity to escape my situation. If my husband was not going to kill me, I was probably going to kill him. . . . My problems with him were so heavy. He was abusive. He always beat me up, and my parents wanted me to leave him for a long time. My children, I left with my sister. I asked my husband for permission to leave the country, and I told him that I was going to be gone for only two years. . . . I was just telling him that so I could leave the country peacefully. . . . On the plane. . . I felt like a bird whose cage that had been locked for many years had just recently been opened. Nine years he abused me. He was very strict, and he tried to control every situation. Often, I could not leave the house. When I was able to escape, I felt free and felt so loose. Deep inside, I felt homesick for my children, but I also felt free for being able to escape the most dire problem that was slowly killing me.

These disturbing testimonies from the 1990s suggest a pattern of abusive male behavior that pushed women to leave the Philippines to escape the debilitating situations in their households. Unfortunately, this still seems to be the case. For instance, a great number of women I interviewed in Dubai had been victim to domestic violence prior to migration. And in Rome, the problem of domestic violence remained a prominent cause of migration among some newcomers I encountered in 2011.

According to British sociologists Sylvia Chant and Cathy McIlwaine, institutionalized practices of "male superiority within the Filipino household include the practice of wife-beating. Domestic violence is viewed as 'ordinary' and 'normal' within the context of marriage and stems from the polarized socialization of men as aggressive and assertive and women as passive and submissive" (1995: 13). As the Human Development Network notes, "Recent estimates in the Philippines show that anywhere from one to six out of every ten women face physical, sexual, and psychological assaults in the home. . . . the study also found that the most common perpetrator of assaults on women were their male spouses or partners, accounting for more than half of the abuses" (2010: 38). The problem of domestic violence in the Philippines truly establishes that gender cannot be reduced to economics. Patriarchy persists despite Filipino women's higher level of educational attainment and high rate of formal labor-market participation (Eviota, 1992; National Statistical Coordination Board, 2013).

Women, at least those with resources (such as networks and funds) emigrate instead of facing ostracism in the community for getting a divorce or separation, for which they are more often blamed than men (Israel-Sobritchea, 1990).[2] Divorce is not a legal option for couples in the Philippines, even though legal separation can now be granted on the basis of physical violence and incest. Moreover, legally separated individuals do not have the option of remarriage. Legal restrictions and the burden of cultural expectations (for example, the tremendous value placed on family cohesion for the children's benefit and the immense influence of Catholicism) constrain the options women have for leaving abusive spouses permanently. Chant and McIlwaine add, "It should also be noted that grounds for separation on the basis of sexual infidelity are strongly weighted in favour of men, in that a wife only has to have sexual intercourse with another man for this to be granted, whereas a charge of adultery against a husband has to involve concubinage" (1995: 14–15). It is not surprising, then, that some women believe that they can escape their marriage only by taking advantage of the migrant networks and agencies that are well in place in the Philippines.

Other interviewees decided to emigrate after their husbands abandoned them and left them to raise children on their own. Jennifer Jeremillo, for example, sought the higher wages of domestic work in Italy because she could no longer support her children with the wages she earned as a public school teacher:

After three years of marriage, my husband left me for another woman. . . . My husband supported us for just a little over a year. Then, the support was stopped, everything was stopped, the letters stopped. I have not seen him since. . . . I think of my children's future. There I would be the only one working, without a husband and supporting my children on my own. I knew that my salary was not enough for their future, for their schooling and everything. So I decided to come here even though I had to borrow a lot of money. It cost me 200,000 pesos [US$8,000] to come here. Just to pay for the agency was 150,000 pesos [US$6,000].

Although on the surface women who are abandoned by their husbands seem to be motivated solely by the economic benefits of migration, that motive cannot be situated only in the overarching world-system of global capitalism. It must also be placed in the context of gender inequalities that have shaped their experiences and positions as single mothers. Because husbands are more likely to abandon their wives than vice versa, it is important to emphasize how this is caused by double standards in male and female sexual practices in the Philippines.[3] Thus, it is this gender inequality that places these women in a position of needing to migrate for economic reasons.

The case of married women in Rome is actually not reflected in my Los Angeles sample, which includes only two women who cited similar reasons for migration. This is not caused by social differences between the two groups but is likely the case because it is more difficult to migrate to the United States. More stringent requirements for prospective migrants delay the migration of women who want to leave the Philippines quickly.

My findings in Rome are supported by the observations of Linda Layosa, the founding editor of *Tinig Filipino*, a now-defunct publication once based in Hong Kong and Italy that featured the writings of Filipina domestic workers across the diaspora:

In my casual talks with lots of my fellow women overseas contract workers especially the married ones, I found out that there seems to be a certain common factor that binds them—that leaving their families for overseas gave them temporary relief from the sacrifices that go with their marriage. Others are blunt enough to share that their main reason for coming abroad is not merely to earn money but to escape from their bitter relationships with their husbands. Very rightly so. For no mother could ever afford to leave her young children and her home if the situation at home is normal. (Layosa, 1995b: 7)

Given these realities, I argue that theoretical discussions of the causes of migration must consider the system of gender inequality in the Philippines, which, in the case of these women, manifests in the limited options they have for divorce and the double standards in male and female sexual activities. Highlighting the gender relations and divisions in the Philippines complicates discussions of migration. Patriarchy, as it operates within a discrete system in the sending country of the Philippines, is a hidden cause of migration for women. And although this system must be included in any formulation of the macrostructural reasons for female migration, we must equally consider the system of gender inequality in receiving countries. Migrant Filipina domestic workers depart from a system of gender stratification in the Philippines only to enter another one in the advanced capitalist and industrialized countries of the United States and Italy. In both sending and receiving nations, they confront societies with similar gender ideologies; that is, reproductive labor is likewise relegated primarily to women. Yet racial, class, and citizenship inequalities aggravate their position in receiving nations.

THE RACIALIZED GENDER INEQUALITIES
OF REPRODUCTIVE LABOR

Migration initiates Filipina domestic workers' incorporation into the transnational labor market not only to serve the needs of the highly specialized professionals in "global cities" but also to relieve their mostly white female employers of household work. In the industrialized countries of Asia, the Americas, and Europe, the number of gainfully employed women has climbed dramatically in the last forty years (Licuanan, 1994; O'Connor, 1996; Padavic and Reskin, 2002). In the United States, women represented 46.5 percent of gainfully employed workers in 1992, a considerable increase over 32.1 percent in 1960 (Reskin and Padavic, 1994: 24–25). Scholars predict the continued convergence of men and women's labor-market participation, as shown by the further increase of women's labor-force participation to 60 percent by the end of the twentieth century (Padavic and Reskin, 2002: 26). By 2000, mothers with children in the United States under eighteen years of age had an employment rate of 78.1 percent, though only 56.5 percent worked year-round (Bianchi et al., 2006: 44). In Italy, the downward trend in women participating in the labor force from 1959 to 1972 has since gone in the reverse direction (Meyer, 1987). In fact, Italy has incorporated an increasing number of married women into the labor force, but surprisingly the number of younger single women engaged in paid work has declined (Goddard, 1996). In the case of Italy, it has been argued that women are turning away from reproducing families and concentrating on their advancement in the labor market (Specter, 1998).[4] However, women in Italy do far more household labor than men do, including domestic work, child care, and adult care (Fondazione Giacomo Brodolini, 2009). Likewise, so do women in the United States (Bianchi et al., 2006). In both Italy and the United States, elder care should also be included in the long list of women's household responsibilities. Due to advances in medicine and nutrition, the elderly make up a rapidly growing population (Abel, 1990: 73; Beck and Beck-Gernsheim, 1995; Specter, 1998).

Women's increased participation in the labor force coupled with their continued housework responsibility raises the question of how women cope with the doubling of their responsibilities. As Suzanne Bianchi and her colleagues found in the United States, they do not necessarily take on a "second shift" (Bianchi et al., 2006). Instead, they do less paid work while doing more unpaid work than men; women tend to log fewer paid hours than their male counterparts (Bianchi et al., 2006). The same is the case in Italy, where studies show that market work and household work are strongly differentiated by gender (Fondazione Giacomo Brodolini, 2009). According to Bianchi and her colleagues, men have responded somewhat to the increase in women's labor-market participation with an increase in household work. However, the hours they log at home and at work do not equal those of women. In other words, the increase in men's housework does not correlate with the increase in women's participation in the labor market. The casualty in all of this is the time that couples spend doing housework, particularly cleaning, cooking, and other non–child-related reproductive activities (Bianchi et al., 2006: 89–112).

Although a higher joint income does not guarantee a more egalitarian distribution of housework between the sexes, it does give families the flexibility to afford the services of other women. Household work is commodified as families increasingly turn to day care centers and family day care providers, nursing homes, afterschool babysitters, and also privately hired domestic workers to balance work and family (Glenn, 1986; Hochschild, 1989; Rothman 1989a, 1989b; Nelson, 1990; Glazer, 1993; Reskin and Padavic, 1994). Often, it is immigrant women of color whom they hire to do this work (Romero, 1992; Glenn, 1992). As Joy Manlapit, a provider of elder care in Los Angeles, observes, "Domestics here are able to make a living from the elderly that families abandon. When they are older, the families do not want to take care of them. Some put them in convalescent homes, some put them in retirement homes, and some hire private domestic workers."

Fitting Glenn's schema of the "racial division of reproductive labor," the incorporation of migrant Filipina domestic workers into the labor market constitutes a hierarchical and codependent relation with their mostly white female employers. They free their female employers of housework, allowing them to avoid demanding a fairer division of labor with their partners and at the same time enabling them to participate in the labor force. In Italy and the United States, they join the ranks of other groups of working-class and immigrant women of color who have historically performed the reproductive labor of more privileged women.[5] As Glenn points out, women of color help more privileged women negotiate the unequal gender division of labor in their families. Thus, Glenn's formulation of the racial division of reproductive labor suggests that the economic demand for the low-wage labor of domestic workers arises not solely from the concentration of highly specialized professional service workers in "global cities" but also from persisting gender inequalities in the families of these professionals.[6] To fully consider the politics of reproductive labor in migration, I now expand and reformulate the concept of the racial division of reproductive labor by placing it in a transnational setting. In doing so, I situate the increasing demand for paid reproductive labor in receiving nations in the context of the globalization of the market economy.

THE INTERNATIONAL DIVISION OF REPRODUCTIVE LABOR

In globalization, production activities in one area cannot be understood solely from a unilocal perspective but must be situated in circuits of labor, goods, and capital across nations. Likewise, reproduction activities, especially as they have been increasingly commodified, have to be situated in the context of a global economy. Like production activities, reproduction activities in one area have concrete ties to reproduction activities in another. With the feminization of wage labor, global capitalism is creating links among distinct systems of gender inequality. Moreover, the migration of women connects systems of gender inequality in both sending and receiving nations to global capitalism. All of these processes occur in the formation of the international division of reproductive labor.

This division of labor places Glenn's (1992) concept of the racial division of reproductive labor in an international context under the auspices of Sassen's (1984) discussion of the incorporation of women from developing countries into the global economy. It is a transnational division of labor that is shaped simultaneously by global capitalism and systems of gender inequality in both sending and receiving countries of migration. This division of labor applies to different geopolitical scales of migration, including regional migration, for instance linking households in Hong Kong and the Philippines; south-to-south migration, tying families in Kuwait and the Philippines; and lastly south-to-north or global migration, connecting women, households, and families between the Philippines and various nations in the Global North.

Under the international division of reproductive labor, Filipina domestic workers perform the reproductive labor of class-privileged women in industrialized, or richer, countries, while they leave their own dependents to be cared for mostly by other women in the Philippines. This international division of labor refers to a three-tier transfer of reproductive labor among women in two nation-states: middle- and upper-class women in receiving countries, migrant Filipina domestic workers, and Filipina domestic workers, or poorer female relatives, in the Philippines who are often too poor to migrate.

In the article "Economy Menders," Linda Layosa, the editor of *Tinig Filipino*, gives a partial description of the international division of reproductive labor:

Indeed, our women have partially been liberated from the anguish of their day-to-day existence with their families and from economic problems, only to be enslaved again in the confines of another home, most of the time trampling their rights as human beings. . . . We have to face the reality that many of our women will be compelled to leave the confines of their own tidy bedrooms and their spotless kitchens only to clean another household, to mend others' torn clothes at the same time [that they] mend our tattered economy. (1995a: 7)

In her description, she falls short of mentioning who takes up the household work that migrant Filipina domestic workers leave behind on migration. Most likely, they are other female relatives and less privileged Filipina women who cannot afford to seek employment outside of the Philippines. Under the international division of reproductive labor, women's migration from the Philippines is embedded in the process of global capitalism. At the same time, gender is made a central factor of their migration; the process involves escaping their gendered responsibilities in the Philippines, easing the gender constraints of women who employ them in industrialized countries, and finally relegating their familial responsibilities to women left in the Philippines.

The international division of reproductive labor refers to a social, political, and economic relationship between women in the global labor market. This division of labor is a structural relationship of inequality based on class, race, gender, and (nation-based) citizenship. In this division of labor, there is a gradational decline in the worth of reproductive labor. As Rothman (1989a: 43) poignantly describes, "When performed by mothers, we call this mothering . . . ; when performed by hired hands, we call it unskilled." Commodified reproductive labor is not only low-paid work, but it declines in market value as it gets passed down in the international division of reproductive labor. As care is made into a commodity, women with greater resources in the global economy can afford more expensive care for their family. Conversely, the care given to those with fewer resources is usually worth less.

Consequently, the value of family life progressively declines as care is passed down the international division of reproductive labor. Freed of household constraints, those on top can earn more and consequently afford better-quality care than can the domestic workers they hire. With their wages relatively low, these domestic workers cannot afford to provide the same kind of care for their family. They, in turn, leave them behind in the Philippines to be cared for by domestic workers who are paid even less or by unpaid female family members, many of whom feel overworked (Parreñas, 2005). Relegated to the bottom of the three-tier hierarchy of reproductive labor, women in the Philippines have far fewer material resources to ensure the reproduction of their own family.

In the international division of reproductive labor, Filipina domestic workers do not just ease the entrance of other women into the paid labor force; they also assist in the economic growth of the receiving countries. Patricia Licuanan, in reference to households in Hong Kong and Singapore, explains:

Households are said to have benefited greatly by the import of domestic workers. Family income has increased because the wife and other women members of working age are freed from domestic chores and are able to join the labour force. This higher income would normally result in the enlargement of the consumer market and greater demand on production and consequently a growth in the economy (1994: 109).

By spurring economic development, the international division of reproductive labor retains the inequalities of the global market economy. The low wages of migrant domestic workers increase the production activities of the receiving nation, but the economic growth of the Philippine economy is, for the most part, limited and dependent on the foreign currency provided by their low wages.

A similar observation can be made of the employing families. Freed of reproductive labor, the family employing the migrant domestic worker can increase the productive labor generated in their household. The mobility of the Filipina migrant domestic worker and her family is, for the most part, dependent on the greater mobility of the employing family. The same relationship goes for domestic workers in the Philippines and the migrant domestics who employ them. The case of Carmen Ronquillo, whom I interviewed in the mid-1990s, provides a good illustration of the international division of reproductive labor. Carmen is simultaneously a domestic worker for a professional woman in Rome and an employer of a domestic worker in the Philippines. Carmen describes her relationship to each of these two women:

When coming here, I mentally surrendered myself and forced my pride away from me to prepare myself. But I lost a lot of weight. I was not used to the work. You see, I had maids in the Philippines. I have a maid in the Philippines who has worked for me since my daughter was born twenty-four years ago. She is still with me. I paid her 300 pesos before, and now I pay her 1000 pesos [US$40].

I am a little bit luckier than others because I run the entire household. My employer is a divorced woman who is an architect. She does not have time to run her household, so I do all the shopping. I am the one budgeting. I am the one cooking. [Laughs.] And I am the one cleaning too. She has a twenty-four and a twenty-six-year-old. The older one graduated already and is an electrical engineer. The other one is taking up philosophy. They still live with her. . . . She has been my only employer. I stayed with her because I feel at home with her. She never commands. She never orders me to do this and to do that.

The hierarchical and interdependent relationships among Carmen, her employer in Italy, and her domestic worker in the Philippines comes from the unequal development of industrialized and developing countries in transnational capitalism, class differences in the Philippines, and the relegation of reproductive labor to women. Carmen Ronquillo's case clearly exemplifies how three distinct groups of women participate in the international division of reproductive labor. Whereas Carmen frees her employer (the architect) of domestic responsibilities, a lower-paid domestic worker does the household work for Carmen and her family.

Wage differences of domestic workers illuminate the economic disparity among nations in transnational capitalism. A domestic worker in Italy such as Carmen could receive US$1,000 a month for her labor:

I earn [US$1,000], and she pays for my benefits [for example, medical coverage]. On Sundays, I have a part-time; I clean her office in the morning, and she pays me [US$200]. I am very fortunate because she always gives me my holiday pay [August] and my thirteenth-month pay in December. Plus, she gives me my liquidation pay at the end of the year. Employers here are required to give you a liquidation pay—equivalent to your monthly salary for every year you worked for them, but they usually give it to you when you leave. But she insists on paying me at the end of the year. So, [in] December, I always receive [US$3,600].

Carmen's wages easily enable her to hire a domestic worker in the Philippines, who usually earns below-poverty wages. Moreover, the female domestic worker in the Philippines, in exchange for her labor, does not receive the additional work benefits, like medical coverage, that Carmen gets for the same labor. Not surprisingly, migrant Filipina domestic workers, as shown by their high level of educational attainment, tend to have more resources and belong to a more comfortable class than domestic workers do in the Philippines. Such resources often give women like Carmen the option of working outside of the country.

THE OVERLOOKED PARTICIPANTS: CHILDREN AND WOMEN IN THE PHILIPPINES

The private world remains devalued, as poor people become the wives and mothers of the world, cleaning the toilets and raising the children. The devaluing of certain work, of nurturance, of private "domestic" work, remains: rearing children is roughly on a par—certainly in terms of salary—with cleaning the toilet. (Rothman, 1989a: 252)

Although the devaluation of "rearing children" could be lamented as a tragedy for children in general, we should distinguish among the experiences of the different groups of children (and elderly) in the international division of reproductive labor—those who are cared for and those who are not, and those who regularly see their parents or children and those who do not. The fact that "rearing children is roughly on a par . . . with cleaning the toilet" means that the meager wages migrant Filipina domestic workers receive usually do not cover the higher costs of maintaining a family in an industrialized country. In the United States, where women of color have traditionally been caregivers and domestic workers for white families, mothering is diverted away from families of color. Sau-ling Wong defines "diverted mothering" to be the process in which the "time and energy available for mothering are diverted from those who, by kinship or communal ties, are their more rightful recipients"

(1994: 69). Historically, a married black domestic worker in the United States "typically saw her children once every two weeks, leaving them in the care of the husband or older siblings, while remaining on call around the clock for the employer's children" (Wong, 1994: 71). Although now in an international context, the same pattern of "diverted mothering" could be described for Filipina, Latina, and Caribbean domestic workers, as many are forced to leave their children behind in their country of origin (Colen, 1995; Hondagneu-Sotelo and Avila, 1997). The question is, then, who cares for these "other" children?

In the Philippines, it is unusual for fathers to nurture and care for their children; but, because not all migrant Filipina domestic workers hire their own domestic workers, some men are forced to renegotiate the household division of labor. Yet, in my observations of twenty-six transnational households of migrant mothers in the Philippines, I found that fathers who stay behind rarely did housework or child care (Parreñas, 2005). More specifically, only four fathers could be described as their children's primary caretaker. The rest relied on other women—eldest daughters, extended kin, or paid household help—to do the housework and child care for their families. A few men assisted these women, but many more had been absentee fathers. My observations agree with studies on dual-earning families in the Philippines, where, according to Chant and McIlwaine (1995), older (female) children, not fathers, are more likely to care for younger siblings while their mothers work.

Female relatives are usually the ones who take over the household work of migrant Filipinas. In these cases, nonegalitarian relations among family members should be acknowledged, considering that for female family members who remain in the Philippines, "the mobility they might achieve through migration is severely curtailed" (Basch et al., 1994: 241). However, hired domestic workers—a live-in housekeeper or *labandera* (laundry woman)—also free migrant Filipina domestics of their household labor. Almost all of my interviewees hire domestic workers in the Philippines. This should not be surprising considering that, as I have already noted, the average wage of domestics in the Philippines is considerably less than the average wage of migrant domestics.

Women who cannot afford to work as domestic workers in other countries should not be considered equals of those who do. Maya Areza, who dreams of retiring in the Philippines after a few more years in Los Angeles, reminds us of the structural inequalities characterizing relations among women in developing countries when she states:

When I retire I plan to go home for good. I plan to stay at my parents' house. . . . I would just lounge and smoke. I will get a domestic helper whom I can ask to get my cigarettes for me. . . . My children and my cousins all have domestic workers. You can hire one if you have money. It's cheap, only 1,000 pesos [US$40]. Here, you earn $1,000 doing the same kind of work you would do for 1,000 pesos there! I won't have a problem with hiring one.

Because migrant Filipina domestic workers are usually in the middle of the hierarchical chain of caretaking, they maintain unequal relations with less privileged women in the Philippines. Under the international division of reproductive labor, the unequal economic standing of nation-states prominently distinguishes the position of female low-wage workers in advanced capitalist countries like the United States from that of their colleagues in developing countries like the Philippines. Migrant Filipina domestic workers surely take advantage of these differences in wages and maintain a direct hierarchical relationship with the domestic workers they hire in the Philippines.

THE PROBLEM WITH THE "CARE CHAIN"

In my initial discussions of the political economy of domestic work, I interchangeably used the terms *international transfer of caregiving* and *international division of reproductive labor*. Yet, I primarily refer to this hierarchical relation among women as a "division of reproductive labor," one that I recognize takes place via a transfer of caregiving, so as to foreground social and political-economic inequalities. This is because I found that care, as opposed to reproductive labor, is an inadequate concept for analyzing the inequalities constituted in domestic work, whether they are local, transnational, or global. Reducing the international division of reproductive labor to a "care chain" simplifies the concept, resulting in its misunderstanding, as the analysis of Nicola Yeates (2012) points out. This relation of inequality among women, Yeates argues, does not sufficiently examine local inequalities based on race and ethnicity, for example, in its more narrow focus on inequalities across nations. Yeates's critique is in itself problematic, as it ignores the foundational roots of the concept, which is Glenn's classic discussion of the racial division of reproductive labor. Still, Yeates's criticism calls for the need to further clarify the concept of the "international division of reproductive labor," which requires an explanation of why care, as opposed to reproductive labor, is an inadequate framework for examining women's paid and unpaid work in the family.

Care work, according to Paula England and her coauthors (1992), entails face-to-face contact and refers to the provision of a service that develops the human capabilities of the recipient. In contrast, reproductive labor encompasses the "array of activities and relationships involved in maintaining people both on a daily basis and intergenerationally" (Glenn, 1992: 1). Reproductive labor is a more expansive concept than care work, as it entails the work of sustaining a population instead of just one person. As such, reproductive labor entails a wider array of activities than care work does; it includes purchasing household goods, preparing food, laundering clothes, dusting furniture, sweeping floors, maintaining community ties, caring for adults and children, socializing children, and providing emotional support. Much of the work done by migrant women is actually nonrelational and would therefore not fit the traditional definition of "care work," suggesting that the "care chain" ignores the bulk of the work that migrant care workers actually do: performing the dirty work of cleaning households. As Mignon Duffy observes, "A theoretical focus on [care] privileges the experiences of white women and excludes large numbers of very-low-wage workers" (2005: 79).

The concept of reproductive labor enables us to better account for racial inequalities among care providers and care recipients. For one, we can more fully account for the range of tasks performed by migrant domestic workers and the division of labor in the social reproduction of the population, allowing us to take note of who does menial and nonmenial labor and nurturant and nonnurturant work in caring institutions, including households, hospitals, and schools. In domestic work, "spiritual" labor like reading books and providing emotional support is mostly done by employers (Roberts, 1997); menial work, including nurturant (such as cleaning soiled pants) and nonnurturant tasks (such as sweeping the floor), is mostly done by migrant women and women of color (Glenn, 1992; Romero, 1992).

Simultaneously accounting for transnational and local inequalities in our discussions of the reproductive labor of migrant workers is a challenge that seems to have emerged in the application of the "care chain." Yet, returning to the conceptual origins of the "care chain" or "international division of reproductive labor," Glenn's 1992 seminal formulation of the "racial division of reproductive labor" can help us restore the documentation of local inequalities when situating the labor of migrants in a "care chain." The "racial division of reproductive labor" offers an integrated model of race and gender; it accounts for the racial and ethnic hierarchies that define not just domestic-service arrangements but also various service institutions. Thus, focusing on reproductive labor as opposed to care work allows us to frame our discussion outside the context of the family and to also look at the caring and reproductive work done in other institutional settings. Whereas women of color and migrant domestic servants do more laborious tasks in the household, so do their counterparts in the hospital, where cafeteria workers, janitors, and lower-level nurses tend to be nonnative or nonwhite women. According to Glenn (1992), documenting the hierarchy of reproductive tasks and the distribution of such tasks across various institutions, along with accounting for who gains and who loses from paid reproductive labor, consistently reveals a "racial division of reproductive labor," one in which women of color usually perform menial tasks.

As noted earlier, the concept of the "international division of reproductive labor" (Parreñas, 2000) merely places Glenn's theory in an international context, accounting for the costs of migrant reproductive labor to families and communities in countries of origin and juxtaposing such costs to the gains made by the employers' households in the host countries. The research informs us that such work concerns not just local but also transnational inequalities, and that service work also shapes political-economic ties between nations. This disrupts the assumption that the manufacturing of goods is the only relevant labor that links nations to each other.

THE QUESTION OF MEN

The international division of reproductive labor, or more directly, Arlie Hochschild's discussions of the "care chain," has also been critiqued by many for reifying the notion that only women do care work (Yeates, 2012: Kilkey et al., 2013). Such a critique presumes that men also perform care work. To make this point, studies repeatedly cite the work of Alicia Pingol (2001), who documents the increasing caring labor that men have taken on since their wives emigrated from the Philippines. Yet, her findings are notably exceptional and do not agree with larger-scale studies on the division of labor of families in the Philippines (Illo, 2010; Human Development Network, 2010). Additionally, studies claim that migrant men also do care work, describing the work of Polish handymen (Kilkey et al., 2013), yet such a categorization downplays how this work would fall into the reproductive labor category of "nonnurturant labor" (Duffy, 2005).

A pressing question that remains is whether or not migrant men do caring work. Statistical evidence indicates that only a very few do. Using national labor surveys, the ILO found that the overwhelming majority of domestic workers across the globe are females: 94.1 percent in Israel, 90.9 percent in Spain, and 92.4 percent in Argentina (ILO, 2010: 6). Belize has the highest rate of male domestic workers at 25.8 percent, where they are not likely to be "care workers," but chauffeurs, gardeners, and guards (ibid.). Few men do "care work." In Italy, I found that the handful of men who do work inside the home are relegated to the nonnurturant work of housecleaning. When they do provide nurturant work, they usually care for elderly men, a job that entails the masculine task of heavy lifting, or they work in tandem with their wife to care for a family.

Although the "care chain" may reinforce the notion that care is inherently a woman's responsibility, it does also remind us that men rarely provide care. Insisting on studies on the caring work of men (Yeates, 2012; Kilkey et al., 2013) may inaccurately suggest that men perform more care work than they actually do. It may also lead to the romanticization of the few men who do housework, failing to consider how their performance of such work does not necessarily entail the provision of nurturant care (Duffy, 2005). Instead of calling for studies on the care work of men, perhaps we need to document how the labor of migrant women not only relieves other women but also provides "benefits to men, other family members, and society as a whole" (Duffy, 2005: 80).

If we are to include the work of men in discussions of caring labor, it would be more accurate to frame it in the increase in social reproduction work outside of private household settings. As janitors, cooks, waiters, teachers, and nurses, men do the cleaning and maintenance tasks of reproductive labor in institutional settings (Duffy, 2005). Some of this work, although not all, is nurturant (hence feminine) and involves the provision of care, suggesting a disruption of the gender order when performed by men. Yet, for the most part, men primarily perform what Duffy labels "nonnurturant reproductive labor" (2007: 323) as janitors, food preparation workers, or gardeners, questioning the notion that they do care work. Although we are notably seeing a visible presence of male nurses, for instance in Singapore (Huang et al., 2012), we find they recuperate masculinity and reject femininity by seeking assignments in emergency rooms, intensive care units, and in areas using advanced technologies. For the most part, the nursing work of men downplays the job's caring features (Williams, 1992).

Without question, we need to include men in our discussion of reproductive labor. We need to account for the challenges that men face when they do atypical gender work. Yet we need to include them not only as care providers but also as care recipients. Moreover, our inclusion of men should account not only for the constitution of gender in care work but also document the racial-ethnic makeup of care providers. In postindustrial societies across the globe, the decline of manufacturing has led to an increasing presence of men of color in reproductive labor. However, we should keep in mind that they mostly do nonnurturant work; in other words, they are unlikely to provide care. Still, particular racial groupings of men are more likely to perform atypical gender work than other groups. This suggests that a focus on male reproductive laborers vis-à-vis male nonreproductive laborers can be a springboard to examine the constitution of race and ethnicity across nations.

THE DISLOCATIONS OF REPRODUCTIVE LABOR

The concept of the international division of reproductive labor establishes that women's migration is a movement from one distinct patriarchal system to another, bound by race and class, in transnational capitalism. It tells us that women's migration should be analyzed from a gendered perspective of the political economy. The hierarchy of womanhood—involving race, class, and nation, as well as gender—establishes a work-transfer system of reproductive labor among women. It is a distinct form of transnational division of labor that links women in an interdependent relationship. Filipina domestic workers perform the reproductive labor of more privileged women in industrialized countries as they relegate their reproductive labor to poorer women left in the Philippines. This demonstrates that production is not the only means by which international divisions of labor operate in the global economy. Local economies are not solely linked to global economies by the manufacturing of goods. Under globalization, the transfer of reproductive labor also links nation-states.

The formulation of the international division of reproductive labor treats gender as a central analytical framework for understanding why Filipinas migrate, as it explains employer demand for their domestic labor. It shows that the movement of Filipina domestic workers is embedded in a gendered system of transnational capitalism. Although forces of global capitalism spur the labor migration of Filipina domestic workers, the demand for their labor also results from gender inequalities in receiving nations, for example, the continued relegation of reproductive labor to women. This transfer of labor strongly suggests that, despite their increasing rate of participation in the labor market, women continue to remain responsible for reproductive labor in both sending and receiving countries. At both ends of the migratory stream, they have not been able to negotiate directly with male counterparts for a fairer division of household work; instead, they have had to rely on their race and/or class privilege by participating in the transnational transfer of gender constraints to less privileged women.

A central contradiction in the maintenance of gender inequalities is that they hinder as much as they facilitate the migration of women. In the Philippines, gender stratification spurs women to leave in resistance to male abuse, the double day, labor-market segmentation, and single motherhood; it is a hidden cause of migration. For example, leaving the country alleviates the household reproductive labor of married women, whereas single women escape gender-defined duties in the family. But as they are relegated to domestic work in the labor market, they enter another system of gender inequality. Ironically, women in industrialized (Western) countries are often assumed to be more liberated than women are in developing countries. Yet this is often because women of color are stepping into their old shoes and doing their household work for them. As women transfer their reproductive labor to less and less privileged women, the ideology of female domesticity maintains its stronghold. This is one of the central reasons why there is a need for Filipina domestic workers in more than 100 countries today.

Unequal gender relations in the family represent an underlying dislocation confronted by migrant domestic workers in both ends of the migration process. It is a dislocation they notably share with their female employers. This dislocation drives the formation of the international division of reproductive labor, which results in other key dislocations confronted by migrant Filipina domestic workers. First, being in the middle of the international division of reproductive labor involves experiencing the pain of family separation. Second, being in the middle also means being part of the Philippine middle class. This alludes to the dislocation of contradictory class mobility and the partial citizenship migrants experience in receiving nations that fail to acknowledge their educational training prior to migration. Returning to my analysis of dislocations, the next two chapters address the dislocation of the pain of family separation.

CHAPTER THREE

THE TRANSNATIONAL FAMILY

MOST OF THE DOMESTIC WORKERS I MET in Rome and Los Angeles are members of transnational families. By this I mean that they are part of a family whose members are located in at least two countries. Although not occupying the same residence, family members in transnational households share resources, maintain a sense of collective responsibility for each other's well-being, and uphold the duties expected of them as kin. In these households, migrant domestic workers often act as breadwinners, sending monthly remittances to their elderly parents, children, and sometimes other kin. In my initial study, I found that 77 percent of research participants in Los Angeles and 89 percent in Rome maintain transnational households. While working in Italy or the United States, their families—spouses, children, and/or parents—remain in the Philippines. Twenty years later, migrant domestic workers still maintain transnational families.[1]

Initially documented among contemporary migrants by Linda Basch and her colleagues (Basch et al., 1994), the formation of transnational households is not exclusive to Filipino labor migrants. The burst of studies in the last ten years suggests that transnational families are in fact a norm in migrant communities, including among Mexicans, Salvadorans, and Hondurans in the United States (Schmalzbauer, 2004; Dreby, 2010; Abrego, 2014); Filipinos in the United Kingdom (Madianou and Miller, 2012); migrants in Europe (Bryceson and Vuorela, 2002), and among Indonesian migrants (Silvey, 2006). Yet, transnational families are not particular to present-day migrants. The earliest Chinese migrant workers in the United States, guest workers in Western Europe, and Mexican braceros in the southwestern United States, to name a few examples, adopted this type of household because of disparate levels of economic development between sending and receiving countries and laws against their integration (Glenn, 1983), similar to current conditions. Yet differences do exist between transnational households in the past and present. Whereas those in earlier migrant communities were composed primarily of a male income producer living apart from female and young dependents in the sending country, contemporary transnational households include women migrants (Basch et al., 1994).

Contemporary transnational households also involve a different temporal and spatial experience. They inhabit postmodern spaces as relationships in these families function through the process of "time-space compression . . . , the speed-up in the pace of life, while overcoming spatial barriers so that the world sometimes seems to collapse inwards upon us" (Harvey, 1989: 240). Although transnational family members perform daily activities across vast geographical distances, they overcome spatial barriers through the rapid flow of money and information. Due to advancements in technology, information about family members can be received instantaneously, communication can be constant, and money can be transferred to urban centers of Third World countries immediately (Madianou and Miller, 2012).

Migrants create transnational households to maximize resources and opportunities in the global economy. They mediate unequal levels of economic development between sending and receiving nations, legal barriers that restrict their full incorporation into the host society and polity, and the rise of anti-immigrant sentiments (Basch et al., 1994; Laguerre, 1994; Glick-Schiller et al., 1995). At the same time, transnational households form because of family ties and extended kin support (Foner, 1997). In short, transnational families form from the interplay of structural and cultural factors.

TRANSNATIONAL FAMILY FORMATIONS
IN THE FILIPINO DIASPORA

Although beginning with the household as a central unit of analysis could dangerously promote the assumption that the family represents a singular collective interest and may conveniently mask social inequalities within it, I find that the household provides a useful point of departure for analyzing the complexities of migration (Thorne, 1992). Offering a typology of migrant households will allow me to document how migration reconstitutes households and family relations.[2]

There are generally two types of households in Filipino migrant communities—proximate and transnational. Proximate households contain family members who live in close geographical proximity. In Rome and Los Angeles, the transnational household has historically been more dominant among domestic workers. When I revisited the field in 2011 and 2012, transnational families were still a common strategy of household maintenance among them. In Rome, for instance, many parents still preferred to raise their children in the Philippines due to the limited mobility options for the second generation. As one father told me, "No, I do not want them to join me. I do not want my children to become domestic workers in Rome. I would not be proud." In Los Angeles, proximate households likewise remain a rarity among domestic workers who tend to migrate at a later age, when their children are adults; are often disqualified from bringing their children as dependents if entering with an immigrant visa; or, if entering clandestinely, often cannot afford to obtain a tourist visa for other members of their family.

Proximate households tend to form in temporal stages of migration, with one parent migrating before other members of the family and the rest individually following in different stages. Trina Jusay's family followed this trajectory. A teacher in the Philippines, Trina, a forty-five-year-old domestic worker when I first met her in 1996, followed a female neighbor to Rome in 1981—seven months after the birth of her only daughter and when her two sons were still fairly young, at three and six years old. While Trina's husband followed her the next year, Trina's children migrated much later, the youngest at the age of six in 1987 and the two older children at the ages of sixteen and twelve in 1990. Although Trina's family now manages a proximate nuclear household, this was only after a transnational phase of ten years.

Transnational households can be further divided into three subcategories: one parent abroad, two parents abroad, and adult child(ren) abroad. One parent abroad transnational households are those with one parent—a mother or a father—producing income abroad while other family members carry out the functions of reproduction, socialization, and the rest of consumption in the Philippines. In the second category, both parents work abroad and the children usually reside together in the Philippines under the care of other relatives. Finally, there are adult children whose earnings as migrant laborers provide necessary or additional financial support to relatives in the Philippines.[3]

One Parent Abroad

The most common form of transnational household I found among domestic workers has one migrant parent—usually a mother—working outside of the Philippines for a prolonged period of separation from her or his family. The predominance of this type in my sample not only indicates that many women migrate independently from the Philippines but also suggests the reconfiguration of the gender division of labor in families. The question, then, is whether husbands and fathers left behind in the Philippines nurture the children under their care. Not all do. Instead of providing hands-on care to their children, many fathers who stay behind in the Philippines choose to leave the primary care of their children to other female relatives including older daughters, mothers and mothers-in-law, sisters and sisters-in-law, and aunts (Parreñas, 2005). Sometimes, fathers are altogether absent, as many migrants are single women (including separated and never-married women as well as widows) who had been raising their children on their own even before migration. Yet, as we see from the following story of Vicky Diaz, some fathers do provide day-to-day care. Two stories, one of a woman in Los Angeles and another in Rome, illustrate the struggles transnational mothers face in balancing the emotional and material needs of the children they leave behind in the Philippines.

In 1988, Vicky Diaz—a thirty-four-year-old mother of five children between the ages of two and ten years old—left the Philippines for Taiwan. Vicky had been neither content with her salary as a public school teacher in the Philippines nor comfortable with the insecurities of running a travel agency in Manila. Although made more lucrative by the greater demand for employment outside of the Philippines in the last ten years, the business of travel agencies had not been as profitable in the late 1980s. Lured by the financial rewards of employment outside the Philippines, Vicky decided to move to Taiwan, where doing domestic work would give her a more secure income.

In Taiwan, Vicky worked as a housekeeper and a factory worker, but mostly as a janitor, for which she earned approximately US$1,000 a month. Vicky, who speaks English very well, also subsidized her earnings by teaching English part-time at nights. Although satisfied with her earnings in Taiwan, the greater enforcement of restrictive polices against migrants in the early 1990s drove her to leave Taiwan and return to the Philippines in 1992. However, that trip turned out to be just a stopover before migrating to the United States:

From Taiwan, I stayed in the Philippines for only three months. I used this time to fix my papers to come here. After Taiwan, my real target was the States. It was because I knew that America is the land of promises and the land of opportunities. I had several friends who went to America and never went back to the Philippines. I figured it was because life was wonderful in the United States. . . . So, why not give myself the same opportunity?

Only a few months after her return to the Philippines, Vicky used her savings from Taiwan to pay a "travel agency" US$8,000 to use another woman's passport to enter the United States. As Vicky told me, "You know, in the Philippines, nothing is impossible if you have the money."

Considering her middle-class status after running a travel agency in the Philippines and her ability to raise such a huge sum of money for her trip to the United States, one could easily wonder why Vicky chose to endure such a prolonged separation from her family. When I interviewed her in 1996, Vicky had spent a total of only three months in the past nine years with her husband and children in the Philippines. Clearly an absentee mother for most of her children's adolescence, Vicky explained that it had been for her family's benefit that she opted to work outside the country:

They were saddened by my departure. . . . The children were not angry when I left because they were still very young when I left them. My husband could not get angry either because he knew that was the only way I could seriously help him raise our children, so that our children could be sent to school.

Vicky insisted that her family needed her higher earnings outside of the Philippines. Although aware of her children's persistent requests for her to return to the Philippines, Vicky was not convinced that her family could sustain its middle-class status without her earnings.

In Los Angeles, Vicky was initially employed as a domestic worker, primarily caring for a two-year-old boy for a wealthy family in Beverly Hills. While the mother "just [sat] around, smoking and making a mess," Vicky cleaned, cooked, and cared for the boy for $400 a week, clearly a sharp contrast to the $40 she was paying her own family's live-in domestic worker in the Philippines. Mainly, Vicky did not like being a housekeeper because of the physically demanding load and the excruciating loneliness, heightened by the contradiction of caring for someone else's children while not caring for her own:

Even though it paid well, you are sinking in the amount of your work. Even while you are ironing the clothes, they can still call you to the kitchen to wash the plates. It was also very depressing. The only thing you can do is give all your love to the child. In my absence from my children, the most I could do with my situation is give all my love to that child.

Not completely indifferent to the separation that her family has endured, Vicky did express feelings of regret over missing the formative years of her children's adolescence: "What saddens me the most about my situation is that during the formative years of their childhood, I was not there for them. That is the time when children really need their mother, and I was not there for them." Yet, for Vicky, the economic rewards of separation softened its emotional costs:

In my one year in the U.S., I was able to invest in a jeepney.[4] I wanted to do that so that no matter what happens with me, my husband does not have a hard time financially. . . . *Of course, I have neglected them, and the least I could do to make up for this is to make their lives a little bit easier. I could ease their lives for them materially.* That's how I console myself. . . . Besides the jeepney, there's the washing machine and TV. In the Philippines, it is hard to get to buy these things, right? [Emphasis added.]

To overcome the emotional gaps in her family, Vicky commodified her love and compensated for her absence with material goods. Although Vicky claimed that she worked outside of the Philippines so that her family would not become destitute, it is actually more accurate to say that Vicky worked in Los Angeles to sustain a comfortable middle-class life for her family in the Philippines. Vicky told me that she hoped her family would eventually reunite in Los Angeles because her family's opportunities in the Philippines were dismal. Without legal documents, however, she has not been able to sponsor her family's migration. Obtaining legal status had been the biggest challenge for Vicky and had been the main obstacle blocking the reunification of her family.

Unlike Vicky, Judy Reyes's primary motivation for migrating did not have to do with economics. In the Philippines, she had a rewarding career, a job she loved, and a salary that, along with her husband's, afforded her family a comfortable middle-class life in Manila. Migration had actually been Judy's way of escaping a horrible marriage. Judy went to Rome in 1991, leaving behind three daughters and one son between the ages of two months and nine years old. Although it had been her ambition to go to the United States or Canada, Judy had to settle for the more viable destination of Italy, where she had two sisters who had been working in Rome since the early 1980s. The two-week trip to Italy cost her US$6,400, depleting her savings and leaving her indebted to one of her sisters in Rome.

Life in Rome has been far from comfortable or enjoyable for Judy. Reflecting on her experiences, Judy recounted three major traumas: the harrowing voyage to Rome through a war-torn country in Eastern Europe, her downward mobility from her position as a registered nurse in the Philippines, and the pain she felt over family separation, most especially from the son she had left when he was just a two-month-old infant, four years before our interview. Although she could reconcile the downward mobility in her labor-market status, Judy was still coping with the distress of family separation:

The first two years I felt like I was going crazy. You have to believe me when I say that it was like I was having intense psychological problems. I would catch myself gazing at nothing, thinking about my child. Every moment, every second of the day, I felt like I was thinking about my baby. My youngest, you have to understand, I left when he was only two months old.

Judy carried a tremendous amount of emotional strain—guilt over her absence, especially missing her son's formative years; the burden and anguish over lost time with her children; and the sadness of not being familiar with how her family was developing, such as not knowing who prepared her children's breakfast every morning.

In any given month, Judy sent her children US$300 to $500. Even so, they were forced to live apart in the Philippines due to their father's irresponsibility. The money that she sent to subsidize her husband's income was not enough to keep the children together, as he continued to spend money on "women" and "going out with friends." Judy's children were divided among different relatives—two lived with their father in Manila, another in the province with her maternal grandmother, and the youngest also in Manila but with her sister-in-law.

Due to her husband's irresponsibility, Judy was anticipating their permanent separation: "I have a joint account with my child. It is my secret account so I am prepared no matter what happens to the two of us. I experienced what it was like to take care of my children on my own—financially supporting them with my salary without any help from him. It was hard." Nonetheless, she also held on to the possibility that her husband would somehow change for the better, hoping that her time in Rome would make him see his past errors:

He finally realized that he needs me now that we are apart. [She cries.] . . . I have not shown him any ill feelings. I have been very diplomatic in how I tell him what I did not like in our relationship. People have told me that I am such a martyr. But I tell them that I have four children, and it is important to me that my four children have a relationship with their father.

Once my children can think for themselves, maybe we can separate. But if I cannot bear our relationship anymore, that is when I am going to decide. I need to raise my children first and let them know that they have a father. . . .

He keeps on saying that he wants it to work, but he is with his other family all of the time. I ask him why he even maintains a relationship with us because he hardly gives us any time. I told him that it probably would be better if he packed his clothes and moved to his other family. But he is embarrassed because the other woman is not educated and is a gambler. . . .

His brothers and sisters tell me to have a little bit more patience. They tell me that they know that their brother is wrong, and he will probably change. They have cried to me, asking me to come back, and I told them I will only come back once their brother has changed.

Though her in-laws were trying to convince her to stay in a bad marriage, Judy had a sinking feeling that her husband would never change. To avoid the socially and culturally influenced pressures from family and community to keep her marriage intact—even with an unfaithful husband—Judy planned to prolong her stay abroad. When I met her, she had no immediate plans for reunification but foresaw her maintenance of a transnational family until her children completed their schooling.

Two Parents Abroad

Though less common than one-parent households in the diaspora, I did encounter transnational households with both parents abroad. Two such families, both in Rome,[5] illustrate distinct parental attitudes toward separation: One set of parents consciously tried to ease the emotional tensions in their transnational family, whereas the other was less willing to confront them. These divergent attitudes might have something to do with the difference in their transnational family make-up: In one family all of the children lived in the Philippines, whereas in the other the children were divided between Rome and the Philippines.

With the help of her sisters-in-law, Lolita Magsino migrated to Rome in 1984. Her husband, Antonio, followed her ten months later. When leaving the Philippines, he left four young children between the ages of two and seven years old under the care of Lolita's mother. When we spoke in 1995, Lolita had no regrets about her decision to relocate to Italy:

I have been here for eleven years. . . . It is ingrained in my head when I came here because it reminds me of how many years I have been struggling. . . . I followed my sisters-in-law, who have been here since 1981. Within ten days, I had a job. I knew that it was going to be domestic work because that was the job of my in-laws. . . . I came from a very poor family. I am used to working. It is nothing to me. I lack knowledge, so any job is good enough for me. As long as you are hardworking here, you have money. . . . I came, and my husband followed me after ten months.

In the Philippines, Lolita and Antonio had lived in a nipa hut[6] with their four children, barely making ends meet with the money they earned farming and selling vegetables. They took advantage of the opportunity to go to Italy to secure a more stable future for their children.

Lolita and her husband worked as domestic workers for only five years. Beginning in 1990, she started working as a full-time vendor of Filipino food in Rome. Lolita began selling food near a central bus transfer point where Filipinos and a few Peruvian women stopped between jobs. Very business minded, she and her husband both started businesses to serve the growing migrant community in Rome. While she worked as a vendor, he fixed cars for a living. Profits from their businesses enabled Lolita and her husband to provide a comfortable life for their children. Eventually Lolita was even able to formalize her business and open an actual eatery.

Lolita passed away in 2010. Other members of the community told me she died of a heart attack when visiting her family in the Philippines. When I met Lolita and Antonio in the mid-1990s, they lived with three of their children in an apartment in the center of Rome. But none of these children was among the four she was visiting in the Philippines when she unexpectedly passed away. Since migrating to Rome, she had given birth to three more children, all of whom she decided to raise in Italy. The difference in her relationship with her two sets of children had been very stark—when I met her, Lolita had managed to visit her children in the Philippines just once after more than a decade in Italy. Although she could have attached them to her permit to stay as early as 1990, she chose not to. In fact, her older children in the Philippines had not yet met their younger brothers born in Rome when I had interviewed her in the mid-1990s. When I met Lolita, I was surprised to learn of her "two sets" arrangement:

RP: Do you have children in the Philippines?

LM: Four. We left them with our mother.

RP: Do you miss them?

LM: Yes. We are here sacrificing for them, so that they are able to be educated. That is why we can bear leaving them in the Philippines. We sacrifice for the happiness of our children. We had no resources in the Philippines. If we had stayed in the Philippines, we would not have been able to send our children to school. That is how it was.

RP: I've noticed your children here, so some have been able to follow you?

LM: No, I left four in the Philippines, and three, I gave birth to in Rome. I have seven children.

RP: Can you talk about your children?

LM: My oldest is seventeen years old. He is a boy. Then there is a fifteen-, thirteen-, and twelve-year-old. Here, they are six, three, and one-and-a-half years old. [Long pause.]

I was working in houses until 1989, and since then, selling cooked food has been my livelihood.

When I first inquired about her children, Lolita described them only according to age, pausing for quite a long time, as she seemed to contemplate whether she should continue talking about them. In the end, she opted to redirect the interview toward her work experiences, leaving me to conclude that she had difficulty facing the contradiction of raising two sets of children.

When I continued to inquire about her children, she became uncomfortable, responding coldly and mechanically:

RP: Have your children met?

LM: No. But my children in the Philippines have seen my children here in videos that I have sent home. I talk to my children in the Philippines once or twice a month.

RP: Do you miss them?

LM: Yes.

RP: What does it feel like being apart from them?

LM: After being apart for a long time, you stop being lonely. It is because you have to remember that you are here to sacrifice for them. It is important not to think negatively.

Avoiding discussions about the emotional strains of geographical separation in her family, Lolita argued that focusing on the "negative aspects of their relationship" would not do them any good and would only be self-defeating. Physical distance seemed to have fostered detachment and emotional distance in Lolita's family, a reality underscored in her statement, "After being apart for a long time, you stop being lonely."

When I inquired about her sentiments regarding her children in the Philippines, Lolita opted to redirect our discussion to the material goods she has been able to provide them, becoming much more comfortable and informative:

From coming here, I have been able to have a house built in the Philippines. It is fairly small with nine bedrooms, and four bedrooms we rent out to students. It is close to the private school in our town. . . . We use the money paid by the board-ers to pay for the utilities and the food. But we also send our children money every month. We send them [US$250 to $333] at the end of the month for their schooling, and during Christmas, we send them [US$667]. We send them [US$1,000] at the beginning of the school year, when they have to buy school supplies. They need it to buy things.

Through the years, ties with her children in the Philippines had been com-modified, based mostly on the monthly remittances she was obligated to send.

Lolita had two different plans for her children in Italy and the Philippines. Although she planned to send her children in Italy to college, she intended to give each of her children in the Philippines an inheritance of a plot of land:

I am unable to go home frequently because I have so many children. I have to save every cent I earn for their future. What is important for me is being able to give each one of them land so that, when they do get married, they will have a place to have for themselves. So, I don't know when I am going to go home. I plan to stay here as long as my knees are strong.

Although it seems that her children in the Philippines would always remain there and her children in Italy would stay in Italy, it is important to recognize that she provided for all of them. Lolita did not necessarily abandon any of her children, despite the different ways she opted to parent them. Still, these differences seemed difficult for Lolita to resolve. Long after the interview, during one of my many visits to the bus stop, Lolita surprised me when she brought up her children in the Philippines: "My youngest in the Philippines recently told me: 'Your children over there in Italy are those you love, they are your real children.' It hurts, but you know that you are sacrificing here for them. Everyone struggles here." Both parents and children struggle emotion-ally with the maintenance of transnational households, which is a challenge parents often try to resolve via frequent communication and the provision of material goods. Yet, as suggested by Lolita's comments, material provisions that families secure in transnational households do not necessarily erase the emotional challenges wrought by physical distance.

Likewise struggling with the emotional difficulties of transnational family life, Luisa and Luciano went through a few different family formations before they settled on maintaining a transnational household. In 1981, Luisa—a single woman and the only college graduate in her family—followed her cousin to Rome to help her parents pay for her younger siblings' education. In 1987, she married Luciano, a Filipino domestic worker she had met in Rome. During the first few years of their marriage, both Luisa and Luciano worked as live-in domestic workers and maintained a nontraditional proximate household, seeing each other only on Thursdays and Sundays. After giving birth to her first son in 1987, Luisa continued to live apart from Luciano and, without his assistance, struggled to care for their baby while still having to work as a live-in domestic worker. Juggling two full-time responsibilities proved impossible and left her on the verge of a nervous breakdown:

After I gave birth to my first son, I had some sort of nervous breakdown because the child did not sleep at night. . . . The child would go to sleep at 4 in the morning, and I would have to get up at 6:30 to prepare myself because at 7:30 the breakfast of my employer and the children had to be prepared. During the day, the baby was still crying and crying.

Toward the end, I myself was so depressed. When the baby started crying, I would start crying. Everything I held fell. There came a time that even though I was very, very, very hungry, I could not eat because even as I held a spoon, my whole body would start shaking. I was very exhausted.

My husband, Luciano, lived with his employer, and I lived with mine. And his employer was terrible; he wasn't allowed to sleep outside, not even once was he allowed to come over and help me. I had to look after that kid on my own for twenty-four hours a day, seven days a week, for months. When the baby was almost four months old, I went to see a doctor because I had lost eight kilos in one month. I looked like a corpse. I felt like I was going crazy. When I dropped a glass, I would start crying. When Luciano called and I heard his voice, I would start crying. I felt hopeless. . . . I was just working and working. I did not have time to rest, and I was not eating well.

The demands of domestic work left Luisa physically unable to care for her child. As a family, they had very limited options; they could not live together, and they needed Luisa's second income because they both still had financial responsibilities to relatives in the Philippines. Luisa and Luciano did not have relatives they could rely on for child care or financial assistance in Rome.

Literally on the brink of physical collapse, Luisa had no other choice but to stop working. To finally give her body its much-needed rest and her baby his proper care, Luisa went back home: "So, I decided to go back to the Philippines. I told Luciano that whether he liked it or not, we were going to go home. So, I went to the Philippines and stayed in the Philippines for five months. I rested. Then I came back here and left my baby in the Philippines. Then before the baby was two years old, I took him back [to Rome]." Unable to bear the separation from their young child, Luisa and Luciano decided to bring him back to Rome within less than a year. Although with difficulty, Luisa managed to care for their son while keeping a full workload of various "part-time" cleaning jobs by bringing him to work with her. They were finally able to rent a room in an apartment with other Filipinos. As Luisa was left doubly tired by having their son with her the whole day, Luciano was often in charge of preparing dinner and other housecleaning chores. However, the birth of their second son a year later ended this manageable arrangement of family work. Now with two children in Rome, Luisa and Luciano found themselves shouldered not only with greater child care responsibilities but also with more expenses. Hence, they decided it was best to send their infant son back to the Philippines. They could not afford to live off Luciano's wages alone, and after Luisa's previous experience with their oldest son in Rome, they knew that it would be impossible for her to work and care for an infant at the same time.

After two years of maintaining a transnational household with each child in a different country, Luciano and Luisa decided it would be best if they left both of their children in the Philippines. Unlike Lolita Magsino, Luisa and Luciano were conscious of the detrimental effects that raising children in two different places would have had on the child in the Philippines. "I preferred that both of my kids grow up in the Philippines. . . . To me it's worse for one to be here and one in the Philippines, because then one will have a reason to be jealous of the other. One will think that we care about the other more than we care for him. I don't want one to grow up resenting us."

Luisa and Luciano opted to raise both children in the Philippines and not in Italy largely for practical reasons. Both of them would have to work full-time to afford their higher living costs, but only one of them would be able to do so because of child care demands. Leaving their children in the Philippines would also enable them to provide financial assistance to their extended families. Raising two children in Rome, even if already of school age, was also less of a viable option because of the informal nature of domestic work. Luisa explained:

What I also experienced was when one of my children got sick, I had to stay at home for twenty days. So, I did not work for twenty days, but before those twenty days were over, the other one got sick. So, I had to excuse myself for another twenty days. Forty days I was in the house without any salary. Our work here as a part-timer is "no work, no pay."

As domestic workers, they do not receive employee benefits to ease the costs of reproduction, such as subsidized day care facilities, sick leave, or maternal leave. Family and friends in the community usually work full-time and cannot help the parents with child care. Parents are thus compelled to leave their children in the Philippines or send them back there, where at least they would have the support of a wide kin network.

While her mother took care of their two children in the Philippines, Luisa and Luciano worked part-time for four and two families, respectively. Conscious of the physical toll such a full schedule could take on each other's bodies, they had set up an egalitarian division of labor in which Luciano did more housework because of his lighter workload. Pooling their monthly income of more than US$2,000 in 1996, Luisa and Luciano rented a room for US$400 a month and paid no more than US$267 for household expenses. They sent US$333 to their children in the Philippines, while the rest of their income went to their savings and property investments there. When I met them in the mid-1990s, Luisa and Luciano had modest goals. They hoped to build an apartment complex with four units, three of which they would rent out as their source of fixed income once they return to the Philippines. Although still quite tentative, they planned to eventually reunite as a family in the Philippines. But, until that happened, they made sure that they saw their children regularly, visiting them during life-cycle events like birthdays every year.

Adult Child(ren) Abroad

The subcategory of transnational households with adult child(ren) abroad is where I place most single domestic workers in Rome and Los Angeles. This was Luisa's case when she first moved to Rome, prior to meeting and marrying Luciano. In the Philippines, adult children have the responsibility of caring for elderly family dependents; although they tend to share and divide the work with brothers and sisters, most of the responsibility often falls to single adults without children, particularly women. The identification of this type of household for single adult migrants highlights the deeply instilled cultural value of familism in the Philippines.

Not one of my interviewees has failed to provide financial assistance to his or her family. Although I expected to find strong ties between adult single migrants and parents in the Philippines, I was surprised that family interdependency extends to include financially supporting brothers and sisters, as well as their respective families. Of 105 single women surveyed in 1996, fifty-five sent remittances once a month, twenty-eight every two to three months, and eleven occasionally; only eleven did not remit any funds. Of the women who remitted monthly, the average amount had been US$360. Women who remitted every two to three months sent on average US$489. Those who remitted occasionally sent on average US$667. Fewer of their male counterparts remitted funds regularly, and those who did usually sent less. Of thirty-two single men surveyed in Rome, only eleven remitted funds every month and five every two to three months. Those who remitted monthly on average sent their families US$252, which is significantly less than what women sent.

Single women usually sent more because of the greater cultural expectation of daughters to provide for their families and the more stable employment of women than men. Qualifying these figures, almost all of the female domestic workers I interviewed took the responsibility of covering the costs of at least one younger relative's college education, but more often than not they put at least two relatives through college. Although some send greater remittances than others, and although some limit remittances to life-cycle events or when requested, most send money to families in the Philippines regularly. By adopting the role of income producer for extended families in the Philippines, single adult women such as Valentina Diamante and Maria Batung maintain transnational households in migration. Hence, like most of the single women in my study, they cannot be regarded as single householders.

Now married with her husband and children in Rome, Valentina Diamante was once a single domestic worker who in her mid-twenties followed three aunts and three sisters to Rome in 1990. Her migration was made possible by the female migrant network sustained in her family, with one sister financially sponsoring the migration of a younger sister as one comes of age.

In the Philippines, Valentina had only attended a year of college, majoring in hotel management. Not enjoying school, she decided that she could better help her parents with the schooling of her younger siblings by following her sisters to Rome. When we met in 1996, Valentina worked as a live-in worker for a divorced Italian mother of two children. She earned a monthly salary of US$667. True to her intention of coming to Rome to help her family, Valentina sent almost all of what she earned back to the Philippines: "I send money monthly. It's because the others don't so much because they have their own families. I don't care that I am sending more than them. I think about my family more often than I think about myself. Sometimes, actually most of the time, I send them [US$667]." Most months this left her without spending money, but Valentina claimed that this did not bother her because, as a live-in domestic worker, she had no personal expenses; her employer provided her with food, toiletries, and even clothing. On her day off, she did not even have to pay for public transportation because one of her older sisters picked her up from her employer's house.

Even so, it was still surprising to learn that she did not keep some of what she earned for herself:

That's what my employer told me. She asked me why I don't open a bank account, and I told her that it really is not possible because my sisters and brother are still going to school. Maybe I will start thinking about saving money for myself after one of them graduates. Right now, I have a bank account, but I only have 2,000 pesos [US$80] in it. [Laughs.] It's so embarrassing. I didn't want to actually, but my friend forced me to open one. That's my first bank account. I just opened it this year.

While many adult single women send half of their monthly earnings to the Philippines, Valentina is an extreme example of someone who put aside her own needs for her family.

I actually spent quite a lot of time with Valentina. One day, when I was visiting her at her employer's home, a letter arrived from the Philippines. On reading it, she suddenly became distressed and could not help but comment sarcastically that she always gets a headache when she receives a letter because it is almost always a request for money. I asked to read the letter and found out that her parents were asking for an additional US$200 to pay for her sister's graduation dress, the cost of her other sister's participation as a muse in a town fiesta, and the party her parents felt obliged to give because of their daughter's role in the fiesta. Valentina was upset not about having to send them money but about not having the money to send them. As it was the middle of the month, she had already sent them her entire pay of US$667 two weeks earlier. I asked her why she did not get angry, because the request seemed unfair and frivolous. She explained to me that it was her duty to help them. Besides not needing the money herself, she explained that her parents were not the ones who decided to have their daughter participate in the fiesta. They themselves were being pressured by the community, and it would be an embarrassment for the whole family if they did not throw an elaborate party to celebrate their daughter's selection to represent the town. The townsfolk, who assume they are rich because of their daughters in Italy, would think badly of what they would perceive as her family's selfishness.

I could not believe anyone could be so self-sacrificing and was stunned that she did not seem resentful. That night, as it was her day off, I jokingly gave her US$1.30 to bet in *jueting*, a small-scale lottery run by men in the Filipino community, and told her that maybe she would win the money that she needed to send to her family. Every Thursday and Sunday, people can select two numbers from one to thirty-two and bet US$1.30 to win a pot of around US$300. I got into the habit of betting regularly but never won. To my amazement, Valentina won that night. I figured it was her good karma for all the sacrifices she had made for her family; finally, while she was able to send her family the money they had requested, she also had some to keep for herself.

Another single domestic worker who provided a great deal of support to her family was Maria Batung, who had been working for a Filipino family in the United States for more than twelve years and supported her family in the Philippines with her earnings. Prior to migrating, Maria also worked as a domestic worker—a nanny—because without a college degree or appropriate networks she did not have access to other types of employment in Manila. Maria had actually been attending college prior to entering domestic work, but she had to give up her educational aspirations because her parents, whose sole income had been her father's sporadic earnings as a carpenter, could not afford to send her or any of her five brothers and sisters to school.

In Manila, she usually worked for foreigners, mostly diplomats and businessmen. In 1980, ten years after she started working as a domestic helper, Maria accepted a former employer's offer to move to London with them. Although she could have continued working for the English family, Maria decided, after four years in London, to take up another former employer's offer, but this time for a job in the United States. Her present employers were migrating to the United States to establish an import-export rattan furniture business in Southern California and, by investing capital in the United States, qualified to bring a small number of employees with them, including Maria. They covered all of her travel expenses and the costs of obtaining legal papers. With their sponsorship, Maria was able to obtain a green card to stay in the United States permanently.

Maria was very satisfied with her work, earning far more than she ever did in London (US$150 per month), always having a manageable workload, and not having to deal with demanding or strict employers:

I earn enough so that I could help my family in the Philippines. I get more than $1,000 a month, and everything is free. They pay for my Social Security, and they handled my papers. They pay for my ticket home every year. When I go, they also give me vacation pay for two months. That is why I don't have a problem here. Everything is free, and they also cover my insurance. . . . It is OK. Anytime I want to leave, I can. . . . That is why I lasted long with this family. If that were not the case, I would have probably returned to the Philippines a long time ago.

Of all the employment benefits she receives, the one Maria appreciated the most was her annual two months of paid vacation because it gave her time to spend with her father. Very satisfied with her job, Maria planned to work for her employers until she is old herself.

With no personal expenses to cover, like Valentina, Maria sent most of her earnings to her family in the Philippines. By the time I met her, she had sent numerous relatives to college. Maria invested in the education of her siblings as well as nieces and nephews, because she wanted to make sure that no one else in her family "settled" for domestic work as she was forced to do almost thirty years ago:

I send my father money, and my nieces and nephews I equally sent to school. For every single sibling of mine, I sent one of their children to school. So there is no jealousy. The rest they could send to school on their own, but each one of them I sent at least one of their children to school. . . . So, I am very happy. Although I was not able to finish school . . . I was able to ensure [they] finished their education. It is hard when you don't finish. I told them that they would have a hard time if they did not have a degree and that it was necessary that they finish school.

Because of her remittances, Maria had not accumulated any savings when I met her in the mid-1990s, which had not concerned her. With her legal status, she was secure that she would eventually qualify to receive Social Security benefits once she retires as her employers contributed to this fund every month.

Maria's earnings not only covered younger relatives' college education but also assisted her family with their day-to-day living expenses:

The last time I sent money it was for $500. That is the lowest. It is mostly $1,000 or $600 or $700. So I have no savings. My bank is with all those that I sent to school. I also had a house built in the Philippines where my father lives right now. I had that house remodeled and everything. My father was telling me that maybe when I get older I would regret what I did because they would no longer recognize me. But I told him that they can do what they want to do, but I am happy that I was able to help them.

Maria's generosity had been voluntary, and her most satisfying rewards have been the love of her family and their appreciation for her tremendous financial support. Although very appreciative of the money and material goods Maria has provided them, her relatives want her to come home soon and settle down in the Philippines so that they can build a more intimate relationship based not only on the monthly remittances she sends them. A single adult migrant in a transnational family, Maria Batung worked in Los Angeles to sustain her family in the Philippines. The responsibility for extended kin that Maria maintained through migration is notably not an exception but a trait common among other single migrant domestic workers whom I met in Rome and Los Angeles.

THE POSTINDUSTRIAL FAMILY: STRUCTURAL FACTORS IN TRANSNATIONAL HOUSEHOLD FORMATIONS

Numerous scholars have challenged the monolithic construct of the family as a "firm, unchanging entity, always similar in shape and content"; instead, they posit that the family is a social institution that adopts various strategies in response to external structural, cultural, and ideological forces in society

(Thorne, 1992: 6). Although there are debates on what constitutes legitimate family forms, my discussion of the family avoids questions of legitimacy and morality. Instead, I focus on questions of malleability, particularly highlighting the external forces that mold the formation of families into transnational structures.

Shifts in economic arrangements have historically coincided with shifts in family organization. According to sociologist Judith Stacey (1991), the family can be traced historically from premodern to modern to postmodern structures and arrangements. In preindustrial societies, the essential functions of the family—production, reproduction, consumption, socialization—generally stayed within its institutional boundaries. Typically encompassing wide kin networks, premodern families maintained economically self-sufficient and land-based agricultural units that produced their own food and clothing (Kessler Harris, 1981; Mintz and Kellog, 1988). The coming of the industrial era in the late eighteenth century transformed household arrangements, although slowly, to the modern family. In contrast to the premodern family, it inhabited a private space—a "haven in a heartless world"; sustained a clear-cut division of labor between the (productive) income-generating father and the (reproductive) nurturing mother; and relied on love as its enduring bond and stronghold (Stacey, 1991). In further contrast to premodern families, modern households were typically enclosed and mobile nuclear units. In the late twentieth century, contemporary economic transformations, or global restructuring, led to another shift in household arrangement, this time from the modern to the postmodern family.

According to Stacey (1991), the decline of unionized manufacturing jobs in postindustrial societies has contributed to the breakdown of the family wage system—the backbone of the modern family—and has resulted in greater dependence on the wage earnings of women, the decline of the nuclear family, and the diversification of household forms. Households now encompass varied social arrangements and relations. They include dual wage-earning households, domestic partnerships, single-parent families, and divorced families. Unlike premodern and modern families, the postmodern family is not bound to a definitive model with set characteristics; thus it embraces the diversity of family forms.

Representing a postmodern family, transnational households are one of the many family arrangements that have subverted modern family norms.

Fitting the "two-tier workforce" in the global economy, transnational families include low-wage migrant workers and professionals (Reich, 1991). The latter includes "astronaut families" with "parachute kids," such as children from wealthy families in Asia who are educated in nations with universally recognized educational systems (Ong, 1996). The ability of wealthy transnational families to cross borders freely distinguishes them from those of low-wage migrant workers, whose visits with family members are more sporadic. A lack of funds, job restrictions, or one's undocumented status restrain the movement of low-wage migrant workers, as strict border regulations limit the ability of dependents to join them.

What are the structural factors that propel the formation of transnational households among secondary-tier migrant workers in the global economy? Migrants respond to various social and economic realities of globalization, the first of which is the unequal development of regions. Although the meager wages of low-paid migrant workers afford their families a comfortable middle-class lifestyle in the sending country, they cannot provide a comparable lifestyle in receiving countries. As illustrated by Luisa Balila's decision to leave her children behind in the Philippines, and Vicky Diaz's observations on how much more she can purchase in the Philippines with her low wages, the migrant family transcends borders and the spatial boundaries of nation-states to take advantage of the lower costs of reproducing—feeding, housing, clothing, and educating—the family in the Third World. Its spatial organization directly responds to the forces of global capitalism, as the family's geographical split coincides with the uneven development of regions and the unequal relations of states in the global economy.

As shown by Judy Reyes's concerns over the lack of mobility her children would have in Italy, migrants also form transnational households in response to nativism—"neoracism" and xenophobia—in receiving societies.[7] Nativist sentiments against migrants still brew throughout the United States and the northern region of Italy (Feagin, 1997; Golash-Boza, 2012). For this reason, migrant parents may not want to expose their children to the racial tensions and anti-immigrant sentiments fostered by the social and cultural construction of low-wage migrants as undesirable citizens (Ong, 1996).

Finally, migrants turn to transnational households to negotiate restrictive measures against their integration into the host society. In Italy, the long-term status of Filipino migrants as "guest workers" has encouraged the maintenance of transnational households, as has the disqualification of adult children from joining their parents in the United States. Many of my interviewees in Los Angeles had actually been caught in the legal bind of either being undocumented, like Vicky Diaz, or having obtained legal status only after their children reached adult age, at which point they would no longer be eligible for immediate family reunification. In other words, although they may have wanted to sponsor their children, the laws prevented them from doing so.

The formation of transnational households corresponds with the opposite turns of nationalism in globalization, meaning the opening of borders to goods and labor and simultaneous closing to people (Sassen, 1996). Receiving societies have most likely encouraged the formation of transnational households because they get the benefits of low-wage migrant labor without having to support their reproduction. In other words, although receiving countries need migrants' low-wage labor, they have wanted neither the social nor the economic responsibilities that arise when these workers have children. Thus, transnational households, though themselves a strategy of resistance in globalization, maintain the inequalities of globalization. From transnational families, receiving countries benefit from the minimized wage demands of a substantial portion of their workforce. Such economic benefits translate to increased production, resulting in growth and profits for the higher-tier workers in receiving countries.

Transnational households should not be praised as a small-scale symbol of the migrant's agency against the larger forces of globalization because their existence marks an enforcement of border control on migrant workers. Transnational households signify segregation. They result from the successful implementation of border control, which prevents families from reuniting. Family separation is often prolonged and may even extend to span a life cycle. Among my interviewees, for example, the length of separation between mothers and their now-adult children stretched to as long as sixteen years.

THE PREINDUSTRIAL VALUE SYSTEM: CULTURAL FACTORS IN TRANSNATIONAL HOUSEHOLD FORMATION

Transnational households have come to signify the decline and disintegration of family values. Because they fail to fulfill the ideological notion of a traditional Filipino family, transnational households are considered "broken homes."

Transnational households are considered "broken" in a number of ways. First, the maintenance of this household diverges from traditional expectations of cohabitation among spouses and children. Filipino families are traditionally nuclear in structure. Second, they do not meet the traditional division of labor in the family, as transnational mothers do not live up to the social expectations for women to perform domestic chores. Notably, this expectation still stands despite women's higher degree of participation in the labor force in the Philippines (Medina, 1991). Third, they move away from traditional practices of socialization in the family. Whereas socialization is expected to come from direct supervision and interaction with parents as well as other adults, the geographic distance in transnational households hurts the ability of mothers to directly supervise their children.

At the same time that it is considered a threat to the traditional Filipino family, transnational households can only form because of the strong sense of family allegiance maintained by its members. Notably, the formation of transnational households depends on the persisting cultural value of *pakikisama* (mutual cooperation or familism); that is, sentiments of collectivism and mutual obligation among kin. Transnational households would not be able to form and reproduce without the cultural value of *pakikisama* and the mechanisms strengthening such an allegiance, including mutual assistance, consanguineal responsibility, "generalized family exchange networks" (Peterson, 1993), and fosterage. As such, transnational households reveal the resilience of the Filipino family.

As already mentioned, transnational families rely on sentiments of consanguineal responsibility, that is the extension of responsibility to include parents, siblings, and even nieces and nephews. The high level of interdependency in extended families is first illustrated by the tremendous sense of responsibility that they have for extended kin in the Philippines. Many single domestic workers, like Maria Batung, shoulder the financial costs of reproducing the extended family by investing in the education of younger generations. Although married domestic workers with children usually pay for the schooling of only their own children, those who had migrated as single women support extended kin prior to marriage. Of thirteen migrant workers who at one point had been single women in Los Angeles, five sent at least three or more nieces and nephews to college. Others have also provided valuable financial support to their families. Besides subsidizing the everyday living expenses of elderly parents, some purchased a house where their parents and siblings, including those with children, now live, and sent at least one younger relative to college.

Of eighteen women without children in Rome, five had houses built for their families and still subsidize the day-to-day living expenses of their parents. Others send monthly remittances, anywhere between US\$67 to \$333, with those who send less sharing the responsibility with siblings also working outside the Philippines. Finally, most of them have covered the educational costs of the younger generation in their families. Most feel a strong moral obligation to provide support to their families. As Gloria Diaz told me, "When I don't send money, I feel guilty because my mother is alone, and it is my obligation to help."

As a consequence of their financial contributions, many migrant Filipina domestic workers claim that they have not been able to accumulate a sizable amount of savings. Ruth Mercado, for example, supports her parents and her brother's family in the Philippines with the remittances she sends every month:

I have not been able to save any money at this point (after seven years in Rome). Even though I am the youngest (of four children), I am the breadwinner of my family. I send them [US\$333] every month. Life is hard when you are single. My sisters are married, and so my parents do not expect as much from them. My brother lives with my parents, and he does not have a job, but has a lot of children. . . . So, I support his family. . . . At least I am able to help my family. Let's say I continued my career as a policewoman [in the Philippines], my salary would have just been enough for myself. Even though my life is physically demanding and I am far apart from my family, it's OK because I am able to help them.

In acknowledgment of their extensive support, younger members of their extended family often consider women like Ruth to be second mothers. Nieces and nephews refer to them as "Mama" or "Nanay" (Mom) as opposed to just the customary "Tita" (Aunt). For domestic workers, their financial assistance to the family gives them the most tangible reward for their labor. At the same time, their generosity guarantees them a well-established kinship base if they choose to return to the Philippines. This is premised on the cultural value of *utang na loob*, literally meaning debt of the soul, in which favors are returned with lifelong debt.

Cooperating to send younger members of the extended family to college also operates on the system of "generalized family exchange" among kin (Peterson, 1993). In such a system, the success of one member of the family translates to the success of the family as a collective unit. Peterson defines this family exchange system as an open reciprocal exchange: "Generalized exchanges are those in which A gives to B, B gives to C, C gives to a D, and D gives to an A" (1993: 572). By sending one or more persons to college, domestic workers assume that those they send to school will reciprocate by later supporting the education of their younger siblings and relatives. These younger relatives are then culturally expected to provide care and support for the domestic worker once she chooses to return and retire in the Philippines. Valentina Diamante's migration is embedded in this family exchange system. Valentina managed to relocate to Rome only with the help of her older sister, and in exchange she is expected to provide greater support to their family in the Philippines than the sister who covered the cost of her migration.

The high level of interdependency among extended families is also reflected in the reliance of migrant parents on grandparents, aunts, and other relatives for the care of dependents left in the Philippines. In the Philippines, it is not uncommon for families to take in extended family members whose own immediate families may not be able to provide as much material or emotional security. Fosterage of children is in fact a common practice among extended kin in the Philippines (Peterson, 1993). For example, Cecilia Impelido, a street vendor in Rome, was raised by her grandmother for fourteen years. The arrangement, she claims, strengthened kinship ties to her maternal grandmother in the province, as it eased the financial costs of reproduction for her parents in Manila. As shown by the dispersal of Judy Reyes's children to various households, transnational families are embedded in the cultural practice of fosterage.

Parents outside of the Philippines rely on other relatives to act as their children's "guardians." In exchange, remittances sent by parents to dependents in the Philippines benefit other members of the family. Jennifer Jeremillo's remittances to her children in the Philippines extend to benefit her elderly parents: "Right now, I send [US$333]. I have to pay for the domestic helper, and then I have a regular allowance for my kids, and then the rest is for my mother. I always send that amount, and that's about 8,000 pesos [US$320];

5000 [US$200] is for my parents. My parents are using the money to renovate and expand the house."

Transnational households strengthen extended family kinship, with children (and also elderly parents) acting as the enduring bond of interdependency. Migrants rely on extended kin to care for their dependents, whereas extended kin raise their standard of living with the financial support that migrant workers provide. The extended family bolsters options for individuals otherwise bound by duties and responsibilities to dependents in the Philippines. Thus, transnational households rely on the resilience of extended family bonds. The persisting cultural value of familism assists with the formation of transnational households as much as the structural forces of globalization propel it.

WHEN CHILDREN MIGRATE

In *Families Apart*, the geographer Geraldine Pratt (2012) depicts the reunification of mothers and children in Canadian-Filipino transnational families as one of profound distress. Children suffer when migrating to follow their stranger mother. Their isolation aggravates the cultural challenges of integration, as migrant mothers in Canada work long hours while their recently arrived children struggle in school and long to reunite with family and friends in the Philippines. In Rome, I likewise saw children struggle, sharing the same dilemmas as their counterparts in Canada, but I also saw them thrive. There I found three groups of reunited children: those who migrated as adolescents, those who migrated as teenagers, and those who followed as adults. Their degree of integration largely depended on what point in their lives they migrated. Those who came as adolescents were more likely to attend university or technical school and hold semiprofessional or professional jobs in Italy; those migrating as teenagers became proficient in Italian, gaining access to retail or restaurant jobs; and those who arrived in Italy as adults were likely to face language difficulties and follow their mothers into domestic work. The number of school-age children who followed their parents was relatively small. An elected city councilman in Rome informed me that there are approximately 16,000 Filipino youth enrolled in school in Rome.

According to prominent members of the community, including religious clergy and migrant advocates, most children join their migrant parents as teenagers. They note that rarely do children grow up in Italy from adolescence, as the absence of child care options usually deters parents from raising young children in proximity. Yet, there is a benefit to raising children in Rome, as they are more likely eventually to have access to higher-status employment. However, there are limits in their mobility. Reflecting not only the relatively small number of adolescents raised in Italy but also the racial barriers that Filipinos still confront, the second generation largely remains underrepresented in university. For this reason, rarely has the second generation been able to have access to professional jobs.

One thing that deters the second generation from pursuing higher education is the migration system. Once migrant children turn eighteen years old, they can no longer stay in Italy as their parents' dependents. Those born in Italy, who also grew up and went to school there, can apply for citizenship, but those born to undocumented mothers as well as those who had not been continuously enrolled in Italy's educational system do not qualify. On turning eighteen years old, children must either apply for citizenship or, if unqualified, attain their own residency card, which grants more preferable terms to workers than to students. One thing that encourages the second generation to enter the workforce instead of going to college is the fact that students get a permit to stay for only six to nine months, which is significantly shorter than the two-year residency permit granted to those employed as domestic workers. Although the law inadvertently pushes the second generation to seek low-wage jobs, particularly domestic work, some do attain higher-level employment, but at most become only retail managers, hotel supervisors, or office workers. Yet, despite the glass ceiling, the second generation still see their situation as an improvement from that of their parent's generation, who, according to Myra Mirando, who migrated to Italy at the age of sixteen, have accepted the limits in their mobility: "It is as if our parents surrendered. It is as if they have accepted that they will just be at a certain place, that they can't go any higher than that."

Children are also deterred from pursuing an education by the racism they confront in school. According to Myra, it is not unheard of for Italian students to bully Filipinos in school, especially the newcomers with language difficulties. Perhaps it is for this reason that one often sees groups of Filipino youth hanging around the central train station of Termini during school hours.

One afternoon, one of them sat next to me while I waited for potential interviewees near a McDonald's in the basement of the central train station. Assuming he was in high school, I asked why he was not in school. He told me that
he had cut class that day to avoid being bullied. He explained that there were
only two other Filipino students in his school, and they were his only friends.
Unfortunately, both were absent that day, so he decided to cut class because
being in school without them was "unbearable," in his words.

I did not catch this young man's name, but I recall how his spiked hair reminded me of the hairdos prominent in the 1980s among various pop groups
including Echo and the Bunnymen. He was quite soft spoken. I learned that
he had been what the community refers to as a "packaged child"; he was born
in Italy and then sent back to the Philippines as an infant. According to staff
members of the Philippine Embassy in Rome, an average of two to three in-
fants are sent home to the Philippines every month. The young man I met
returned to Italy at the age of fifteen years old and found himself having to
repeat a grade due to his poor language skills. He admitted that his Italian is
not stellar, so much so that he often did not fully understand the taunts he
received at school. In response to my question of whether he planned to go to
college, this young man, who is now sixteen, told me that he planned to start
working as soon as he finished high school, explaining, "Any job would do, as
I long as I am able to help my parents out financially."

Children who follow their parents as adults or near-adults are often funneled into low-wage jobs. According to Donna Mercado, a bank teller who
had migrated at the young age of ten, "Those who run after family reunification are the ones with greater problems. They face difficulty adjusting to the
language and they have a harder time adjusting to their parents." Near-adult
migrants are those who migrate at seventeen years old, during their last year of
eligibility for family reunification. Although they enter legally as a dependent
of a *carta di soggiorno* or *permesso di soggiorno* holder, these migrants have to
obtain their own residency permit—independent of their parents—after they
turn eighteen years old. Language difficulties deter them from pursuing higher
education, and they almost always end up doing low-wage work.

Luis Flores, who works as a domestic worker in tandem with his wife in
the outskirts of Rome, followed his mother to Italy after he had dropped out
of engineering school at the age of twenty-one. He had, ironically, left behind

two children when he migrated. When I asked why he was not raising his children in Italy, he responded:

What we have seen is that if children are born or raised here, they stop going to school and instead start working when they reach eighteen years old. . . . We want our children to go to college. We do not want them to end up like us, working as domestic workers. We do not care how much they end up earning, if they do not earn enough to support us, as long as they do not end up as domestic workers.

Indeed, many children are reluctant to follow their parents to Rome because they are aware that they would have to give up school once they get to Italy. Jennifer Salaveria was one such reluctant migrant when she followed her parents there at the age of sixteen. She had no intention of migrating to Italy but instead wanted to attend college in the Philippines. Her parents had convinced her to go by telling her she was going to Italy only on vacation. Once there, she learned that they had actually planned for her to stay with them permanently. Though still somewhat bitter about her parent's decision, Jennifer values the labor-market opportunities she has had in Italy. She works not as a domestic worker but as a retail clerk in a fashionable leather goods store in the center of Rome. Her language skills are impeccable, but they did not come easily— she had to attend two years of night classes for five days a week from 4 pm to 8:30 pm while working for seven hours as a nanny during the day.

Interestingly, many of the second generation I met in Rome can be described as reluctant migrants. Many had not been eager to join their parents in Italy and, like Jennifer, were tricked into going. Donna, the young woman who migrated at age ten, still teases her parents about her "vacation" in Italy, often commenting on how long it has been. According to Donna and her peers, parents tell their children that they will be going to Italy only on vacation so as to avoid conflict, because they know that their children often do not want to lose the close ties they had cultivated with family and friends in the Philippines.

The family is not always a source of immediate support for the second generation. According to them, distance can hurt the development of affinity. As Myra describes, "Even if you completed a bond because they came home frequently, called often, there was still a lack. There is something missing. It is not until after one year, or two years, that you feel comfortable enough to chat and joke around with them. . . . I know it is worse for others, those who do not see their parents for nearly ten years." Reuniting with her parents also did not come without conflict for Donna, who resented them for the isolation she experienced after migrating to Italy: "It was difficult at first because in the Philippines I was able to easily go out, visit my neighbors, and play. Here, there was nothing. You go out only to find work. Otherwise, you are just at home."

Despite the struggles of reunification, many children come to appreciate the economic rewards of migration. Many also find resolution after their initial conflict with their parents, eventually learning to appreciate the value that their parents have placed on familial proximity when they forced their migration to Italy. Lastly, they learn to see the formation of the transnational family not as their parents' fault but as a reality imposed by structural forces, including barriers to higher education, racism in the classroom, the absence of public child care support, and their parents' low wages. They come to understand the maintenance of transnational families, and the challenges of reunification, as a struggle they share with their migrant parents.

In 1994, Linda Basch and her colleagues predicted that transnational families will "continue as an arena of social relations" and will remain an intergenerational part of migrant communities as long as migrants face structural barriers to their integration (1994: 242–43). Indeed, this is true. Twenty years after my initial field work in Rome and Los Angeles, I find that migrant domestic workers still form transnational families. Many of their children eventually migrate but often as semiprofessionals or professionals to other destinations in the diaspora, including Singapore, the United Arab Emirates, Saudi Arabia, Canada, and the United States. The continued migration of the children of migrant workers tells us that transnational families often cannot discontinue or decrease their dependence on foreign earnings across generations. Because migrant parents invest most of their earnings in the family's day-to-day expenses, they are unable to invest in income-generating resources (small businesses, for example). Without a sufficient means of productive labor in the Philippines, migrant parents prolong their tenure abroad. The cycle continues across generations, as the earnings of the now-adult children with college degrees cannot cover the costs of reproducing their own families. With forces beyond the control of the individual migrant, the economic insecurities resulting from globalization in the Philippine economy continue to generate transnational families.

The stories that I have featured here illustrate that transnational families represent creative responses to and adaptive strategies against the economic displacement of workers in developing countries. Yet the various forms of transnational households that I have illustrated not only reveal the agency and resistance of migrants against structural forces in society, but they also point to an emotional dislocation that migrants experience. Transnational families are agonizing for both parents and children. To some extent, geographical distance unavoidably engenders emotional distance and strain among members of transnational families. Separation inflicts emotional injuries that family members must cope with in their everyday lives. This is a particular dislocation that should be acknowledged as part and parcel of the migrant experience of domestic workers, and one that I will address more systematically in the next chapter.

CHAPTER FOUR

GENDER AND INTERGENERATIONAL RELATIONS

C HANGES IN HOUSEHOLD STRUCTURE HAVE
a significant impact on the personal lives of migrant work-
ers as well as on those of the relatives they have left behind in the Philippines.
Mothering from a distance has painful emotional ramifications. The pain of
family separation creates various feelings, including helplessness, regret, and
guilt for mothers, whereas children can experience loneliness, vulnerability, and
insecurity. The emotions expressed in the stories we have already read beg to be
understood systematically. As Hochschild (1983) has shown, emotions do not
exist in a vacuum. Instead, they operate within the context of social structures:
"Emotion is a sense that tells about the self-relevance of reality. We infer from
it what we must have wanted or expected or how we must have been perceiv-
ing the world. Emotion is one way to discover a buried perspective on matters"
(Hochschild, 1983: 85). Regulated by "feeling rules," emotions are determined
by ideologies, and in the Filipino family, as in many other families, the ideology of woman as nurturer is a central determinant of the emotional needs

and expectations of its members (Medina, 1991). If that is the case, then how do gendered ideologies of mothering influence parents and children's feelings about separation? To answer this question I analyze the social reproduction of families, emphasizing how mothers and fathers confront different parenting expectations. I address the emotional difficulties mothers and children confront in transnational households and examine how mothers negotiate the pain of family separation. Ultimately, I argue that socialized gender norms aggravate the emotional strains of transnational family life.

TRANSNATIONAL FAMILY REPRODUCTION

There are three main forms of care expected to ensure the reproduction of the family: moral care, meaning the provision of discipline and socialization to ensure that dependents are raised to be "good," moral citizens of society; emotional care, which involves providing emotional security through the expression of concern and feelings of warmth and affection; and material care, which provides for the physical needs of dependents, including food, clothing, and education or skills training to guarantee that they become producers for the family. Expectations of moral, emotional, or material care vary considerably in different societies and cultures. In the Philippines, the family provides for the material, emotional, and moral needs of its members, with limited intervention from the state.[1] Moral expectations are greatly influenced by the values and virtues of Catholicism (honesty, faith, and purity, for example) and a high regard for filial piety—respect for parents and elders in the community. Relations in the family are based on the cultural construct of *utang na loob* (debt of the soul), and, because the gift of life is irreplaceable, children are born with an irreplaceable debt and burden of gratitude to their parents.

Ideological norms, particularly gender ideology, and the location of families in the political economy undeniably determine a parent's ability to meet these care expectations. Can parents in transnational households provide all three basic forms of care? They may be able to do so with the support of extended kin who could, for example, assure the provision of moral care when one or both parents are abroad. In a survey and study of the effects of parental absence on Filipino migrant workers' children, Victoria Paz Cruz of the Scalabrini Migrant Center found that "the great majority of the students in the sample (92.4%) have no special problem which has come to the attention of the guidance counselor or other school official(s)" (1987: 22).[2] In a survey of "solo-parents" and guardians, Paz Cruz also found that children tend to get along better with their siblings, still respect their parents and guardians, continue to practice their religion, and show no health problems (meaning no drastic change in energy level, weight, or appetite). Certainly the continued respect for elders and religious devotion among children indicates that extended kin instill strong moral values and traditions in transnational households.

In contrast, one can easily imagine that the provision of basic emotional care in the family is somewhat inadequate, considering that the emotional support provided by other relatives may not completely replace that of parents. This was demonstrated by the needs of Ruby Mercado's children, as she explained to me:

When I saw my children, I thought, "Oh, children do grow up even without their mother." I left my youngest when she was only five years old. She was already nine when I saw her again, but she still wanted for me to carry her. [Weeps.] That hurt me because it showed me that my children missed out [on] a lot. They did not get enough loving from their parents, the loving they needed as they were growing up.

This example suggests that, although parenting can be transferred to other relatives (Stack and Burton, 1994), the emotional care they provide might not be completely interchangeable with that of a parent. However, the absence of health and psychological problems among children does suggest that emotional care is also subsidized by the tremendous resource of extended kin who act as fictive mothers and fathers. Finally, with the third form of care, the increased income of transnational laborers surely provides families a greater amount of material security.

In general, it is very difficult to imagine a family whose members reside across vast geographical distances. Standard conceptions of the family associate it with proximity. For this reason, transnational households are considered "abnormal," perceived as "broken homes," and thereby viewed as a tragedy in Philippine society (Parreñas, 2005). The question, then, is why this is the case, considering that traditional family values, particularly the collectivism instilled by *pakikisama*, are a foundational backbone for the formation of such families. To address this question, I present the perspectives of both mothers and children, highlighting the underlying gender ideologies that determine and control their feelings and emotions. I show that migrant Filipina domestic workers in the diaspora are reconstituting what it means to "mother" (Hondagneu-Sotelo and Avila, 1997), but traditional ideologies of family life are making this shift difficult to accept.

THE PAIN OF TRANSNATIONAL PARENTING

When the girl that I take care of calls her mother "Mama," my heart jumps all the time because my children also call me "Mama." I feel the gap caused by our physical separation especially in the morning, when I pack [her] lunch, because that's what I used to do for my children. . . . I used to do that very same thing for them. I begin thinking that at this hour I should be taking care of my very own children and not someone else's, someone who is not related to me in any way, shape, or form. Don't we think about that often? Oh, you don't, but we—the Filipino women over here— feel that all the time. The work that I do here is done for my family, but the problem is they are not close to me but are far away in the Philippines. Sometimes, you feel the separation, and you start to cry. Some days, I just start crying while I am sweeping the floor because I am thinking about my children in the Philippines. Sometimes, when I receive a letter from my children telling me that they are sick, I look up out the window and ask the Lord to look after them and make sure they get better even without me around to care after them. [Starts crying.] *If I had wings, I would fly home to my children. Just for a moment, to see my children and take care of their needs, help them, then fly back over here to continue my work.* (Rosemarie Samaniego, widow, Rome; my emphasis)

Migrant Filipina domestic workers like Rosemarie Samaniego are overwhelmed by feelings of helplessness. They are trapped in the painful contradiction of feeling "the gap caused by physical separation" and having to give in to the family's dependence on the money this distance provides. Although they may long to return to the Philippines to be with their children, they cannot because their family depends on their earnings.

Domestic work is both a "labor of love" and a "labor of sorrow," to borrow the words of historian Jacqueline Jones (1985). Often saying that their sole motivating force for seeking domestic work is their love for their children (while ironically being away from these same children), migrant mothers seek every opportunity to maximize their earnings to send more money to dependents in the Philippines. Describing her situation, Clarita Sungkay—who sends her children at least US$500 every month—stated:

My husband has a new family of his own. He has two children, I think. I actually went to their house when I found out that he had sold our house. There I found my two daughters working for them as babysitters. He was basically abusing my children. I cried. I felt terrible, but what could I do? I wasn't going to try to kill myself again because if I did that, then nothing would happen to my family. . . . Now my two daughters live in their own apartment, which I pay for every month. Seeing them made me decide that I could not stop. If I stopped, yes, we would be together, but we would have nothing. We wouldn't have a steady income, and life [would] be very hard. We could be together in the Philippines, but we would not have any money. At least they now have families of their own. The youngest is the only one not married, but if we were together, what could we live off? They tell me that they want us to finally be together, but it's hard.

Like many other Filipina domestic workers, Clarita has worked outside the Philippines for most of her children's adolescence. In this case, domestic service becomes a "labor of sorrow" that requires migrant women to repress their longing to reunite the family because of economic instabilities in the Philippines.

Transnational parenting also involves overwhelming feelings of loss. Because they missed their children's childhood, many mothers are remorseful and admit to lost intimacy in the transnational family. In general, they feel a surreal timelessness during family separation until they are suddenly catapulted back to reality the moment they reunite with their children. As Ermie Contado, a widow in Rome, recounted:

When I came home, my daughters were teenagers already. [Starts crying.] When I saw my family, I dropped my bag and asked who were my daughters. I did not know who they were, but they just kept on screaming "Inay, Inay!" [Mom, Mom!] I asked them who was which, and they said, "I'm Sally" and "I'm Sandra." We were crying. I did not know who was which. Imagine! But they were so small when I left, and there they were as teenagers. [Weeps.] They kept on saying "Inay, Inay!"

Maintaining transnational households is quite agonizing for migrant parents. For them, missing their children's adolescence is an insurmountable loss, which sadly turns into a deep-seated regret over the emotional distance it has caused the family. As Ana Vengco, a single mother working in Rome for almost three years, explained, the small pleasures and familiarities a parent gets from watching her children grow up are irreplaceable: "I really, really miss my daughter. I really regret not being able to see my daughter grow up, learn her hang-ups, how she learned to brush her teeth, walk. . . . I left my daughter when she was not even one year old, and now she is already three years old." In transnational households, the absence of daily interactions denies familiarity and becomes an irreparable gap defining parent–child relations.

Transnational parenting also entails loneliness over the denial of intimacy. Migrant mothers often battle with the grief imposed by constant reminders of their children and the emotional distance engendered by unfamiliarity. Gelli Padit, a married migrant worker in Rome, felt this viscerally. As she explained, "Whenever I receive a letter and I hear that one of my children is sick, oh, but I can't function for a week, and it's like I am also the one who is sick. That's how I feel whenever I hear news that my children are sick. My employer even predicts when I receive a letter that by the next day I will be sick. It's true, and my employer knows it."

When I spoke with Analin Mahusay, also in Rome, she was just beginning to experience life without her children, who did not understand their mother's absence:

My kids are still very young, so they still don't know about my life here. . . . They often ask my husband where I am and wonder why they have not seen me yet, especially the youngest child of mine, the one who was born here. What I really want is to be able to get papers, because I really want to see my children. . . . I always think about my children. I always worry about not sending them enough money. . . . Sometimes when I look at the children that I care for, I feel like crying. I always think about how if we did not need the money, we would all be together, and I would be raising my children myself. . . . That's what is really hard about life here, being away from one's own family. Without your family, you are just so much more vulnerable.

As we see repeatedly, family separation aggravates the hardships of migrant life, highlighting the helplessness parents already feel because of the material constraints that force them to live apart from their children.

The pain of family separation is further intensified by caregiving tasks in domestic work. Taking care of children becomes very difficult when, in the process of doing so, one cannot take care of one's own. This contradiction accentuates the pain of family separation and consequently results in an aversion to this job. As Ruby Mercado stated, "Domestic work is depressing. . . . You especially miss your children. I do not like taking care of other children when I could not take care of my own. It hurts too much." Yet others, including Trinidad Borromeo, find themselves resolving this tension by "pouring [their] love" into their wards. As she explained, "When I take care of an elderly, I treat her like she is my own mother." In doing so, they are able to feel less guilty for leaving their families behind in the Philippines.

With feelings of loss and loneliness defining their day-to-day migrant experience, how do mothers strategically negotiate the pain of family separation? I found that they do so in three key ways: through the commodification of love, the repression of emotional strains, and the rationalization of distance.[3] They do this either by justifying that the material gains far outweigh the emotional costs to the family or by reasoning that physical distance is a manageable challenge that can be eased by regular communication. In general, individual women use all three coping mechanisms, although not always consciously. For the most part, mothers justify their decision to leave children in the Philippines by highlighting the family's markedly visible material gains. Vicky Diaz and Lolita Magsino repeatedly did this during our interviews. Mothers also struggle to maintain a semblance of family life by rationalizing distance; Judy Reyes and Luisa Balila phone their children in the Philippines regularly. More recently, families have been able to interact daily with the advancement of technology (Madianou and Miller, 2012). They communicate via text messages, Skype, Facebook, and Internet voice calls, allowing the cultivation of close relations and familiarity across distance. Although a few women deny the emotional strains of transnational family life, most cannot.

How does one show and give love across vast geographical distances? In the field, I often heard women say, "I buy everything that my children need," or "I give them everything they want." They knowingly, or unknowingly, have the urge to overcompensate for their absence with material goods, as Ruby Mercado revealed:

All the things that my children needed I gave to them and even more, because I know that I have not fulfilled my motherly duties completely. Because we [have been] apart [for twelve years], there have been needs that I have not met. I try to hide that gap by giving them all the material things that they desire and want. I feel guilty because as a mother I have not been able to care for their daily needs. So, because I am lacking in giving them maternal love, I fill that gap with many material goods. I buy them clothes, shoes; when they say they want a computer, I tell them to go ahead and buy one. They don't demand too much but often just ask for things that they may need.

Unable to provide their children with daily acts of care, transnational mothers such as Ruby tend to rely on commodities to establish concrete ties of familial dependency.

Although transnational mothers have regrets over separation, they withstand this hardship by thinking about the financial gains they have achieved in migration. As Incarnacion Molina, in Rome, admitted, "I have been lonely here. I have thought about the Philippines while I am scrubbing and mopping that floor. You cannot help but ask yourself, what are you doing here scrubbing and being apart from your family? Then, you think about the money and know that you have no choice but to be here." Working abroad guarantees mothers such as Incarnacion the financial resources they need to ensure that their children eat daily meals of meat and rice instead of "dried fish" or "fried stale bread with sugar," attend college, and reside in their own home as opposed to a relative's.

Though many migrant laborers outside the Philippines had attended some years of postsecondary schooling, they were not able to achieve a secure middle-class lifestyle in the Philippines. So why do they bother to invest in their children's college education? Why not just have them work outside the country? Migrant parents see the education of their children as a marker of status and security. Clearly, education is a central motivating factor for migration. As one domestic worker states, "*The intelligence of my children would be wasted if they don't attain a college degree*; that's why I made up my mind and I prayed a lot *that I [might] have a chance to go abroad for the sake of my children's education*" (Acgaoili, 1995: 14; italicized words translated from Tagalog to English). Parents believe that the more educated children are in their family, the greater the family's resources and the less its members will depend on each other, which means that there would be less of a need for one to seek the higher wages of domestic work outside the Philippines to support other members of the family.

By operating under this mind-set, parents can rationalize the need to sacrifice intimate familial bonds for the collective family's material well-being, but at the expense of having to do a great deal of emotional work. Yet, instead of paying children for their emotional debt with more time together, they purchase love with American or Italian designer clothing and school supplies. Parents weigh the pros and cons of transnational parenting and systematically conclude that the material benefits of their earnings compensate for the emotional toll separation inflicts. Maya Areza, for instance, underscores the mobility that a transnational family arrangement garners her children:

My children understand our situation. Before, they could not understand life, what was going on, but now they understand why I was here and there. They know it was for financial reasons. [Starts crying.] They were studying, but you know . . . the guidance of the mother is different from the guidance of the aunties. They missed out in a way not having parents around. I suffered, but to me it was more important that they did not suffer the way I did. I did not want them to do the work that I had to do because I had only a high school education. I don't want them to live not being able to have what they want because the financial situation is not enough. (Maya Areza, separated, Los Angeles)

Besides highlighting the material gains that they have achieved by sacrificing family intimacy, migrant mothers also cope with the pain of family separation by repressing their emotions and rationalizing distance. This came through in Joy Manlapit's explanation of why she decided to migrate to Los Angeles for work:

After I had four children, I was teaching. But the money that I made as [a] teacher was not enough. Number one, there the children need education, clothing, and food. My salary was really not enough. That is why I decided to come here. . . . I used to send my children $1,000 a month, but I stopped sending money when they all graduated from college three years ago. Now I send them $500 once in a while, and they divide that among themselves. . . . You ask yourself why you left your children, and then you think about their future so that you can be strong [that is, to withstand the geographical distance]. So, I have regrets but no regrets. . . . You [ask yourself] why you left them, but then you think that if you did not leave them, they would not have a future. My only real regret is leaving the youngest when she was still young.

Many women spoke in a detached manner when directly asked about their thoughts and feelings over family separation. They avoided confronting their feelings, consciously underplayed the gaps caused by prolonged separation, and through it all emphasized the material gains that the family now enjoys. Furthermore, many, like Mimi Baclayon in Los Angeles, noted that they can communicate from a distance:

It is just like shutting one part of yourself and going to another place in your life, which is just temporary anyway. [Pauses.] If you think about it, you have more to gain. You have much to lose but so much more to gain. . . . You are here for only a short time, and at least you can communicate. There are letters, and I make long distance calls every week.

When I asked Mila Tizon, also in Los Angeles, if she missed her children, she responded, "Of course." She paused, and then added, "It is hard, but when you think about how much you are earning, you forget the loneliness. You can also call them on the phone." Similarly, Tessie Mandin in Rome, explained,

I miss my children of course but I am tranquil because I know that I am doing what God has set out for me to do. So, I know that God is extending his love to them. I have the assurance that how God takes care of me, he takes even more care of my children. . . . We usually call my children monthly. Then, we call them on their birthdays. We also communicate by letter. They do the same.

Despite their tendency to downplay the emotional tensions of transnational family life, migrant mothers cannot deny the loss of intimacy in migration.

Migrant mothers try to convey love, affection, and care from a distance. They create "bridges" that compress the space that plagues their family relationships. As a writer in *Tinig Filipino* states, "If our relationship with our loved-ones is on the stage of collapse, let's try our best to save it. If it is still possible. Let's try to construct a bridge for others to reach us—a bridge which is not a structure made of steel or concrete, but one whose foundation has its maximum strength where no storm or any other natural calamities nor human forces could destroy" (Balangatan, 1994: 10). Viewing physical separation as just one of the many challenges of contemporary family life, parents compress time and space and alleviate the physical distance in the transnational family by phoning or writing letters and more recently via texting and using the Internet (Hondagneu-Sotelo and Avila, 1997). In the process, they keep abreast of their children's activities and at the same time achieve a certain level of familiarity in the family. As Patricia Baclayon in Los Angeles commented, "There is nothing wrong with our relationship. I pay a lot for the phone bill. Last month, I paid $170, and that's two days of wages. They write too. Last week, I received four letters."

Regardless of whether they successfully rationalize the geographical distance that characterizes their family life, why do some mothers repress the feelings of pain invoked in separation? Why do some downplay the emotional distance in the transnational family? Considering that larger structural forces of globalization constrain their ability to reunite the family, they sometimes cannot afford to confront their feelings. In other words, the structural constraints that limit their options for raising their children do not allow them to confront the emotional distance that plagues their intergenerational relationships. As Dorothy Espiritu—a domestic worker in Los Angeles who left her now-adult children at the ages of nine to eighteen—explains, lingering over the painful sacrifice of separation only intensifies the emotional hardships of transnational family life:

> RP: Has it been difficult not seeing your children for twelve years?
> DE: If you say it is hard, it is hard. You could easily be overwhelmed by the loneliness you feel as a mother, but then you have to have the foresight to overcome that. Without the foresight for the future of your children, then you have a harder time. If I had not had the foresight, my children would not be as secure as they are now. They would not have had a chance. [Pauses.] What I did was I put the loneliness aside. I put everything aside. I put the sacrifice aside. Everything. Now, I am happy that all of them have completed college.

Many parents are like Dorothy; they can tolerate their family's geographical distance only by consciously, but more often unconsciously, repressing its emotional costs.

Emphasizing one's own suffering also helps parents cope with transnational parenting; this was the case for Joy Manlapit in Los Angeles:

> RP: Is it difficult not seeing your children for a long time [ten years]?
> JM: It is hard on my heart to be away from my family. At first I could never resolve being apart from my children, but my friend told me that they are

older now. They have all finished college, so that's it. . . . They got married. They got married—the second and third got married before they finished college. That was another burden. You have to make them finish school, then you have to make their spouses finish. Yeah, you have grandchildren, and you have to support them too. Because you are here, they think that you have a lot of money. Because they think of how much you earn and calculate it in pesos. They do not realize that you eat, sleep, and do everything in dollars as well. That is where they are wrong. They write and ask for money. You are angry, but then you are also concerned. You get mad because when they write they don't say, "Mama, thanks for everything." Instead, they say, "Mom, this is what else I need." [Laughs sarcastically.] I need this, I need that. They don't bother asking you how you are, how you make a living, what you have to do to send them that money. Nothing.

Once while attending a standard Sunday mass in Rome—paying only half-hearted attention to the ceremony that I already knew by heart thanks to my Catholic upbringing—I was suddenly caught off guard. It happened during the Responsorial Psalms, the part in which churchgoers pray collectively with the response, "Lord hear our prayers," when the woman deacon stated, "So that our families we have left in the Philippines understand our hardships and that they learn to be frugal." What struck me about this blessing was not its confirmation of the presence of transnational households in the community but its illumination of the migrant worker's perspective on the issue of family separation. It clearly centered on material benefits and the hardships that they personally undergo. Instead of praying for the safety and emotional security of family members, especially young children who were far from them, migrant workers worry that their families in the Philippines are neither spending their hard-earned money wisely nor appreciating the sacrifices that they have made for the sake of the family.

Although most of my interviewees do recognize the difficulties children might experience and the need to consciously weigh that against the material gains of transnational family life, some completely deny the emotional costs of separation. Not surprisingly, this was demonstrated primarily by parents whose children were located in both the Philippines and abroad and who preferred not to discuss intergenerational relationships. For example, after providing rich and descriptive anecdotes about her experiences migrating to and working in Rome, Incarnacion Molina—who at the time of our interview had a newborn son in Italy and twelve- and fifteen-year-old daughters in the Philippines—transformed completely. She became evasive when I asked her about her relationship with the daughters she has not seen for more than five years:

RP: Do they know that you have another child here?

IM: In a letter, I told them that I was pregnant. [Pauses.]

RP: Did they respond?

IM: Yes. They said that what is done is done, so what could they do about it. [Pauses.]

RP: Are they jealous?

IM: Of course they are. They can't help but know that my devotion will be divided. [Pauses.]

RP: Are they upset?

IM: Probably.

RP: Do you want your children to come over here?

IM: Maybe.

Incarnacion's short responses and long pauses reflect her discomfort. Disconcerted by the jealousy engendered by the birth of her son, Incarnacion admitted that she could not "afford to think about it" when questioned about her feelings concerning her two sets of children. She then became very guarded for the rest of the interview, avoiding my questions about the effects of separation on her daughters and redirecting our discussion to the US$600 she sends them every month.

Similarly, Jovita Gacutan—a domestic worker in Los Angeles with children in both the United States and the Philippines—would rather not have discussed her relationship with the youngest child she left in the Philippines:

RP: How old was your youngest child when you left the Philippines?

JG: Thirteen years old. It was very hard leaving him.

RP: How is your relationship?

JG: I have been back four times.

RP: Do you think he has some resentment?

JG: I don't think so.

RP: Do you think it is hard for him?

JG: Ummm. . . .

RP: Do you talk about it?

JG: That is why I want to go back home.

RP: What does he tell you?

JG: Nothing really.

RP: Do you feel less close to him than your older children?

JG: No, no! I have been home four times, and I would stay there for two to three months.

RP: Do you plan to petition him to the United States?

JG: No, I cannot. He is too old. He has to be younger than eighteen. I have not applied for citizenship yet.

RP: What are your plans?

JG: I have no plans right now. I really don't know.

Aside from giving vague responses, Jovita became agitated when probed about her son. Moreover, she denied even the slightest possibility of an emotional rift developing in her family. Like Incarnacion, Jovita struggled to rationalize her relationship with her youngest son in the Philippines, which cannot be placed outside the context of the different dynamics she has with the children who live with her. For Incarnacion and Jovita, the different relationships that they have developed and maintained with their two sets of children are inexplicable. It is a source of tension they are unable to confront.

Although the majority of the mothers in my study have left young children in the Philippines, three women in Los Angeles stand out for waiting to migrate until their children were much older. As parents, they believed that the emotional gaps caused by separation would have been too great a risk to impose on the family. Libertad Sobredo in Los Angeles explained:

In the early 1980s, my sister had already invited me to join her in the United States. My children were still young then, and I told my sister that I could not afford to leave them. I could not turn my back on my children. Money can be earned anywhere, but if your children grow up undisciplined and neglected, they might grow up to be good, but they might also grow up to be bad. If that happens, then that would be your fault as a parent. *Taking care of children is primarily the mother's role. The father is the person who is supposed to leave and make a living. He comes home only at night, but mothers are needed to always be there for their children.* . . . It came time [when] my children were older. I figured my youngest was twenty years old. My small business could be managed by my children and husband on their own. I thought it was the right time for me to come here. [My emphasis.]

Significantly, gendered expectations around motherhood caused a small number of women in my study to delay migration, which in turn underscores the fact that most women had *not* felt constrained by gender norms in the Philippines. Instead, most women made a conscious decision to escape them.

From the commodification of love to the "technological" management of distance, mothers find ways to justify family separation and obscure the emotional costs of transnational parenting. Although they ease the spatial barriers imposed on intimacy with communication, most parents do admit that technology cannot replace the familial intimacy that only a great investment in daily interactions can provide.

THE PAIN OF GROWING UP IN TRANSNATIONAL FAMILIES

Regardless of household structure, whether it is nuclear, single parent, or transnational, intergenerational conflicts frequently arise in the family. In the case of transnational households, the children left behind in the Philippines, I found, are racked with loneliness, insecurity, and vulnerability.[4] They also crave greater intimacy with their migrant parents, as children participating in Paz Cruz's survey expressed in the following statements: "I want them to share with us in our daily life, and I want our family to be complete"; "We can share our laughters and tears"; and "I miss him/her a lot" (1987: 43).

Three central conflicts plague intergenerational relationships in transnational families. First, children tend to disagree with their mothers that commodities are sufficient markers of love. Second, they do not believe that their mothers recognize the sacrifices that they as children have made toward the successful maintenance of their families. Finally, while they appreciate the efforts of migrant mothers to create "bridges" of affection and care, they still question the extent of these efforts. They particularly question mothers about their sporadic visits to the Philippines. As I noted, most of the documented migrants I interviewed returned to the Philippines infrequently, about once every four years.

Children recognize the material gains separation provides. Paz Cruz's survey indicates that about 60 percent of the children do not want their parents to stop working abroad. However, in contrast to their mothers, they are less convinced that the material security that their families have achieved has alleviated the emotional costs of separation.[5] Claribelle Ignacio, a thirty-six-year-old domestic worker in Rome, had been raised in a transnational family by a migrant mother in the United States. Too old to qualify for family reunification by the time her mother obtained legal residency, Claribelle relocated to Rome as an adult. From her experience, she believes that the "material stability" brought by her mother's migration could not have replaced the intimacy that her family lost in her absence:

My mother went to the United States and worked as a domestic worker. . . . She went to the States for a long time, when I was still young. I was separated from her for a long time, but she did go home every year. She just wanted to go to the States to be able to provide a good future for us. . . . I can say that it is very different to be away from the mother. Even if you have everything, I can say your family is broken. Once the father, mother, and children no longer have communication, even if you are materially stable, it is better to be together. If a child wants material goods, they also want maternal love. That is still important. When I was a kid, I realized that it is better if we stayed together and my parents carried regular day jobs. . . . It is best if the family stays whole, as whole as it can be. . . . Here it is hard. . . . Filipinos are blinded by material goods. That is not good for me. It is better if they are together, with the family whole, because even if you have money, you cannot replace the wrongdoing that it caused and did to your family.

For children left behind in the Philippines, "staying together" and "keeping the family whole" is a greater priority than the achievement of material security. However, children can make such sweeping claims more easily, because the material security provided by migrant parents affords them the luxury of demanding greater emotional security; it is highly unlikely that impoverished children would make similar demands.

The magazine *Tinig Filipino* included letters written by children that usually conveyed a longing for mothers to return "home" to the Philippines. This desire is usually placed in either/or terms: "money or family" (Aratan, 1994: 34). For example, a letter written by a son to his mother in Hong Kong reads, "Mom, come home. Even if it means that I will no longer receive new toys or chocolates. Even if it means that I won't get new clothes anymore, just being close to you will make me happy. Dad and I are so lonely here without you around" (Daguio, 1995: 40, translated from Tagalog to English). The binary construction of "money or family" suggests that children consider these two to be mutually exclusive choices for migrant mothers.

Moreover, there is an underlying suggestion that mothers have wrongfully chosen money over family. This line of reasoning disregards the fact that mothers migrate to provide money to the family. A letter written by Nina Rea Arevalo to her mother indicates that children recognize that mothers do sacrifice the intimacy of family life for their children's material security. Despite this fact, children like Nina still demand for their mothers to return home. They reason that the emotional gratification that the intimacy of everyday life provides is worth more than material security:

My dear mother:

How are you over there? Us, we're here wishing you were with us. . . . Mom, I was still very young when you left me with Kuya [older brother], Ate [older sister] and Dad. I still did not know the meaning of sadness. . . . Do you know that they would cry when they read your letters? Me, I would just look at them. I grew up actually believing that letters are supposed to be read while crying. . . . Mom, I am older now, and I know how to read and write. . . . I am getting older, and I need someone guiding and supporting me, and that is you. I don't want to be rich. Instead I want you with me, Mom. Doesn't God say that a family should always be together through hardships and happiness? But why are you far away from us? . . . Kuya and Ate read somewhere that Filipino workers in other shores are the heroes of our country. But, Mom, come back, and you will be the queen that I will be with every day. My wish is that you come home this coming Christmas.

Your youngest child, Nina Rea (Arevalo, 1994: 28,
translated from Tagalog to English)

The poignant letter expresses how children in transnational families hunger for emotional bonds with absentee parents and wish for the intimacies of everyday interactions.

Children want their mothers to return to the Philippines to amend the emotional distance wrought by separation. For many, such as Evelyn Binas, geographical distance created an irreparable gap in intergenerational relations. After graduating from college with a degree in computer science in 1994,

Evelyn joined her mother in Rome, where they lived in a room no bigger than the size of a walk-in closet in the home of her mother's employer. Left in the Philippines at the age of ten with her father, brother, and sister, Evelyn continued to resent her mother even after she followed her to Rome:

> *RP:* Are you close to your mother?
>
> *EB:* No. There is still a gap between us. We got used to not having a mother, even my brother and sister in the Philippines. . . . I was independent. I always felt that I didn't need someone guiding me. . . . Even though we are [now] living together, there is still this gap. . . . My mother came home when I was in my second and fourth year of high school and then fourth year of college. . . . When my mother was home, we felt that our house was too crowded. We never stayed—we always went out. Whenever she was there, we never stayed home.
>
> *RP:* Do you think that you will ever be close to your mom?
>
> *EB:* No, not really. I don't think that I will really know how to open up to her. . . . *She should have gone home more frequently.* At Christmas, I hated the fact that our family was not complete, and I would see other families together. I don't think that we needed to come here to survive as a family. I see the homeless surviving together in the Philippines, and if they are surviving, why did my mother have to come here? My classmates were so jealous of me because of all my designer things. They tell me that they envy me because my mom is abroad. I tell them, "Fine, she is abroad, but we are not complete." Since the fourth grade, this is the first time that I actually spent Christmas with my mother. [My emphasis.]

In contrast to other children, Evelyn asserts that she never looked forward to seeing her mother, yet she still thought that, in her words, "she should have gone home more frequently." Hurt and still feeling somewhat abandoned, Evelyn resented her mother for what seemed to be the relegation of their mother–daughter relationship to a few infrequent visits. Although unable to fully explain her feelings, Evelyn often cited the presence of a "gap" that hindered her ability to communicate with her mother. Bitter about her mother's prolonged absence from her life, Evelyn sadly conceded that there would always be a permanent emotional distance between them.

Although the emotional insecurities engendered by geographical distance can be eased by a mother's efforts to communicate with and visit her children regularly, they can also be tempered by the support that extended kin provide. Jane Sapin, for example, grew up with her grandmother from the age of six, when her mother, followed by her father two years later, began working in Italy. She did not follow her parents until she was almost eighteen years old. Still, Jane describes her childhood as "not so bad" because of the support and security her extended family in the Philippines provided:

It was not hard growing up without my parents because I grew up with my grandmother. So it wasn't so bad. . . . I wasn't angry with them. At that early age, I was mature. I used to tell my mother that it was fine that we were apart because we were eventually going to be reunited. . . . I see my mother having sacrificed for our sake so that she could support us financially.

From a young age in the Philippines, Jane acknowledged the sacrifices her parents were making, particularly her mother, and had been secure with the knowledge that her parents sought employment abroad not just for their personal interest but for the collective interest of the family. In contrast to Evelyn, Jane does not resent her mother for visiting the family infrequently; instead, she recognizes the financial struggle involved in making those few visits, the first being when Jane was already ten years old.

The extended family provides tremendous support to transnational families. As I noted earlier, it is mostly other female relatives, not fathers, who care for the children left behind in the Philippines. Of those in Los Angeles with young dependents, seven had their children cared for by other relatives, usually grandparents or female relatives, and five by fathers. In Rome, nine women left their children with fathers, and seventeen left them with other relatives. However, even in the presence of relatives, children left behind in the Philippines can still feel insecure. As the stories of Cesar Gregorio and Gay Villarama illustrate, children experience anxiety and abandonment while also feeling deprived of parental love. Cesar Gregorio, a college student, migrated to the United States with his brother in 1990, five years after his parents. Left in the Philippines with his grandparents at the age of five, Cesar recalls feeling insecure growing up, not knowing when he was going to see his parents again:

For a long time, I was questioning the love of my parents. . . . Finally, when I got to go to this country, I was looking forward to establishing a relationship with my parents and receiving affection, you know. So I just fell when I saw the baby. The least they could have done was to make sure that my brother and I were brought over before the baby was born. It would have made a difference. The fact that they can do this when they had two sons they have not spent time with for more than four years in another continent . . . I don't know. So, my wanting to make sure they really cared was impossible. But at least they took us out and did a lot of things with us our first few years, but there is still this question about what they were thinking and feeling about us while putting all this energy to their new child.

Adding to his emotional strife was his regret over his parents' absence during his formative years:

My parents and I are close. That's not weird because I have lived more with them than I have been separated from them. So, they have seen me grow up. But [there are] a few things in our relationship that [have] a gap, but it doesn't make us not close. It's more like this absence in that period of my life that should have included them but didn't. . . . Okay, like my first day in school or my first Holy Communion, important events that they did not see, that I do not remember, that an adult is not there to tell me about what I was like, what stuff I did that [is], I guess, funny kids' stuff we hear about once in a while.

In Cesar's perspective, his family can never make up for the loss in intimacy caused by the many years they had spent apart.

Besides emotional distance in parent–child ties or feelings of insecurity among children, vulnerability to abuse also plagues children in transnational households. Sensationalist stories circulate around Filipino migrant communities about abandoned, lost, and abused children of overseas workers. Although an extreme case—but definitely not unheard of in the field—Gay Villarama's life in the Philippines before following her mother to Rome at the age of twelve illustrates the heightened vulnerability of children in transnational households and the social costs of migration:

My mother has been here for fifteen years, and she left me in the Philippines when I was only five years old. . . . It was OK because she came home every year, sometimes on Christmas and other times during our school vacation when we weren't doing much so she was able to take us out a lot. However, we did miss her. It is true that life is sweeter when you are with your whole family, even if you are experiencing hardships. At this point, you can't really say that we are rich. You can only say that we went up just a little bit. However, this was at the cost of my family separating. What happened was that my sisters got married very young. I am the only one not yet married. My two siblings here are living with their partners, and so they are not actually married-married. One has two children and met her partner in the Philippines. The other one met her partner here in Rome.

Although this had been Gay's response to my question concerning the cost of family separation, one would definitely say that another cost had been her vulnerability to an abusive father, whose relationships with other women had been the significant push factor for her mother to consider employment outside of the Philippines:

I matured very fast when my mother left us. I grew up with my father, but he was very irresponsible. He did not really look after us well. [Pauses.] When I was ten years old, I was a victim of rape. [Pauses.] I was raped by my father. That's why I decided I had to come here. I could not take what my father did to me any longer. [Pauses.] You know why he did it? I look like my mother when she was younger. My father told me that when he sees me, he sees my mother when she was still young. That is why he did that to me. For me, I wonder why? I am his own child. I am not someone that he just found somewhere. For me, I wish he did it to someone else. During the time that he did that to me . . . the youngest in our family saw it, and that is why he has had some psychological problems since then. . . . I think my father has a lot of anger toward us, his children . . . . Our life is messy. [Laughs.] Thank God my brother has somewhat recovered. I sent him to a doctor when I went home. In school, he does well. He wants revenge and wants to be a lawyer.

When my mother and I went back to the Philippines, we took the case to the authorities. I did not take it to Manila but just in the provinces. When I saw my father, I told him that I was grateful that I am in this world but I am just unlucky to have him as a father. I told him that if I really wanted to kill him, I could do it, but I was just going to go through it legally for the sake of his [second] family and his new children. I feel sorry for his kids. I told him that I hope to God that he does not do what he did to me to his young daughter. . . .

But can you imagine what he did to me? I was only ten years old when he hurt me. And to top it all off, he pointed a gun at me. He tied my feet at the edge of the bed that he slept on. I couldn't tell my mother immediately after I came here. I counted three years until I told her . . . . It was all too much for me, so I finally told her. . . . I was actually scared, though, because my father told me that if I told any-one, he was going to kill me.

Gay was very stoic when she described her experience with her father, leaving me speechless and even more surprised when she told me that she "moved the lawsuit" to grant him an early release from prison (ironically, for the sake of his younger children).

The stories of Cesar, Evelyn, and Gay illustrate the vulnerability and inse-curity children can experience in transnational families, raising the question of how they cope with the situation. Gay, even with all the heart-wrenching struggles, was consoled by her family's slight upward mobility and her own early maturity and independence:

I have experienced the hardships of the Philippines in [their] extreme. I experi-enced [this] when I was so young. I remember not eating throughout the afternoon and evening. We wouldn't eat. Then, the following day, we would eat old bread. [Laughs.] We would fry it and top it with sugar. That was what I would take to school for lunch. Our life in the Philippines was difficult. Even though my mother was already here, it was hard because at first she could not send us any money. She was still new then, and she was saving money then because she really wanted to build our own house. Now, we have a house there. . . . *Our life slightly improved since we came here. . . . You have to understand that when my mother left us, we matured im-mediately. We learned to live without our mother being around for us. We learned to make do with what we had, and we did not, could not, rely on our father. We bought our own food and made money when we could. That's what is nice about our situation. We learned to survive without her.* [My emphasis]

Claribelle Ignacio, who was raised by her grandfather while her mother worked in the United States, saw the "pain and hardships" of her childhood as positive lessons that better prepared her for the harsh realities of adulthood:

It is better I realized to experience pain and hardships instead of just relying on my mother always. They say that a mother should protect [her] children from all the pain and hardships, but I realized that it is also good for children to experience some pain and suffering. For me, it made me a better person afterwards. Instead of just being irresponsible your whole life, I realized that if you get used to a life without problems, when you do have your first problem, you fall flat on your face. It's better to be exposed to some suffering while you are young. It makes you a better person when you get older.

Women like Claribelle Ignacio and Gay Villarama can only make the best of their situation and, as a coping strategy, must convince themselves that some good comes out of "suffering while you are young."

Because of her "early maturity" and "independence," Gay started working as a domestic worker in Rome at the age of thirteen. Even after reuniting with her mother, Gay was still denied a secure childhood free of adult responsibility:

> *GV:* I got my first job from my mother when I was almost thirteen. I would give my mom money at the end of the month, but I would keep some for myself to go shopping with. When I was young, the employers did not want to take me because of my age. I had to look after this child, and they were worried that I wasn't going to be able to look after the child properly. They did not care about the housework. The child is the most important. . . . I was making [US$800] a month working a "day job" from 8 am to 7 pm or to 8 pm. Then I went to [language] school at around 8:30 pm.
>
> *RP:* You were only twelve, and you were already attending evening school?
>
> *GV:* Yes.
>
> *RP:* You were riding the buses on your own?
>
> *GV:* Yes. I would get home at midnight because it was almost a two-hour bus ride from the school to my house. When I got home, I would not talk to anyone. I would just eat and then go to sleep. [Laughs.] . . . It was not regular school because I did not want to be a burden on my mother if I could earn my own money. She only insisted that I go to school once, but I had tasted how good it feels to make money. [Laughs.] I can buy what I want and do what I want to do. What is important is that there be a limit.

Although Gay could have finally had a "regular" childhood in Rome— especially after her personal struggles with her father in the Philippines—she continued to set aside her own needs. Gay worked so as not to become a burden on her mother.

Like their migrant parents, children endure transnational family life by prioritizing the family's material security over physical intimacy. By putting aside feelings of emotional distance and bearing the insecurity their parent's absence might invoke, children are making sacrifices for the success of their family arrangement. Yet children also want parents to recognize the relentless sacrifices that they make and commit to keeping the family intact through separation:

But I don't blame my parents for my fate today, because they both sacrifice just to give us our needs, and I just got my part. . . . And now, I realize that having a parent abroad may be a financial relief. But it also means a lot more. The overseas contract worker suffers lots of pain. They really sacrifice a lot. *But, hey, please don't forget that your kids also have lots of sacrifices to give, aside from growing up without a parent. Specifically, for those who thought that sending money is enough and they've already done their responsibilities, well, think again, because there are more than this. Your children need your love, support, attention, and affection.* You can still be with your children although you really are not. You can let them feel you can be their best friends. And that you're still beside them no matter what, because distance is not a hindrance to a better relationship. . . . *It's not only one person who suffers when an overseas contract worker leaves for abroad. All his or her loved ones do. And the children are the first on the list. The whole family bears the aches and pains just to achieve a better future.* (Gonzaga, 1995: 13; my emphasis)

To resolve the insecurities caused by geographical distance, children need concrete reinforcements of parental love. According to Junelyn Gonzaga, parents can do just that by creating "bridges" of constant communication.

When describing their position and experience growing up in a transnational household, children were stoic when they told me, "My parents had to do what they had to do," or "I understand why they had to leave us." The attitudes of children in transnational families reflect those of the working-class children in *Worlds of Pain*, Lillian Rubin's 1976 study of working-class American family life. As opposed to middle-class children, Rubin found "no complaints from the working-class child. . . . Children in all families frequently are 'lonely or scared,' or both. But the child in the working-class family understands that often there's nothing his parents can do about it" (1976: 27). Finding consolation in the belief that separation is not a choice but a parental sacrifice for the reproduction of the family, children in transnational households, like the working-class children in Rubin's study, feel an immense gratitude to migrant parents and recognize the hardships that they endure "for the sake of the children." Now parents just need to acknowledge the equally relentless sacrifices children in transnational families make.

Even though children recognize their mothers' efforts to provide emotional and material care from afar, and even though they appreciate the monthly remittances and frequent telephone calls, the bottom line is they still want their mothers to return to the Philippines. This is regardless of their mothers' efforts to maintain ties with them. For example, both Claribelle Ignacio—whose mother returned to the Philippines every year—and Evelyn Binas—whose mother returned far less frequently—shared the opinion that they would rather have had their mothers work in the Philippines. They both insisted that, by not returning home, mothers are not recognizing the emotional difficulties wrought by their prolonged geographical separation.

Based on the writings in *Tinig Filipino* and my interviews with children, it seems that children are not convinced that extended kin, the financial support of migrant mothers, and weekly telephone conversations can meet all their emotional care needs. As an eighteen-year-old female college student in Paz Cruz's survey suggests, only "family togetherness" can provide complete "guidance, attention, love, and care":

I will tell my friend to convince her mother not to go abroad but to look for a profitable means of livelihood such as planting, embroidery, etc. Two years being with the family is more worthy compared to the dollars she might earn abroad. Is it enough to show our love in terms of wealth? I think it's not. We need the warmth of love of our fellowmen, especially our parents. We need their guidance, attention, love, and care to live happily and contented. I will make her mother realize the value of family togetherness. . . . If only all Filipinos aim to have a simple life, not the luxurious one, then, there is no need to leave our country to earn more money. (1987: 42)

Despite the fact that children seem to recognize their mothers' efforts to provide love and care from afar, for the most part they have this ingrained desire for their mothers to return "home." Underlying this demand is the suggestion that their mothers are somehow at fault for working abroad. As I go on to reveal, the tendency of children to view transnational mothering as an insufficient strategy for the provision of emotional care in the family emerges from socialized expectations of traditional mothering. I argue that the traditional ideological system of the patriarchal nuclear family aggravates the intergenerational conflicts engendered by emotional tensions in transnational households.

GENDER AND PAIN IN TRANSNATIONAL FAMILIES

The thrust of the problem is to ask to what degree the central emotional and material moment found in each society is ideology, to what degree the ideology is accepted and plays a role in sorting out material and emotional interests of the participants. (Medick and Sabean, 1984: 19)

The material and emotional interests in the social institution of the family are shaped and guided by an underlying ideological system, as Medick and Sabean postulate. Ideology, according to Stuart Hall, refers "to those images, concepts, and premises [that] provide the frameworks through which we represent, interpret, understand, and 'make sense' of some aspect of social existence" (Hall, quoted in Espiritu, 1997: 12). Indeed, in the case of the children I spoke with, as I will argue, their emotional interests are ideologically determined. This is a springboard to further explore the feelings of pain that both parents and children feel in transnational households. Here I argue that patriarchal gender norms in the Filipino family, with its basic framework being the division of labor between fathers and mothers, fuel the emotional stress in the transnational families of migrant women. Although it is true that feelings of pain in transnational families are fostered by separation, they are undoubtedly intensified by children's unmet gender-based expectations for mothers (and not fathers) to nurture them, as well as mothers' self-imposed expectations to follow culturally and ideologically inscribed duties in the family.

As more women leave the Philippines and relegate traditional responsibilities of mothering to fathers (who do not necessarily perform them) or other relatives, migrant women—especially the mothers who constitute a visible portion of female migrants—are judged and scorned by the family, community, and the nation on their insufficient performance of ideologically determined family work. In fact, the denial of maternal love is considered child abuse in the diaspora. As a domestic worker writing in *Tinig Filipino* states, "Just [by] leaving [children] in the custody of fathers or relatives, we have already abused them. We have denied them their right of a motherly love and care" (Mariano, 1995: 26).

Between the early 1970s and 1980s, when men still dominated migration flows out of the Philippines, the traditional ideological foundation of the family remained stable. Migration did not question the division of labor in the family, as husbands continued to sustain the family economically while mothers nurtured it. The spatial division of labor remained unchanged, with the father earning wages outside the home and the mother nurturing the protective environment of this space. It was only in the mid-1980s, when the flow of female migration increased, that the "problem" of the "broken home" turned into a national crisis. The outmigration of women that included many mothers caused the family to topple over.

A striking image on the December 1994 cover of *Tinig Filipino* shows a Filipino family surrounded by traditional holiday decor. The father, clutching a sleeping baby with his right hand, raises the traditional Christmas lantern by the window as his other son, who looks about five years old and holds on to a stuffed animal, is next to his older sister in her early teens. The family portrait evokes a feeling of holiday celebration as the caption states: *"Pamilya'y Masaya Kung Sama-Sama"* (The family is happy when everyone is together). The picture, however, is not supposed to call forth an image of celebration but of a "broken family," as a very small highlighted subcaption strategically placed next to the family portrait asks in Italian *"peró dov'é mamma?"* (but where is mama?). The subcaption reminds readers that a mother, not a father, is supposed to be rocking her children to sleep. The image is supposed to invoke a feeling of loss as the man, not the woman, cares for the family. The magazine's editor, Linda Layosa, confirmed this negative construction of the transnational family:

I am certain, all of us have experienced similar incidents wherein abnormalities in our relationship with the members of our family are felt. A [*Tinig Filipino*] contributor stated that her son, instead of asking his [overseas contract worker] mother to sew his pants, he called his father instead. And since he is used to utter the word "Papa," he always said the same word even if he meant "Mama." (1994: 13)

Because the formation of female-headed transnational households leads to the reconfiguration of gender relations in the family, such households are generally considered "broken" and "abnormal," even in migrant communities. This is regardless of the fact that the family now can and does hire domestic workers and, more often that not, rely on other female relatives to reproduce the family.

Although the prolonged absence of either a father or a mother can have a negative impact on intergenerational relations, the transnational family with women working outside the Philippines is often construed as more pathologi-cal. Paz Cruz (1987) found that 82.8 percent of the 302 students in her survey would advise their friends to "allow your parents to work abroad," but the breakdown of responses actually shows that 59.5 percent would advise friends to allow their fathers to go abroad, 19.7 percent would advise friends to allow both parents to migrate, and only 3.6 percent would advise friends to allow their mothers to work abroad (1987: 38). Paz Cruz's finding that most children "would allow parents to work abroad" should be clarified. Most children seem to be comfortable only with the idea of a father working abroad.

The youths' responses to the question of what advice they would give friends whose parents are considering employment outside the country also seem to fall within the grid of traditional gender norms in the family:

The mother is the nurturer:
I'll advise my friend not to allow her mother to go abroad. It's better that her father go because mothers can't do what fathers do. Mothers are closer to their children than the father. She's always present in times of difficulties and problems. (eighteen-year-old in Paz Cruz, 1987: 42)

The father is the breadwinner:
I'll try to make her understand that it is the obligation of the father to provide for the family. With the present situation of the country, it's understandable that the father will look for greener pastures. They want the best for their children. I'll tell her she's lucky—her father is sacrificing to give them a good education and a good home. (seventeen-year-old in Paz Cruz, 1987: 40)

It's good that the father will be the one to go abroad because he is the man. He will manage our money. He is stronger than a girl and man is the one who is talented. (thirteen-year-old in Paz Cruz, 1987: 40)

In articulating their expectations, wants, and desires, children follow the gen-der division of labor in the family. Importantly, the ideological construction of the family controls not just their opinions but also their feelings and emo-tions concerning family separation.

In my study, most families with young children fall under the category of transnational households with one parent abroad. With the exception of the families of widows, this suggests that a father is usually left behind in the

Philippines. Still, despite the presence of fathers in the Philippines, children regularly claim that the migration of their mothers has resulted in a deficiency in their emotional care. Expressions of emotional insecurity from children raise the question of why fathers are not easing the emotional tensions of transnational family life especially as women are financially sustaining the household. The question then is whether fathers in the Philippines are able to provide the "maternal love" sorely missing from the lives of children, if women are capable of assisting men with their ideologically prescribed role as income-producer.

What happens if fathers do provide emotional care to their children? Although I do not want to underplay the pain of children in transnational households, I question the poignant pleas for emotional security of those whose fathers are present in their everyday lives. Begging her mother to finally return to the Philippines, Nina Rea, the young child who had grown up without her mother since before she learned to read and write, mentions having been left in the Philippines with her father. "*Mom, I was still very young when you left me with Kuya [older brother], Ate [older sister], and Dad. . . .* Mom . . . I am getting older and I need someone guiding and supporting me, and that is you. I don't want to be rich. Instead I want you with me, Mom" (my emphasis). As she asks her mother to return to the Philippines and finally provide her with the guidance and support she has long been denied, I have to wonder what the father in the Philippines is doing. Why does he not give her the much-needed support? Why can she not turn to him for the guidance expected of parents? Is he not even trying to provide care, or does his daughter not recognize the care that he gives?

Unlike Nina Rea, Evelyn Binas recognized how her father had nurtured and emotionally cared for her since the fourth grade, but nonetheless she still failed to appreciate her mother for economically sustaining the family with her earnings as a domestic worker in Rome:

> *EB:* Since the fourth grade, my mother has been here in Rome. My father looked after me. I remember when there were school functions with mothers. I would worry about not being able to participate. I always thought that I was different. Everyone had a mother, whereas I was the only one without one. It was only my father around for me. Like at graduation, it would be my father putting the medals on me. I remember my father always being there for me. During lunch, he would bring me over some food.

RP: Did he work?

EB: No. He sometimes did some work. We had some land with fruits and vegetables. He would go there to harvest. . . . So, he would do that work but not all the time.

Underlying her long enumeration of all the family work her very caring father did was her silence about her mother's contributions to the family and the suggestion that her mother somehow failed to perform the work that she should have done. Evelyn scorned all the material benefits that she had gained from her mother and wished that her mother had returned to the Philippines more frequently so that she could have received the "maternal love" that her very caring father had been unable to give her. Evelyn insisted that her family is "broken" and "incomplete." In families such as Evelyn's, I have to wonder whether a shift or breakdown of ideological norms would lead to a different take on the emotional costs of separation.

In sharp contrast to Evelyn's continued resentment of her mother, even though she was raised by a very loving father, is the Rodney Catorce's more blasé attitude, a child of a migrant father raised in a transnational family. He writes in *Tinig Filipino*:

I have always thought about it, my dad being so far away from us for more than ten years now. I mean, how could he? I was barely eight years old when he left us to work abroad. He had to because he and Mom were having a hard time trying to make both ends meet for our family. . . . The night after he departed, I could sense the feeling of emptiness in our home, despite the fact that everybody was trying to pretend that nobody left. . . . But while we were praying the rosary, the tears rolled down from my mother's cheeks. She wept, and it was all my dad's fault. Days after that memorable night (memorable because that was the first time I saw my mom cry), we learned to accept that Daddy was away, had to be away. And for us here, life had to continue. From now on, pen and paper would be our means of communication. . . . Sometimes I wonder what if Dad didn't gamble his luck abroad? What if he didn't pursue his dream of giving us a bright future? What would have happened if he preferred to stay with us? Well, undoubtedly, we would not have missed him that much. He would not have missed us that much. He would have celebrated the Christmases and New Years with us. He would have been present through all those birthdays. He would have attended all those graduations. He would have seen us grow up. Too bad, he was not able to. But then again, we would not be where we are now. We would not be living in our own house. . . . I and my brothers and sisters would not be studying in great schools. Daddy would not have been a good provider. . . . Worst, we would not have been eating three meals a day. All these considered, I am glad he did. True, he is away, but so what? (1995: 9)

Recognizing his father's economic contributions to the family while benefiting from the presence of his mother in the Philippines, Rodney did not witness a breakdown of the traditional division of labor in the family, a fact that seemed to allow him to pose the question, "My dad is away, but so what?" quite easily.

The reconstitution of family gender ideologies would not decrease the sacrifices that children in transnational families have to make, but it could temper the pain of separation. By this I do not mean to imply that a shift in gender ideology would eliminate the emotional difficulties of separation. Instead, I wish to suggest that children may come to appreciate more fully their mother's efforts to provide material care as well as a reconstituted form of emotional care from a distance. Moreover, they may begin to demand less family labor from their migrant mothers. For instance, they would not expect mothers to be primarily responsible for both the material and emotional care of the family. At the same time, they may achieve greater emotional security from the care provided by extended kin and from some fathers left behind in the Philippines. The impassioned pleas of children for emotional care have to be understood within their ideological framework, which surprisingly has remained intensely traditional even through the drastic shifts in the gender division of labor instigated by the migration of women in so many families.

A PAINFUL PARADOX

As this and the previous chapters have shown, although enabling Filipina domestic workers to maximize their earnings, the formation of transnational households also involves emotional upheaval in their lives and those of the children they leave behind in the Philippines. A central paradox in the maintenance of transnational families is the fact that the achievement of financial security for the sake of the children goes hand-in-hand with an increase in emotional insecurity, an impact that nonetheless could be softened by a breakdown of the persisting ideology of women's domesticity in the family. Material rewards contradict starkly the loss of intimacy in many families in Filipino migrant communities. Yet migrants continually suppress this contradiction, either by denying the emotional tensions in transnational families or by overriding emotional costs with material gains. Overall, this shows that the ways in which migrant Filipina domestic workers confront the pain of family separation also maintain this dislocation. Continuing with my discussion of dislocations, I turn my attention in the next chapter to the struggles faced by migrant Filipina domestic workers in the workplace. I focus specifically on the constitution of class in migration, examining how highly educated domestic workers cope with the decline in their social status when they do domestic work.

CHAPTER FIVE

CONTRADICTORY
CLASS MOBILITY

M IGRANT FILIPINA DOMESTIC WORKERS define their sense of self and place in the global labor market from the subject-position of contradictory class mobility. This contentious location refers to their simultaneous experience of upward and downward mobility in migration or, more specifically, their decline in occupational status and increase in financial status. This is the central dislocation that defines their experience of domestic work, in addition to the contradiction of caring for someone else's children and/or parents while not caring for one's own, as discussed in previous chapters. What does it mean for migrant Filipina domestic workers to be dislocated in terms of class? First, I found that it is very difficult for them to accept the low labor-market status of paid domestic work and to resolve the discrepancy between the social status of their current job and their actual training. In addition, they are frequently reminded of the contradiction of both having a maid and being one. As Genny O'Connor explained to me in Los Angeles:

I was crying all the time. [Laughs.] When my employer gave me the bucket for cleaning, I did not know where I had to start. Of course we are not so rich in the Philippines, but we had maids. I did not know how to start cleaning, and my feelings were of self-pity. I kept on thinking that I just came to the United States to be a maid. So that was that. I would just cry, and I wanted to go home. I did not imagine that this was the kind of work that I would end up doing.

For migrant Filipina domestic workers, the sharp decline in their occupational and social status aggravates the stigma of domestic work. They also tend to consider domestic work to be a deskilling process, as Vanessa Dulang in Rome lamented:

I regret not using my education. I invested years in my studies, and for what? The only thing that's going to happen to me is to be a maid. . . . If you don't use your education, you lose it, and you become stupid after a while. The only thing in your mind is mopping and mopping and mopping. You become stupid from your work. You don't use your brain.

Further capturing this anguish is the view of domestic work as *nakakabobo*, meaning a process that makes one stupid. Like Vanessa and many others, Giselle Aragon in Rome feels a tremendous sense of loss for failing to use her higher level of training:

Sometimes I say that I am tired. It's very different when you don't get to use your education. It gets rusty. [Laughs.] I plan to review my accounting when I go back to the Philippines. I miss what I had left. I want to review my knowledge of the subject, and I want to see if I still remember my training. What you learn just does not stay with you forever. It has been a long time. Since 1985, I have only been a domestic worker who has not done anything but scrub and scrub. You don't use what you learn in college. . . . Even here sometimes, I don't remember my English. If I am not speaking to someone who is fluent, I am not able to speak English.

Underemployment is such an excruciatingly painful experience that migrant Filipina domestic workers often spoke of it with great bitterness.

The dislocation of contradictory class mobility is a concrete effect of the larger structural forces of globalization. It emerges from the unequal development of regions, including the nation-based hierarchy of educational qualifications, the devalued accreditation of degrees from the Third World, and the limits of mobility in the Philippines. As Vanessa Dulang in Rome described, migrant Filipina domestic workers suffer from the limited options of either staying in the Philippines or working as a domestic worker outside of the country:

Life is hard in the Philippines. You don't earn enough. Nothing will happen to you if you stay there. Even though you are a maid here, at least you are earning money. What I couldn't buy in the Philippines, I could buy here. . . . You can buy something you really want, but there you can't. . . . But work here is difficult. You bend your back scrubbing. You experience what you would never experience in the Philippines. [There], your work is light, but you don't have any money. Here you make money, but your body is exhausted.

With the unequal development of regions, the achievement of material security in the Philippines means having to experience downward mobility in other countries. For migrant Filipina domestic workers, shifts in status from the sending to receiving nations define their sense of place in the global labor market.

The pain of contradictory class mobility is tempered by its financial gains. Low-wage service workers are willing to suffer a decline in labor-market status because in the Philippines the middle class does not have financial security. Lorna Fernandez, who has cared for the elderly for almost ten years in Rome, put it in these terms:

You have to understand that our money has no value. It is very low. In the Philippines, I was making almost 10,000 pesos a month [US$400], and that was even in the provinces. I lived with my parents, and I had no housing expenses, but still I was not able to save any money. If I had not left the Philippines, I would not have been able to have a house built for my parents. You might be able to save 2,000 or 3,000 pesos [US$80 or $120] here or there, but still goods are very expensive in the Philippines.

Wanting to hold on to their financial gains, migrant Filipina domestic workers negotiate the dislocation of contradictory class mobility by maximizing its material advantages and rectifying its emotional disadvantages.[1]

To analyze these dynamics it is important to have a deeper understanding of the daily duties and routines Filipina domestic workers navigate in their contradictory class mobility. As we will see, the everyday relations of power between domestics and their employers aggravate this dislocation. In my discussions with Filipina domestic workers I discovered that they tend to diffuse their experience of contradictory class mobility by using and manipulating various signifiers of inequality in the organization of paid domestic work. First, they perform domestic work under the fantasy of reversal; in other words, they dream of eventually returning to the Philippines to be served by their own domestic workers. They also downplay their decline in status by emphasizing the higher racial status that employers accord them over their black and Latina counterparts. A third way they deal with the difficulty of class mobility is by de-emphasizing their unequal relationship with employers by embracing intimacy, which, ironically, is a source of authority for employers.[2] Employers, for instance, use the construction of domestic workers as "one of the family" to maximize the labor of the worker for the most minimal of pay (Romero, 1992). Finally, they follow the script of "deference and maternalism" (Rollins, 1985) in the process embracing their subservience, but only so they can manipulate employers whenever they go off script. In other words, they do a good job of abiding by the script of "deference and maternalism" so as to achieve greater control of their labor. Although these tactics may desensitize Filipina domestic workers to the pain of this dislocation, ultimately they do not challenge the larger structural inequalities that have put them in a position of contradictory class mobility.[3]

THE EVERYDAY DOMESTIC ROUTINE: PART-TIME WORK, ELDER CARE, AND LIVE-IN HOUSEKEEPING

My interviewees performed three types of domestic work—part-time, elder care, and live-in housekeeping—each with its own particular difficulties and satisfactions. Providers of elder care generally believe that they hold the most respectable form of domestic work because their job grants them autonomy and requires special medical skills. Live-in housekeepers, although they may not like the social isolation of domestic work, often claim to be averse to elder care or the added pressures of part-time work—running from one job to the next—and prefer this job for the opportunity it gives them to save money. Finally, part-time workers claim to have the most rewarding job of the three because they earn more money and are not socially isolated like those who live in their employer's home.

Part-time workers hold a series of day jobs or part-time jobs with a number of employers. I call them "part-time workers" instead of "day workers" because that is the term Filipina domestic workers use. Unlike live-in workers, part-time workers are usually paid by the hour, and because they are not physically trapped in the workplace, they tend to have more control over their work schedule. Rome has a larger concentration of migrant Filipina part-time workers than I found in Los Angeles.[4] Most part-time workers had started as live-in workers but later sought part-time work to have greater control over their time and labor. For instance, Nilda Cortes, a mother of three working in Rome since 1992, left live-in work because there was no clear demarcation between working and nonworking hours. She explained, "I worked as a live-in, but I did not like it. I got sick from being awake at midnight. You can't go to sleep until they do. You have to be awake before they are because you have to bring them coffee to their rooms." In contrast, when a part-time worker's shift ends, so does her work. As Ruby Mercado noted, "Part-time is better. You work for three hours, and at the end of the three hours you are done no matter what, even if the job is not done." By having control over their work hours, part-time workers are able to set their schedules, maximize their number of employers, and increase their earnings.

However, part-time workers discussed the physical toll of their labor much more than other groups of domestic workers did. This is not surprising given the faster pace and heavier workload. Part-time workers generally have more floors to scrub and more clothes to wash and iron than live-in workers do. For example, Rowena Chavez, once a bank teller in the Philippines and now a part-time worker for three families in Rome, described what she was expected to complete at each of her jobs:

I wash their clothes, wash the plates, clean the house. I mop the floor on my knees. See, employers here have a disease, it's a disease of cleanliness. Everything has to be clean. They're too much. There are employers who look for something to clean even when the house is already clean. For example, this morning, the woman had to point out that I still had to wipe this one table even though I was already on my way out. I told her: "Signora, I'll just do it tomorrow because I am already running late." She then told me that it was okay as long as I don't forget about it tomorrow.

Part-time work generally entails intensive cleaning. As Ana Vengco described, each of the numerous cleaning tasks expected of them is strenuous on its own:

I do cleaning, and this is from morning until early evening. Every day is the same. It is physically exhausting. Especially when I am mopping, my back aches, and I get calluses on my hands. After ironing, you are just exhausted, and then you do something strenuous again like washing piles of dishes. Sometimes you feel numb all over from your hands to your feet. You are standing the whole day. We also do lifting, like heavy chairs, mattresses, rugs. You have to roll those rugs and take [them] outside to the balcony and bang on [them.]

A few employers also require child care, but often as an additional responsibility to the already laborious cleaning tasks.

Further intensifying the routine of part-time work is the hustle and bustle of running from one job to the next, especially for domestics like Ruth Mercado, whose employers live quite far from each other:

I am so sick of it. I get up at 7 in the morning and leave for work, which starts at 8:30. I am there until 12:30. Afterwards, I go to my next job, which is an hour away by bus. It starts at 2 in the afternoon and ends at 6. Most days I can't go home to eat lunch. So, I always eat pizza for lunch. Then, when I go home at 7 or 7:30, that is when I cook to eat a real meal. That's it.

The distance between jobs consumes any time for rest and extends an eight-and-a-half-hour work schedule, such as Ruth's, to twelve hours. This intensifies the physical ailments associated with domestic work. Vanessa Dulang, who worked for eight employers at the time of our interview, complained:

You don't have time to eat. For example, you start at 8, and that's four hours, let's say, so you get off at 12 noon. Then right afterwards, you have to chase your other employer where you start at 12 and end at 3. At 3 o'clock, you have to chase another employer where you have to start at 3. That is what is hard. You forget to eat because the only thing you think about is getting to your next employer on time. The work is exhausting, but I am used to it.

Despite the more onerous routine that women described as "exhausting" and "expensive" (due to the cost of living), many women in Rome prefer part-time work for the autonomy it gives them. Although I had expected to find a concentration of younger women in part-time work given its physical demands, I actually found no age difference between live-in and part-time workers. This is not the case with elder care; younger domestic workers seemed to have an aversion to elder caregiving, as the youngest woman I found holding such a job was thirty-six years old.[5]

Elder care is a somewhat specialized domestic job. Its primary duties include the provision of companionship and/or care to an elder. Whereas tasks often include the traditional housework associated with domestic employment such as cooking and cleaning, providers of elder care tend to make a concerted effort to distinguish their jobs from other types of domestic work. First, they claim that their employers' physical dependence gives them greater control of their work routine. Second, they argue that this dependence garners them more autonomy. Elder care providers generally believe that their work is more respectable than other types of domestic work, requires more skills, and involves a more egalitarian relationship with employers.

The formation of an immigrant niche in nursing among Filipino Americans has led to the conception of elder care as a skilled job in Los Angeles, one requiring special "medical" skills like monitoring blood pressure. In the community, any job in the medical field, including those in the lower ranks, is considered respectable. Further supporting the conception of elder care as a skilled occupation is the possibility of receiving certification as a nurse's aide. Many Filipina workers who care for the elderly in Los Angeles use a nurse's aide certificate to negotiate for higher wage rates. In the 1990s some women claimed that after they were certified as a nurse's aide their wage requirements increased from $60 to $90 a day. By 2013, that rate had increased from $125 to $150 a day.[6]

In Rome, elder care providers agree that their duties require more skills than other domestic jobs do. In contrast to their counterparts in Los Angeles, however, they believe that they, along with other domestics, still occupy a low position in society because of their segregation from the formal labor market. For example, Lorna Fernandez, not unlike other care providers in Rome, was keenly aware of her subordinate status: "They still see me as a maid. There is no improvement. You make good money, but they still call you a *ragazza* [girl]. When you are a *ragazza*, you are a maid." Yet in both Rome and Los Angeles, the perception of elder care as a job requiring more skills is supported by the fact that cleaning is considered secondary to the primary responsibility of providing care. For this reason, Eva Regalado, who has worked in Rome for more than ten years, limited her job selection to elder care: "Now I only get work with an older person because . . . it is not compulsory to clean. There is not too much to clean. Caretaking is more skilled." To establish that elder care is a "skilled" occupation, those who care for the elderly often refer to wards as "patients." Not surprising, then, is the fact that in Rome trained medical workers—nurses and midwives—prefer elder care over other types of domestic work. In Los Angeles, trained medical workers, in contrast to their counterparts in Rome, are not likely to pursue any type of domestic work for long periods of time because of the greater integration of immigrants in the U.S. labor market.[7]

Because they do not have the same opportunities as migrants in Los Angeles, trained medical workers in Rome seek employment in elder care. They see this as dignified because it allows them to use some of their skills and training. However, employers benefit much more than workers do, considering the services, like physical therapy, that employers receive for free. Employers take advantage of migrant Filipina domestic workers' skills often without increasing their wages. Judy Reyes, for example, saves her employers in Rome at least US$390 a week: "They have actually saved a lot of money. They don't pay me to give the man therapy, but before, they were paying an actual therapist [US$130]. The therapist used to visit three times a week. Now I massage him twice a day—evening and morning—for one hour. . . . Their children love me." Judy claims that she does not mind not being financially compensated for her added services because the similarities between her duties as a nurse in the Philippines and a care provider in Rome make her "feel better" about doing domestic work.

Elder care providers in both Rome and Los Angeles are also more satisfied with their jobs because it offers them more control of the job than do other types of domestic work. Elderly wards often depend on the physical assistance of care providers. Lorna Fernandez, who was once a midwife in the Philippines, explained, "With my present employer, I wake up at 7 in the morning. . . . By 8 o'clock, I have to give everything to the older person. I wake her up, feed her, clean her, bathe her, change her. She is totally dependent on me. She can still walk, but she can do so only when you hold on to her. You have to assist her." Employers usually acknowledge this dependency. Thus, providers of elder care believe that, compared to other domestic workers, employers treat them with greater respect. Those who care for the elderly also believe that they have greater control of their labor because of their decision-making power. According to Maya Areza in Los Angeles:

I choose only elder care. What I don't like are jobs with children. No, I don't like that because you are required to do the work they are requiring of you. It is not like that with an elderly person, because it is just you and the elder. You know when to feed them, bathe them. . . . These people are easy to adjust to, you just have to get to know their attitude and personality. The one I am taking care of is ninety-six years old, and so you have to kind of discipline [her,] saying "no, no, no." . . . I am the one who decides everything, if I should take her to the hospital, if I need to call the doctor.

As Maya's situation suggests, although domestic workers have to take orders in other jobs, often that is not the case when providing elder care. Comparing her previous job as a live-in housekeeper to her present job caring for the elderly, Judy Reyes, for instance, described the former as having been much worse, "They never run out of orders, they do not want to lose any money but get their money's worth." In elder care, she sets her own schedule and knows more about the needs of her "patient" than his children do, and thus she has more autonomy. Mimi Baclayon of Los Angeles concurred with Judy's preference for providing elder care. As she stated, "No matter what, there is no god telling you what to do. You are the one deciding what you should be doing."

However, elder care also has its pitfalls. In comparison to other kinds of domestic work, this job often requires twenty-four hours of labor. For example, Trinidad Borromeo, a sixty-eight-year-old woman in Rome, describes having to take care of a bedridden woman in her late eighties nonstop:

I begin at 7 in the morning. I change her, feed her, give her all of her injections and medication. Then I clean the apartment. When you take care of an elder, the first thing you have to have is patience. If you don't have it, you won't last. For example, when you feed her, it can take up to an hour. It gets hard when they don't want to open their mouth or swallow the food. But taking care of an elder like this one is better than a mobile one. Those ones are demanding. You wipe them already, then they want you to wipe them again. They have no shame. These types are better . . . .

You just move them around from the bed to the chair. You have to just clean her bed every day because it will smell like pee around the house if you don't. . . . I wake up at 4 in the morning just to check that the woman is still alive. Then if there is no problem, I sleep until a little bit before 7, and I am done with her by 9. I just serve her coffee and biscuits. I sleep around midnight or 1 in the morning.

While the most stressful part of providing elder care is its time demands, a distant second is the absence of privacy. As Lorna Fernandez explained, "I do everything. I brush her teeth, brush her hair, clean her Pampers. I do everything. The job is nonstop. . . . Our beds are next to each other, and if she cannot sleep then I cannot sleep. I sleep when she starts snoring. Her snoring is music to my ears." Becoming an extension of the dependent employer, providers of elder care do not usually have a space to call their own. Lastly, a frequent complaint about elder care is the isolation and loneliness of the job, which is echoed by live-in domestic workers.

Because more than half of my interviewees who "live" with their employers, excluding providers of elder care, have the dual responsibility of child care and housecleaning, I include housecleaners and child care providers in the "live-in" category. Of the three types of domestic work, live-in housekeeping offers the fewest rewards; these workers have less control over their schedules and, like those who care for the elderly, are subject to social isolation and an unset work schedule. Yet unlike those who care for the elderly, live-in housekeepers are also subject to more control by their employers. Most migrant Filipina domestic workers in Los Angeles are live-in workers. None of them would even consider part-time work because the living expenses would leave them with less money to send to their families in the Philippines and/or fewer savings. In Rome, live-in workers are often deterred from part-time work by its faster pace and heavier workload. Michelle Alvarez, for example, switched to live-in work because the more strenuous demands of part-time work aggravated her heart problem: "I really can't do part-time work. I've always had a heart problem in the Philippines, and when I came here, it was made worse by my workload." In Rome, women without children also seem to be averse to the isolation of live-in employment. Although there is a mixture of women with and without children among part-time workers in my sample, only four of the women without children in Rome have chosen live-in work.

In both Rome and Los Angeles, the routine of live-in housekeeping usually allows women to set a slower pace for themselves. Live-in work is often described as less strenuous, with specific responsibilities delineated as primary tasks. Cleaning is usually a secondary responsibility for child care providers. Marilou Ilagan, a domestic worker for more than twenty years in Los Angeles, gives most of her attention to her two wards and does not have to worry about other domestic responsibilities such as cleaning and cooking:

I wake up in the morning, around 6 am, and I take a shower. By 6:45 I am in the kitchen, fixing the children's lunch. They just have sandwiches. I check if they are getting dressed. Then when they are ready, we leave. They don't have breakfast usually, but sometimes they do. Then, I drive both of them to school. Afterwards, I come back here and clean their rooms. After that, I come down here [the kitchen]. It is not too hard to clean their rooms. . . . Then I pick them up from school. Usually, they have after-school activities, like one has a tutor three times a week . . . and then the younger one has acting classes every Tuesday. Then, when they have doctor or dentist appointments, I take them. When they want to go shopping, I take them. Then we go home, and I [am] done with my work. I don't have to worry about their dinner. I am free at night.

Luzviminda Ancheta, also working for a wealthy family in Los Angeles, worries only about her main tasks of cooking and cleaning:

I wake up at 5:30, and I heat the heater in the Japanese teahouse [located in the gardens of her employers' home] because the woman [a psychiatrist] usually has a patient there by 6:30 in the morning. . . . Then, one hour later, I prepare their breakfast, but usually it is only cereal. That's it. Then I clean when I feel like cleaning. It is [up to] you to know what and when you need to clean. No one tells you how and when you are supposed to clean what. There are a lot of employers like that, but not mine. You know your routine, and so it is just right that they don't tell you what to do. I clean in the mornings and cook in the afternoons. That is my routine. For dinner, I usually cook them fish—just salmon. They don't like a variety, just salmon, and they like it tasteless. . . . Besides cooking, I fix up their room everyday. I fix their bed. I also take care of their laundry. I don't think it is difficult. They are not fancy like other bosses. Some want their sheets ironed, and here they don't. They don't expect me to iron the polyester. [Laughs.]

Given certain tasks as their primary responsibility, Marilou and Luzviminda appreciated their employers' willingness to ease their load. Yet as most families hire only one domestic worker, most women's everyday routine entails a fairly demanding schedule. Nonetheless, live-in workers still tend to have a less physically demanding work routine than do part-time workers.

Live-in domestic workers, however, have to cope with the social isolation of working in a private home much more than their part-time colleagues do. Often feeling trapped, they cannot help but see the enclosed space of the employer's home as a prison. With no communication outlet, Lelanie Quezon, a sixty-eight-year-old grandmother who had been working for a middle-class Filipino family in Los Angeles for more than four years at the time of our interview, described how she felt in her employer's home:

I felt like I was in prison. I wanted to cry. . . . Now I have gotten used to it. But I used to look out the window and wonder why I never see a single person in the middle of the day. It is just a bunch of houses. But after a while, the baby got older, and now I have someone to talk to. Her grandmother was telling me that now I have someone to talk to and I won't get bored anymore. I have someone to talk to no matter what.

Considering that many women's outlet for communication is limited to their very young wards, it is not surprising to hear that counting the days until their day off is part of the everyday routine of live-in work. All of the women in my study described domestic work as painstakingly boring, but live-in workers were more emphatic. Vicky Diaz of Los Angeles, for example, described the isolation she felt when employed as a live-in domestic for three years: "A housekeeping job—there are times at night when you cannot sleep from crying and crying the whole night. The job is boring. You do not see anything except your employer sitting there in front of you. . . . It is boring." The social isolation of domestic work highlights the mundane nature of the job. Consequently, it more than reminds them of their decline in status on migration.

Live-in workers also complained about their employers' authority more than others did. Without set working hours, live-in workers can receive orders from employers at all times of the day or night. Although they may develop a certain amount of control over their work routine, they cannot fully prevent employers from imposing more tasks. Analin Mahusay in Rome, for instance, complained of having to work much later when her employers entertained guests: "As a live-in, one works from 8 o'clock in the morning until 9:30 in the evening. But if there are guests, one can be working until one in the morning, washing the heavy silvers and putting them back in their place." Analin's complaint illustrates that the lack of regulation in domestic work leaves live-in workers in the position of having to deal with their employers' idiosyncrasies more than other domestics do.

As we can see, various conditions in the everyday work routine of each of the three types of domestic employment can add more stress to domestic workers' experiences of underemployment. For part-time workers, the laborious monotony of cleaning more than reminds them that they are not using their educational training. Whereas providers of elder care can claim to use a certain degree of their training, the loneliness and isolation of their job emphasize their decline in status on migration. These conditions contrast quite sharply with their more socially and intellectually fulfilling occupations of teacher, student, business owner, and office worker in the Philippines. Finally, live-in workers contend with their decline in authority, having to cope with isolation and their employers' whims. For child care workers, their young wards' authority over them further aggravates this decline. Jerissa Lim in Los Angeles described the humiliation: "Would you believe, you would hold onto him in public and he would say, 'No. Stupid, idiot.' I could not take that, being told off by a little kid in public. I had to tolerate it. I was so patient for that one year."

EMPLOYER–EMPLOYEE RELATIONS

Documenting the inequalities reflected in the work process and the employer–employee relationship, many studies have concluded that paid domestic work is an inherently oppressive occupation, whether because of the feudal roots of domestic service (Rollins, 1985), the ghettoization of women of color into domestic work (Cock, 1980; Glenn, 1986), the social construction of employers as superior (Rollins, 1985; Constable, 1997), or the "structure of exploitation" (Romero, 1992: 142) implicit in employer–employee relations under capitalism.[8] Such unequal relations of power between domestics and their employers aggravate the experience of contradictory class mobility. Building from other studies on domestic work, here I show how the work organization, which is similar in the United States and Italy, exacerbates the pain this dislocation inflicts. Given that domestic work is set as wage employment in a private home there is an incongruent distribution of authority in the workplace. Because there is no set standard of employment, domestic workers are vulnerable to arbitrary and unregulated working conditions. As Mary Romero states, "Private household workers lack authority and must therefore rely on the employers' cooperation to change the structure of the work and social relationships" (1992: 158). My analysis shows that the authority employers have over migrant Filipina domestic workers stresses the vulnerability of underemployment and often forces the latter into a position of deference. Such conditions reinforce their subordinate position and consequently intensify their experience of downward mobility.

The enclosure of the work setting in a private home results in the absence of regulation (Hondagneu-Sotelo, 2001). Employers of domestic workers usually have "enormous leeway to determine the working conditions by setting wages, establishing job descriptions and determining the work structure" (ibid.: 120). Live-in domestic workers, for example, often complain about the absence of set parameters between their work and rest hours. However, in Italy, employers usually recognize the two-hour-long "rest hour" required by Italian labor law. In Los Angeles, employers usually leave their domestics alone after dinner, except when they are entertaining guests. Though employers have become increasingly sensitive to limiting their employees' hours, it is up to employers to monitor their own authority.

Consequently, migrant Filipina domestic workers must find accommodating employers to secure fair employment conditions. Like the African American domestic workers in Dill's 1994 study, Filipina domestic workers consider their employer's attitude to be a measure of working conditions. They are more content with work if they are fortunate to have found "nice" and "good" employers, meaning employers who are not exceedingly demanding. Domestic workers who report no work-related problems attribute their general satisfaction to having found "good" employers. In response to the question "What problems have you encountered at work?," the answer given by Michelle Alvarez echoes the general sentiments of her counterparts. She said, "Nothing really because my employers have been very nice." Having "nice" employers is so important that some women have even accepted a lower salary in exchange for "good" employers. However, finding accommodating employers can be very difficult.

This is true in both Rome and Los Angeles. Though the domestic workers I interviewed tend to be satisfied with their employers, at one point most had to tolerate stricter and more demanding employers. During the first few years, they often changed jobs regularly

To a certain extent, migrant Filipina domestic workers have come to view their employers as "nice" because these workers have accepted certain low standards of employment. One of these standards is what Judith Rollins refers to as "spatial deference" in the workplace, meaning, "the unequal rights of the domestic and the employer to the space around the other's body and the controlling of the domestic's use of house space" (1985: 171). Employers control the spatial movements of domestic workers in the workplace because they determine the domestic worker's integration in or segregation from the family. More often than not, they prefer segregation as they tend to hire those "who will demand very few of their resources, in terms of time, money, space or interaction" (Wrigley, 1995: 26). The domestic worker's access to household space is usually far more constrained than the rest of the family's.

This spatial inequality signifies the lower social status of the domestic worker. Consequently, it reminds them of their decline in labor-market status. In both Los Angeles and Rome, Filipina domestic workers, including nannies and elder care providers, have regularly found themselves subject to food rationing, prevented from sitting on the couch, provided with a separate set of utensils, and told when to get food from the refrigerator and when to retreat to their bedrooms. Domestic workers describe these attempts to regulate their bodies as part of employers' larger efforts to control them.

With such established spatial deference, Filipina domestic workers are often startled when employers fail to enforce segregation. We can see this in Luzviminda Ancheta's surprise over what she sees as her employers' "odd" behavior. "Here they are very nice. In other households, the plates of the maids and the cups and glasses are different from the employers. Here, it is not. We use the same utensils and plates. They don't care. . . . They even use the cup that I have. They don't care. [Laughs.]" Her astonishment over her employer's lack of concern for crossing the boundaries of spatial deference is telling of its established pattern in the workplace. Notwithstanding its reflections of inequality, spatial segregation can also be a source of comfort for Filipina domestic workers who do not always appreciate employers' efforts to rupture patterns of spatial deference. For example, Marilou Ilagan, a domestic worker for a family in the exclusive Los Angeles neighborhood of Brentwood, chose to maintain boundaries:

> *MI:* I don't want to eat with them, and that is why I eat here [the breakfast room] on my own while they eat in the dining room. But we eat at the same time and the same food. My employer asked me if I wanted to eat with them, but I told her that I would be so much more comfortable if I were just by myself. I would rather be by myself. That was OK with her. She told me that was fine with them if that was what I preferred.
>
> *RP:* Why are you not comfortable?
>
> *MI:* I don't know. . . . This is where I sleep, but it is not the same as being in your own home. You cannot feel as comfortable as being in your own home.

This discomfort could have something to do with her being conscious of the Filipina domestic worker's lower status in race and class hierarchies.[9] According to Shellee Colen, "Eating is a materially and symbolically important arena for dehumanization and lack of consideration" (1989: 181), reflected most clearly in the "classic" situation of domestic workers eating separately from the rest of the family. Though choosing to eat on their own could be seen as an example of conformity to the dehumanization of the domestic worker, it can also be seen as an act of reclaiming one's own space from the employer's, where her identity is that of a perpetual domestic worker. Confining herself to her own space within the workplace could be a creative act of retreat—a break—from her role as a worker.

Generally, Filipina domestic workers do not perceive eating on their own as a signifier of their lower status in relation to the employer. To them, it does not emphasize servility. Instead, the following situations were noted as clearer markers of dehumanization and servility: domestic workers having to eat less expensive food, having to stand by the dinner table during meals, and being allowed to eat only after the employers have finished their own meals. In these cases, differences in eating practices are far more difficult for domestic workers to rationalize, and they reinforce their decline in social status.

Further compounding the authority of employers is the migrant status of domestics. One of the ultimate goals of migrant Filipina domestic workers in Italy and the United States is legalization, the achievement of which often depends on employer cooperation. This leaves domestics in a more vulnerable position. In the United States, obtaining a green card through employer sponsorship has been described as "a form of state-sanctioned, indenture-like exploitation" because "the worker is obligated to stay in the sponsored position until the green card is granted (often two or more years) in spite of any abuses to which she may be subjected" (Colen, 1989: 173).[10] Obtaining a green card through employer sponsorship took an average of ten years. For example, Luzviminda Ancheta, who began working as a domestic in Los Angeles in 1987, was petitioned by her employer in 1990. When I interviewed her six years later she still held only a work permit, which legally bound her service to the sponsoring employer. Today, domestic workers, including caregivers and house-cleaners, no longer qualify for employer-sponsored residency. Only cooks do. Yet, some domestic workers in the United States still find themselves bound in servitude to employers. As discussed in Chapter One, temporary migrant domestic workers, specifically "servants" of former expats, diplomats, and employees of international organizations, are not granted employer flexibility but are instead legally bound to work for their sponsoring employer (Glenn, 2012).

In most other countries, employers can impose lower standards of employment, revoke visas without notice, and leave migrant Filipinos scrambling for new "hosts" to sponsor their stay in the country. In Italy, illegal migrant workers have been known to settle for lower wages in exchange for a permit to stay. In 1995, many employers who sponsored their domestic workers for legal status lowered their wages by 20 percent or expected the worker to cover the advance payment of six months of income-tax contributions that employers are required to pay. Domestic workers had the same complaint in 2012.

Unfortunately, employers sometimes take advantage of the dependency of their domestics for legal status and intentionally mislead them. In Rome, numerous domestics complained about reneged promises to sponsor their stay under the November 1995 amnesty. Many employers informed them of their lack of intention to sponsor them only near the amnesty's closing date (March 1996), not leaving them with much time to seek employers who were genuinely interested in granting them legal status. In Los Angeles, Cerissa Fariñas was misled by two of her employers about processing her papers. After they promised to sponsor her application for a green card, they did not inform her of their lack of intention to do so until after two years of service, during which time they had found other reasons to delay filing her application. Cerissa's employers took advantage of her dependency, which guaranteed them her loyalty and dedicated service. However, the threat of "getting caught" does loom over employers who take advantage of undocumented workers.

The emotional work of deference is another aspect of the job that emphasizes an employer's authority over domestic workers. Judith Rollins, in her insightful examination of the politics of everyday interaction between domestics and their employers (1985), builds from Irving Goffman to identify "deference and maternalism" as the central script controlling the behavior in this relationship. Domestic workers must act with deference—they cannot talk to but must be first spoken to by employers, they must engage in "ingratiating behavior," and they must perform tasks in a lively manner.[11] An employer's control penetrates the bodily movements of domestic workers in myriad ways, including patterns of speech, gestures, spatial movements, and the "attitude and manner with which the individual performs tasks" (Rollins, 1985: 158). Concomitantly, employers validate their higher social status through maternalism, acting "protective" and "nurturing" to the "childlike" domestic worker. According to Rollins, the script of "deference and maternalism" perpetuates nonegalitarian relations in domestic work by affirming the employer's superiority.

The attitude and behavior of employers often disregard the experience and capabilities of domestic workers (Rollins, 1985; Wrigley, 1995). As a result, their actions, like the need to constantly supervise domestics, remind migrant Filipinas of their subordinate status. Because this tendency magnifies the inequalities between domestics and employers, it also denigrates a domestic worker's intellect. Mila Tizon in Los Angeles complained,

I know what I need to do because I know what they do not like. But before I get a chance to do what I know I need to do, the younger sister of my employer will be yapping away about how I did not clean that corner, this table, etc. etc. She always complains about everything she knows she can complain about. She criticizes me all the time.

Such behavior further aggravates the sense of loss in social status for domestics. Rowena Chavez in Rome stated, "I regret not using my education, especially when I am doing something and then they order me to do something else. When they order me around is when I cannot stand being here. It is not like I do not know what I need to do. Being ordered around is what I cannot accept at all."

Also exacerbating the various emotional tensions in domestic work is the "emotional labor" expected of domestic workers. Coined by Arlie Hochschild, the term *emotional labor* refers to the expectation of employers to "produce an emotional state in another person" through "face-to-face" interaction (1983: 147). It indicates the control of the employer over the emotional activities of the worker. In domestic work, following the protocol of deference demands the emotional labor of smiling. Domestic workers have to disregard their true feelings, be they boredom, anger, or exhaustion, and carry attitudes reflecting the idealized (that is, pleasant) environment of the home. Multiple women described this to me:

Even when you are fatigued, feeling feverish, feel terrible, you can't stay in bed, you have to get up and work. Then you have to be smiling and acting happy. (Girlie Belen, Rome)

At the end of the day, you are so tired, and they want you to smile. If you don't, they wonder why you are not smiling as you had been in the beginning of the day. (Evelyn Binas, Rome)

Even when they are angry with you, you still have to be smiling. Even if they are serious, you have to joke around with them. (Michelle Fonte, Rome)

Though I present only three examples here, all of the women in my study complained of the strains imposed by their emotional labor at work. The job expectation of having to smile intensifies the emotional tensions wrought by domestic work, including the strains brought by their experience of underemployment.

As we have seen, certain labor conditions aggravate the dislocation and vulnerability of contradictory class mobility that migrant Filipina domestic workers experience. These include the unregulated authority that employers exert over their employees, the legal dependence of sponsored migrants, and the emotional displays expected by employers. Migrant Filipina domestic workers negotiate their experience of downward mobility and attempt to subvert the pain inflicted by their decline in social status in numerous ways. Though they may seem paradoxical, these strategies include accepting the racialization of domestics, embracing the setting of intimacy in the workplace, and, less frequently, incorporating acts of resistance into the performance of domestic work. Unfortunately, I found that the central means by which migrant domestic workers ease their pain do not question but instead maintain the relations of inequality established by employers in the organization of domestic work.

RECONCILING CONTRADICTORY CLASS MOBILITY

To reconcile the contradictions in their class mobility, migrant Filipina domestic workers emphasize the gains this dislocation has brought them. Although domestic work involves downward mobility, at the same time it constitutes a certain degree of upward mobility, not just because of their higher wages but also because of the higher social status they gain in the Philippines from their identity as a "migrant worker" (Goldring, 1998). Migrant Filipina domestic workers consequently stress their higher status over poorer women in the Philippines and engage in the fantasy of reversal—that someday they will have and be personally served by their own domestics once they return to the Philippines. By situating their identities in a transnational context (Basch et al., 1994), they resolve the loss of class status in the receiving country with the assurance of the greater standing they have in the Philippines.

As Joy Manlapit told me in Los Angeles, "When I go back, I want to experience being able to be my own boss in the house. I want to be able to order someone to make me coffee, to serve me food. That is good. That is how you can take back all of the hardships you experienced before. That is something you struggled for." Gloria Yogore, her counterpart in Rome, found similar comfort in knowing she would be on a higher rung of the social ladder once she returned to the Philippines: "[There] I have maids. When I came here, I kept on thinking that in the Philippines I have maids, and here I am one. I thought to myself that once I go back to the Philippines, I will not lift my finger, and I will be the *signora*. [Laughs.] My hands will be rested and manicured, and I will wake up at 12 o'clock noon." Ironically, Gloria and many others I spoke with mitigate their contradictory class mobility by looking forward to being served by poorer women who are less fortunate than they are in the Philippines. Acknowledging the option migrant Filipina domestic workers have to participate in global capitalism as transnational players is, therefore, critical to understanding their structural position. Their ability to secure access to the higher wages of migrant employment directly contrasts with the insecurity of those who cannot afford to work outside the Philippines.

Despite the fact that race and class differences between Filipina domestics and their employers heighten feelings of social decline, many I spoke with used racialization as a way to negotiate their loss of status. They did so by claiming and embracing their racial differentiation from Latinas and blacks and highlighting their specific distinction as the "educated domestics." Numerous scholars have illustrated the production and reproduction of race and class inequalities among women in the daily practices of paid household work.[12] Documenting the hierarchization of womanhood in the United States in the pre–World War II period, Phyllis Palmer (1989) describes the reflection of race and class hierarchies in the division of labor between "clean mistresses" and "dirty servants." According to Palmer, the more physically strenuous labor of the servant enabled the mistress to attain the markers of ideal femininity— fragility and cleanliness. This hierarchization actually continues today, as the most demanding physical labor in the household is still relegated to the paid domestic worker.

To enhance their own status, employers often assign tasks to their domestics that they would not want to undertake themselves (Rollins, 1985; Romero, 1992). In Italy, domestic workers are expected to scrub the floor on their knees. When performing the same task, employers, the domestic workers noticed, do not scrub but instead mop the floor. The distinction of appropriate household labor enforces race and class hierarchies, as tasks that are unacceptable for employers are acceptable for domestic workers, most of whom are women of color. This division of labor is also reflected in child care. In a study of child care providers and their employers in New York and Los Angeles, Julia Wrigley (1995) found that employers usually assign the most demanding child care duties to domestics and keep physically lighter work, such as reading and shopping, to themselves.

Another employer strategy for reinforcing racial and class differentiation is the preference for hiring "less-educated and poor domestics" (Rollins, 1985: 195), because less-educated women are expected to be more deferent.[13] Yet, Filipina domestic workers claim that their employers would rather hire educated domestic workers. Giselle Aragon, a housecleaner in Rome, stated, "Filipinos are much preferred in domestic work because employers say that

we are . . . educated. Other nationalities are looked at differently. I consider
them underdogs." In Los Angeles, many women made similar claims. This
discrepancy raised numerous questions about the difference between blacks
and Filipina migrants in either the United States or Italy, where Filipinas are
supposedly preferred over other domestic workers of color. Are employers' expectations of domestic workers determined by the racial construction of Filipinos in both Italy and the United States? For example, does the stereotype of
Filipino Americans as meek and compliant eliminate any possible threat that
their high educational level might pose? Does their undocumented or "guest
worker" status make them less threatening? Or are these claims of Filipina
domestic workers even true? Are they just a fantasy that they entertain to differentiate themselves from other women of color doing domestic work? Regardless of their truth, the fact is that migrant Filipina domestic workers in both
Rome and Los Angeles believe that employers distinguish them racially from
other domestic workers because it helps ease their pain of underemployment.

Assuming that employers do differentiate Filipinos by race, what about
Giselle's claims about how the high level of education of Filipinos affects hiring
preferences? Wrigley (1995) distinguishes two main types of child care workers in the United States—low-status and high-status employees. Low-status
employees are considered "socially subordinate" workers who are generally
assumed to be noneducated migrant women from developing countries. The
services that they provide are considered "low quality" because these workers
are perceived to have minimal skills and inferior cultural practices and beliefs.
In contrast, "quality care" is provided by "educated, culturally similar caregivers" (1995: 48). Some employers seek "high-quality" domestic workers, usually European au pairs who demand higher wages, to avoid cultural conflicts
with migrant women from developing countries.

Failing to recognize the high level of education that most Filipina domestic workers have achieved, Wrigley, in her discussion of one Filipina domestic
worker in her sample, categorically places their services under "low-quality
care" (1995: 92). In recognition of their high level of education, I believe that
it is more accurate to place them in between high- and low-status caregivers.
Although Filipina domestic workers in Rome and Los Angeles do not have the
autonomy and racial equality that high-quality caregivers enjoy, they claim
that employers distinguish them from other migrant domestic workers. For

instance, Genelin Magsaysay described the in-between location that they inhabit in Italy:

Italians have a low opinion of us Filipinos because we are all domestic workers, and we are foreigners. That's why you can't blame them for not looking at us as their equals. Filipinos look better than other foreigners do, though. My employers have said that Filipinos are better, compared to other foreigners in Italy. One time, when my employer was hospitalized, the doctor told me that Filipinos are the best and that there's nothing bad to be said about them.

Although Italians do not consider Filipina domestic workers their peers, they still distinguish them from and place them above other migrant groups. This suggests that the experiences of domestic workers vary considerably depending on their racialization and structural location. These factors shape the employer's perception of the domestic worker.

In Italy, Filipina domestic workers claim that they are preferred over other immigrant domestic workers because they are hardworking, honest, clean, and educated. By embracing these stereotypes to be true, by default, they imply that other domestic workers are not. Thus, they distinguish themselves racially from their international counterparts and support the hierarchization of racial subordinates in society. This translates to a wage gap. Filipinas in Italy during the 1990s received on average a higher rate of US$6.67 to $8.00 an hour for day work in comparison to the US$5.33 hourly rate paid to women from Peru, Cape Verde, and Poland.[14] Twenty years later, Filipinos still earn more than other groups of domestic workers. Significantly, the nation-based racial categorization in Italy distinguishes Polish women as "lesser whites" and marks them as socially inferior to Italians and Northern Europeans.

How do migrant Filipina domestic workers in Italy justify their higher wage rates? Vanessa Dulang credited them to a supposedly better work ethic:

Italians prefer Filipinos to others because we are supposedly hardworking, trustworthy, and nice. We are clean, and we are not robbers. Even though Filipinos ask for a higher rate, they still prefer us Filipinos. For example, Polish workers ask for [US$5.33] an hour and Filipinos ask for [US$8.00], and Italians will still hire the Filipinos even if they have to pay more. It's because they say they trust us more, and they are more satisfied with our work.

Although it is highly unlikely that Filipinas are nicer and more hardworking than other domestic workers, the attachment of these stereotypes to Filipinos has made them a "status symbol" for employers. When I asked Jennifer Jeremillo to compare Filipinos to other foreigners in Italy, she responded:

We have the same kind of work; we work in the house. The employers much prefer Filipinos because they see Filipinos as honest and dependable. They much prefer them to other nationalities that are stereotyped as the types who would steal. Here, if a family employs a Filipina, it shows that they are rich because Filipinos get paid a lot more than Bangladeshis and Peruvians, for example. Other groups would work for as little as [US$467]. A friend of my employer, for example, told my employer that she was rich when my employer told her about me. She asked my employer, why not pick a Peruvian or Polish, why did she need to get one that asked for a high salary? Filipinos are a status symbol.

According to migrant Filipina domestic workers, although Italian employers do not consider them their peers, they do distinguish them from other migrant groups because they are expected to provide better-quality services. Often unable to speak English, Italian employers are impressed with Filipinos' command of the English language. Employers with children usually rely on Filipina domestic workers to tutor their children and to assist them with homework—tasks that are, following Wrigley's definition, never entrusted to low-status domestic workers. This differentiation does point to a certain racialization of Filipinos, one that is segmented by a glass ceiling and should not be celebrated by migrant Filipina domestic workers. At most, a high level of educational attainment has only elevated them to the status of "better-than-low-quality" domestic workers, which is only a slight differentiation from other groups of migrant domestics.

Just as Filipinos in Italy claim to be the Mercedes Benz of domestic workers, those in Los Angeles similarly profess to provide better services than Latina domestic workers do. Moreover, they contend that the "higher-quality" services that they offer—from housecleaning to providing elder care—are reflected in their higher pay rate. When I asked Genny O'Connor if she thought employers respected her education, she responded:

I really think so. I really think it just shows in the pay rate. With Mexicans usually, they work for a lower rate, like $250 a week. Once in the bus stop in Bel Air, there was this group of women speaking Spanish, and I know how to speak Spanish. They were telling stories about how much they made—comparing salaries. One was happy with $250 a week, and one was $120 a week, and she had to clean every corner in the house. Then she works for longer hours. It was just abuse! I think that here they have tremendous respect for Filipinos because they know that most of us are educated. Often, when they look for employees, they ask for Filipinos.

Other domestic workers second Genny O'Connor's claim, attributing the preference for Filipinos to their higher level of education and greater command of the English language. Joy Manlapit, for example, explains that it is critical for providers of elder care to know the English language in case of medical emergencies:

As a caregiver, you have a lot of responsibility. You have to have knowledge and skills. You have to know what to do in case of emergency. You have to be able to call a doctor and explain what happened. That is why they do not hire someone who cannot speak English. The only thing they care about when hiring is that you know how to speak English. That is what they like. I am also proud to tell you that they prefer Filipinos [over] Latinas. It is because the second language of Filipinos is English. That is why we don't have a hard time speaking English and understand them right away. It is also because most of the Filipinos are professionals, even if we enter domestic work.

Based on these comments, it is possible that employers meet the higher wage demands of Filipina domestics because they find some sort of reassurance in the belief that they are receiving higher-quality service from these workers.

The different reception and the distinction of Filipina domestic workers from blacks and Latinos in Rome, which also seems to hold true for those in Los Angeles, point to their different racialization. Aihwa Ong's identification of the "bifurcation of Asian immigrants" in the contemporary United States is relevant in this case. She argues that although Hmongs are constructed as "undesirable citizens," and "ideologically blackened subjects manipulating state structures in order to gain better access to resources," middle-class Chinese immigrants are considered "desirable citizens . . . caught between whitening social practices and the consumer power that spells citizenship in the global economy" (1996: 751). The pattern of racial differentiation that Ong found among Hmong refugees and Chinese immigrants parallels the differentiation of Filipina domestic workers from Latina and black domestic workers in Rome and Latina domestic workers in Los Angeles. There seems to be a bifurcation of domestic workers of color into better-than-low-quality and low-quality workers. It is a differentiation that Filipinas openly accept because it works in their favor; they get greater respect and higher wages. Moreover, it is one that they emphasize to highlight their high level of educational attainment. This bifurcation thus salves their painful experience of contradictory class mobility.[15] Likewise, migrant domestic workers turn to a particular relational dynamic with employers to downplay their dislocation of contradictory class mobility. They specifically aspire for a semblance of familial ties with employers in order to achieve dignity in the workplace.

THE POLITICS OF INTIMACY

There is consensus in the literature on domestic work that the perception of domestic workers as "one of the family" enforces, aggravates, and perpetuates unequal relations of power between domestic workers and their employers.[16] First and foremost, it is rooted in the feudal conception of domestic workers as servants bound to the master for life. Second, it clouds the status of the domestic worker as a paid laborer, so employees are less able to negotiate for better working conditions. Their duties become conflated with "family" obligation and considered by employers a "labor of love" because of their close relationship (Romero, 1992; Gregson and Lowe, 1994). Third, employers can manipulate the use of family ideologies to extract unpaid labor, for example, the emotional labor of affection and attachment to their wards (Romero, 1992). Lastly, it obscures the existence of their own families (Bakan and Stasiulis, 1997b).

Although I do agree that the myth of being "like one of the family" perpetuates inequalities, I found that domestic workers use this myth to manipulate employers and resist the inequalities that this myth perpetuates in the workplace (Young, 1987). In fact, migrant Filipina domestic workers in Rome and Los Angeles embrace the notion of being "like one of the family" and the intimacy resulting from this construction to de-emphasize servility. They reason that, as "one of the family," they are not servants but instead like the more respected au pairs in Wrigley's 1995 study. Moreover, they use intimacy to increase the material advantages of domestic work and, in the process, maximize the benefits of their contradictory class mobility. Thus, domestic workers have a dual purpose for intimacy: to decrease the emotional pitfalls of contradictory class mobility while increasing this dislocation's corresponding material benefits. In making this assertion, I do not intend to argue that domestic workers achieve egalitarian working conditions when embracing the intimacy that employers selectively promote. Instead, I want to highlight the agency of domestic workers and at the same time provide an empirical illustration of power's complex operation; as Foucault (1983) has argued, it does not operate only in a descending order. Thus, I wish to show, as the migrant Filipina domestic workers I observed and interviewed revealed to me, that various emblems of inequality in domestic work have not simply resulted in adversities.

Like the Chicana domestic workers interviewed by Romero (1992) and the black domestic workers in Dill's 1994 study, Filipina domestic workers "feel like a person" when considered "one of the family." One domestic worker in Los Angeles told me, "I like my job because my employers treat me like a human being." Another, Helen Gambaya, who worked in Los Angeles in 1988–1989 and has been in Rome since 1990, used very similar wording when she told me, "I am lucky that I have good employers now. They are professors. They don't look down at us. So, I am very happy with my present employers because I am treated like a human being." When I asked Helen and many other women what it means to be treated "like a human being," they enumerated the following: (1) when their skills and "brain" are recognized by not being ordered around constantly; (2) when they are not distinguished as different by being made to wear a uniform; (3) when their social needs are acknowledged by allowing them to have visitors and partners to spend the night; (4) when their physical needs are recognized by making sure that they rest—for example, by encouraging day workers to ease their pace; and (5) when their presence is acknowledged by acts like being offered food when they first come in and being invited to sit down and chat (while they are on the clock). Lastly, being treated "like a human being" also means being considered "one of the family."

When domestic workers are not seen as "one of the family," they consider it to be a marker of their lower status as a person. Claribelle Ignacio in Rome, for example, considered being "treated like a slave" the opposite of being treated "like one of the family." When I asked her if she liked her job, she responded:

Yes. Because my employer right now is a very good employer. They are kindhearted and treat me like one of the family. That is the one thing that is important to me. I want to be treated like a person. Not all employers are good; some are very bad. You can have a high salary but get treated like a slave. I don't care about the high salary as long as I am treated as a person, part of the family, and I get along well with my employer. It is important to have a good rapport and work relationship. What I found among us in Italy, many are unhappy and not content with their employers.

Why do Filipina domestic workers equate being a human being with being "one of the family"? Romero found that Chicana domestic workers have a tendency to contrast "treatment as a 'non-person' versus treatment as a 'family member'" because they seek respect and dignity in the workplace. But this psychological desire makes them more vulnerable, as efforts to please employers usually take them "above and beyond the standard contractual relationship" (1992: 125, 126). Diverging from Romero's observation, I found that migrant Filipina domestic workers consider not being treated like "one of the family" inhumane simply because being treated more coldly by the employer in the intimate space of a private home contrasts with how other inhabitants are regarded and thus labels the domestic worker as inferior by default.

Migrant Filipina domestic workers actively seek to be treated "like one of the family." Reminiscing about an elderly employer who had recently passed away, Jovita Gacutan in Los Angeles proudly described the familial relationship she had with her employer:

"We were like a mother and daughter. We had our fights. We would have different opinions. But of course I could not look at her as a mother completely because no matter what she was still my employer. But our relationship was one of honesty and compassion. Like a family." Although aware of the possibility of being manipulated when demanding to be treated "like one of the family," Filipina domestic workers still prefer it, in contrast to the emotional distancing Romero (1992) found among Chicana domestic workers. A less rigid and more familial-like work environment is desired by Filipina domestic workers for it allows them to have flexible work standards, which enables them to get away with occasional slipups. As women explained, day workers might enjoy occasional breaks while still on the clock, and live-in workers can ease their work pace and workload. For these reasons, Filipina domestic workers do not enforce distance but instead seek intimacy.

Despite the intimacy they might be able to achieve with the employing family, Filipina domestic workers never lose sight of their status as a worker. For instance, migrant Filipina caregivers tend to measure the quality of their labor in terms of the standards they hold for their own families. In Rome, Girlie Belen's case is an example:

I had an employer with two young children. . . . They called me *zia* (aunt) because they could not pronounce my name. . . . I took care of them for two years. . . . The love that I had for my child [in the Philippines], I poured to these two young children. . . . I clothed them, bathed them, taught them how to pray. . . . [Because] I was paid to do it, I gave the children all of my love and attention.

Many domestic workers like Girlie tend to describe the very familial act of "pouring love" into their wards as a central duty of caretaking. This emotional bond, however, is not easy for employers to manipulate. Because it is part of the job, domestic workers can maintain a certain degree of distance from this emotional labor. More often than not, the act of pouring love leaves them physically exhausted. This, in turn, serves as a strong reminder of their wage-based relationship. As Gloria Yogore in Rome explained,

I would wake up at 6:30. I make breakfast, feed the baby, then after they have breakfast and leave for the offices, I take care of the baby, take the baby to the park, and then when I go back, I cook and bathe the baby. . . . There is a seven-year-old daughter whom I have to pick up from school every afternoon at 4:30. Even if the baby is sleeping, I have to wake the baby up to pick up the sister. I cannot sleep. I cannot rest. I cannot breathe at night anymore. I can hardly feel my heart pumping. I am exhausted; from the baby to the household cleaning, doing it at the same time is a hard job.

The physical exhaustion imposed by domestic work is difficult to ignore. Thus, in the field, when listening to domestics talk among themselves, I was not surprised to never hear them talk about the employing family with affection or reverence. Instead, I often heard complaints.

Another reminder of their status as a paid employee amid their emotional attachment to the employing family is the clear difference between their physical state of exhaustion and the female employer's well-rested body. Jerissa Lim, in Los Angeles, described her situation:

It was very difficult. If the child is awake, you have to be awake as well. Sometimes I worked for over sixteen hours. I would wake up at 6 or 7 in the morning. That is when the boy wakes up, and so I have to watch over the boy and make him breakfast and see to his other needs. I start cleaning the kitchen. My employers would wake up at around 12 or one. . . . When they woke up, they would just shower and leave.

Domestic workers often cannot help but compare their activities to those of their employers and in the process notice that one of their main duties is to free them of their time to spend on leisure, rest, and relaxation. This difference reminds them of their status as an employee of the family. This came through when Luisa Balila described her employer in Rome: "The woman was a spoiled brat. She can sleep until 10, 11, 12 in the afternoon without thinking about her two children. I am the one that looked after the children—did everything, spoon-fed them. . . . When she woke up, I even brought her breakfast in bed."

No domestic worker I spoke to believed that she was actually a member of the family. Yet, they all still considered only those who treated them "like one of the family" to be "good employers." Behind their incorporation into the family lies the knowledge that they are paid employees. This is a status that is hard for them to forget, because they know that behind an employers' positive attitude are high expectations. As one interviewee told me, "They love you if they are satisfied with your work, and when they cannot get everything they want from you, they become very dissatisfied."

As Wrigley has argued, it is in the best interest of employers to treat domestic workers with dignity and respect: "Just as sociologists have found that the kind of work people do affects the behavior they encourage in their children, so too this can apply among caregivers" (1995: 19). There seems to be a cycle of dependency defining employer–employee relations in domestic work. By treating domestic workers "like a human being," employers can induce domestic workers to "do a good job." Some Filipina domestic workers, such as Ana Vengco in Rome, also recognize this cycle of dependency in domestic work: "They treat me well because they need me." Generally, Filipina domestic workers with "good employers" credit the positive attitudes of employers to the quality of their work. However, when they are not treated like a human being, they do not consider it to be a sign of doing a bad job.

An employer's terrible attitude makes domestics less invested in their work. Due to her bad treatment, Mimi Baclayon in Los Angeles, for example, did not think twice about leaving her difficult employers in the lurch:

They were too strict with the caregiver, and that is not the kind of environment you would appreciate. You would want your work, even though it is just that, you would want your environment to be right. So, I gave up that job even though the pay was good. It was for $100 a day . . . so after my cousins picked me up for my day off one day, I decided not to return anymore.

Although it can be argued that power inequalities would make domestic workers more dependent on employers, the latter also have a great deal to lose if they do not treat their domestic workers "like one of the family." For instance, employers are made vulnerable by their welcoming of a stranger in the intimate space of a household, which encourages the humane treatment of the worker.

Still, employers do not always reward domestic workers when they do a good job. In Rome and Los Angeles, many employers did not treat domestic workers in a way that reflected the quality of their labor. Jennifer Jeremillo in Rome explained:

Sometimes I wish all of them are like my employers. . . . I often hear from my friends about problems that they have with their employers, how their employers refused to pay them at the end of the month. . . . Some complain about how they did not get out on their day off because their employer had work for them to do. Many of us live-in workers don't stay with our employers for a long time because we are not treated well; for example, in eating, we do not get to eat the same food.

Supporting Romero's 1992 observations that authority clearly lies with employers, the efforts of many migrant Filipina domestics to do a good job do not always result in trust, respect, or humane treatment. This indicates that migrant Filipina domestic workers' use of the myth of being "like one of the family" to mitigate the pain of contradictory class mobility still maintains the employers' authority, which is one of the greatest factors aggravating this dislocation.

Myth or not, domestic workers—in particular, live-in workers—may manipulate the attachment that develops from the closeness between employers and domestic workers who are "like one of the family." Wards and employers can also become attached to the domestic workers, as Jovita Gacutan's and Maria Batung's stories show:

They [the children of her elderly ward and her ward] kept on calling me in the Philippines, and after I came back, she was already different. She had been affected by the separation. I realized then that it is not advisable for your ward to get too attached to you. (Jovita Gacutan, Los Angeles)

If you could have only seen them when I was about to go home. In the airport, all the other passengers were looking over at us because one was hugging me, one was tugging me [on] the right. They were all crying . . . . My employers told me that they had to take the children out so that they would not cry. . . . It was such a big drama when I went on vacation. Then, when I was in the Philippines, soon after I landed they started calling me long distance. They asked me when I was coming back, and I told them that I just got there. (Maria Batung, Los Angeles)

As Dill (1994) has observed, intimacy gives rise to a "familial" attachment that domestic workers can take advantage of to cope with the demands of the workplace. An example is the story of Gelli Padit, a domestic worker in Rome. Even after a huge argument ensued between Gelli and her employer of four years, during which Gelli scared her employer "by hitting the wall in [her] room" and "screaming out on the terrace," the employer begged her not to leave when she started packing that evening. The employer told her to just take a few days off but not to take any of her belongings. Although the employer could have been threatened by Gelli's violent reaction, the familiarity that intimacy breeds may have influenced her to suppress any desire to fire Gelli. In both Rome and Los Angeles, numerous domestic workers mentioned how employers who considered them "like one of the family" did not replace them with other domestic workers when they extended their vacations in the Philippines, even up to six months.

However, as other scholars have pointed out, the danger of holding affection for a ward is that it makes it difficult for domestics to negotiate for fair wages or even leave. Lelanie Quezon of Los Angeles wanted to quit her job but felt guilty about leaving her employers in a tight spot. In a similar situation, Valentina Diamante wanted to quit her live-in job but was restrained by her close attachment to the two young girls she had taken care of for more than four years. Even so, Valentina and Lelanie were not completely hindered by their attachment, which only delayed their departure. After waiting to leave until their employers found suitable replacements, they do not believe that their attachment adversely affected them but only made them more considerate. Furthermore, Valentina, who was not satisfied with her new employers despite the higher salary, was immediately rehired by her former employers without any grudge over her decision to leave them.

Lastly, domestics measure the degree of their integration in the family according to the gifts they receive from employers. Many studies of domestic work dismiss gifts given by employers to domestic workers as acts of "benevolent maternalism" (Cock, 1980; Rollins, 1985; Romero, 1992). According to Romero, "When employers grant favors, make promises and give gifts, the employee becomes ensnared in a web of debt and obligation that masks considerations of the employee's rights. . . . Gift giving is simply another employer tactic for keeping wages low and for extracting additional unpaid labor [from] the employee" (1992: 131). Though employers may intend to use gifts as a control mechanism, domestic workers can also gain tremendous material benefits from them. I found numerous examples of employer gifts not only increasing the power of employers but also working to the advantage of employees. Considered "like one of the family," a domestic worker in Los Angeles inherited enough money from an elderly employer to retire comfortably in the Philippines. In at least two other cases, domestic workers persuaded their employers to invest in business ventures in the Philippines. The trust that comes from the intimacy of being "like one of the family" led Jovita Gacutan's employer to co-sign a loan she used to purchase a house in Los Angeles. Consuelo Cabrido of Rome was given two years of payment in advance by one of her four employers so that she could build a house for her family in the Philippines. One can easily argue that, because Consuelo is bound to work for her employer, the loan translates to indentured labor. However, Consuelo, who is consequently freed of rent, considers the loan from her employer a much better option than her only other choice of borrowing money from another migrant Filipina in Italy. Although the standard monthly interest rate for loans in the Filipino-Italian migrant community is 10 percent, her employer did not charge her any interest.

Employers have also helped domestic workers legalize their status. In Rome, Girlie Macabalo, for example, could not convince her new employers to sponsor her legalization. As a favor, a former employer agreed to sponsor her instead.

Michelle Fonte found her permit to stay in Rome threatened after a squabble with her sponsoring employers led her to quit and seek other employment. The employers later reported her to the authorities as an illegal worker, as her work permit required her to work for them for another year. Although her new employers did not want to get involved, a former employer willingly took over the sponsorship of her permit to stay. In both cases, Girlie and Michelle were not obligated to return to their old employers. These examples indicate that the practice of gift giving does not always signify benevolent maternalism. They also suggest that the intimacy of the family can result in the employers placing a great level of trust in employees, which consequently can result in tangible improvements and greater material benefits in employees' lives.

USING EMOTIONS TO CONTROL THE SCRIPT

To improve their work conditions and ease the strains of contradictory class mobility, migrant domestic workers do not only rely on the achievement of a familial-like relationship with employers but also turn to the manipulation of their and their employers' emotions. They do this via "immediate struggles" (De Certeau, 1994). Not to be equated with coping strategies, such as keeping busy to pass time in hopes of easing the boredom of social isolation or the pain of subservience, immediate struggles are ways in which individuals subvert power in their everyday routines. In the case of Filipina domestic workers, they find ways to challenge the authority of employers, improve work conditions, and gain control over their labor in their everyday work routine. They do all of these to reduce their position of subservience and to temper the contradictions in their contradictory class mobility.

This is not a surprising observation. Numerous studies of domestic work have made similar claims. Both Hunter (1997) and Dill (1988, 1994) establish that the everyday acts of subversion incorporated by domestic workers pose a constant threat to the authority of employers. Dill shows that African American domestic workers enforce measures of control over working conditions through the incorporation of various individual acts of subversion, including "chicanery, cajolery, and negotiation" (1994: 50). Likewise, migrant Filipina domestic workers in both Rome and Los Angeles manipulate the script of deference and maternalism as an act of immediate struggle. Performing a balancing act, they simultaneously follow and question the script of deference and maternalism. Although Nicole Constable claims that Filipina domestic workers "internalize a sense of inferiority" (1997: 69) when performing the script, I found them to be more conscious beings who are able to simultaneously hold feelings of attachment for and detachment from their employers, and in the process attempt to subvert the script within the routine of domestic work.

How are migrant Filipina domestic workers able to do this? Individuals, according to De Certeau, function as "consumers" in society, as their everyday practices follow rules and social orders that are inculcated through the use of "the products imposed by a dominant economic order" (1984: xix). At the same time, individuals are not always inclined to abide by society's disciplining measures but tend to subvert them through the use of strategies or tactics. While strategies visibly reconstruct the proper order, tactics represent the incorporation of subversive activities to manipulate that order in the rituals of everyday life (De Certeau, 1984). Tactics and strategies are differentiated by time and place. Tactics are deployed in the location of oppression and involve the manipulation of time through key moments of intervention, whereas strategies require a space in which to strategize and retreat. Strategies are thus acts of resistance by the "strong," meaning those with resources. Examples of strategies are business takeovers and labor unions (because of the power to lobby for workers at the state level and relieve strikes with wage compensations). Tactics are acts of resistance by the "weak" who, without resources, can only inject subversive acts into the circumstances of constraint.

Domestic workers are hammered by rules, particularly the script of deference and maternalism and, as part of the "weak," more often develop tactics when subverting the authority of employers. Strategies like collective bargaining have long been elusive measures of resistance for domestic workers not only because of the informal nature of their job but, in the United States, also because the law has historically banned the collective action of domestic workers (Glenn, 2012). Tactics such as "clever tricks, knowing how to get away with things, 'hunter's cunning,' maneuvers, polymorphic simulations, joyful discoveries, poetic as well as warlike" (De Certeau, 1984: xix), or what Dill calls "chicanery" and "cajolery," are "victories of the 'weak' over the 'strong'" that they incorporate within the boundaries of the rules and order of domestic work. Through tactics, domestic workers take advantage of opportune moments within the daily rituals of domestic work by creatively interjecting subversive acts into everyday routines so as to resist the tedium and disciplinary measures that normalize inequalities between employers and employees.

In the script of deference and maternalism, employers are said to use emotions to control domestic workers (Rollins, 1985). They manipulate the affective aspects of the relationship to elicit additional labor; for instance, they might act kind to make domestics more willing to comply with substandard wages. As a tactic to subvert the control of employers, migrant Filipina domestic workers have also realized their ability to manipulate employers' emotions. For example, by complying with the expectations for domestic workers to act happy all the time, they normalize the deferent behavior that employers demand. They are then able to manipulate its normalization, because employers then notice the smallest deviation from the script. Vicky Diaz in Los Angeles explained:

In domestic work, I always had to be happy. I had to make them laugh, tell stories. They were happy with that, and that is why they liked me. Once in a while I had to frown because the mood of a person is never the same. . . . Sometimes I just wanted to get mad. . . . When [my employer] [saw] that I [was] lonely, she would ask me if I wanted to go shopping. I would say sure.

Ruby Mercado in Rome similarly noted:

Sometimes we chat with our employers. They talk to you if you have a sense of humor. You have to be in a light mood and cheerful; then they talk to you. When you work, you always have to be smiling so that your employers think you are sweet. Even if I am in a bad mood, I am smiling. If I am not smiling, they know that I have a problem because I am always smiling.

As Rowena Chavez of Rome explained, the emotional script of smiling is so well established that it is very clear to employers when domestic workers fail to follow the script: "They always want you to be smiling, even when you are really tired. They always want you to be smiling. If you are not smiling, they always bug you, ask you what's wrong, if you have a problem. If you're frowning because they said something offensive, they feel guilty and apologize."

Aware of the emotional script they are expected to follow, domestic workers have come to realize that they have the ability to subvert the authority of employers by manipulating the script. Doing just that, migrant Filipina domestic workers use the tactical projection of emotions to negotiate working conditions. They go against the script of deference and maternalism by crying, showing anger, projecting a somber mood, becoming very quiet and unresponsive to employers, or simply talking back. Emotional deviation in domestic work has to be rare for it to be effective because it loses its punch when used frequently. Nonetheless, domestic workers have still been able to bargain effectively and make demands on employers through the calculated projection of emotions. This is particularly effective if they can elicit emotional discomfort in employers, such as unease and guilt. Moreover, they manipulate the maternalism of employers by putting them in the position of having to make domestic workers feel better.

In using conscious emotional displays, domestic workers not only challenge the script of deference and maternalism, but they can also ease various challenges of domestic work such as boredom, a heavy workload, or the demeaning attitude of employers. Genny O'Connor, for example, told me that she relies on frowning as a way to ease her workload: "Oh, you have to be smiling all the time. If you are not smiling, they don't like it. They want you to have a jolly face all the time. They don't want to see you frown, but once in while I just have to show them that I am frowning from all the work that I have to do. Especially when I am not used to it and they give me so much work." Genny claimed that her attempts to ease her workload were usually successful, for instance, leading to the extension of time in which her employer expected her to complete a task. Like other domestic workers, however, she was only able to manipulate the rituals of deference to her advantage by going against them sparingly. The women I interviewed used other subversive tactics as well, such as working at a slow pace. Yet when given an unreasonable load by employers, they more often relied on the tactical display of emotions.

I found that other challenging aspects of domestic work were also mitigated through this tactic. To relieve the loneliness and boredom engendered by social isolation in Rome, Janet Sapida would sometimes cry to intimate her desire to visit friends on a workday when she was still a live-in domestic. "When my [previous] employer would come home, sometimes I would be bawling. I would still continue my work, but I would be crying while I did it. I would tell them that I was missing my parents. So, they would take me to the house of a friend." By manipulating her employer's maternalism with calculated crying, Janet was able to arrange a subversive visit with a friend. More often than not, however, the women I interviewed usually coped with social isolation by keeping busy and distracted (for example, by watching television). Other times, domestic workers reveal their anger, irritation, and frustration over a demanding workload or an employer's demeaning treatment more directly. As Claribelle Ignacio in Rome explained, "I always frown and bang things around when I'm mad. . . . It's funny that my employers always try to appease me by giving me presents." Emotional outbursts contradict employers' expectations and leave them feeling uneasy and consequently easier to manipulate. Employers accommodate domestic workers so that they can return to the script immediately.

Although one may wonder why domestic workers do not attempt to speak rationally to employers, the reality is that power inequalities between domestic workers and employers often prevent them from being able to do so. Moreover, domestic workers find the projection of emotions to involve less effort. Incarnacion Molina told me in Rome, "When I do get mad, I just keep it to myself. I don't show it. But when I get quiet, they know it affected me. They know when they offend me. They offend me when they ask me why I have not cleaned something that I have cleaned already. After they know that I am offended, they leave me alone and then talk to me again later." Incarnacion's statement reveals that she does not have to make the effort to explain her dissatisfaction to her employer because she can choose to display particular emotions instead. If that does not successfully send the message about problems with working conditions, domestic workers resort to talking back. This is a more direct form of arbitration, and one that puts their job security at greater risk. Helen Gambaya is one domestic worker who talked back: "My employers always shouted at me. But in a book, I had read 'When in Rome, do what the Romans do.' So, I did what the Romans did, I screamed back at them."

Because domestic workers talk back so sporadically, when they do, it often leaves employers surprised and compelled to listen. Michelle Fonte of Rome finally verbally challenged her employers when they hung up the phone while she was speaking to her mother in the Philippines. "That old employer of mine used to slam the phone on my mother when my mother called me. That's when I got mad at them, and that's when I started fighting back. . . . Then my employer told me I was being disrespectful. I told her that I am disrespectful when she is disrespectful. I am nice when she is nice." According to Michelle, her employers did not dramatically change for the better, but they did recognize her action by never hanging up on her mother again. Although none of the women who rely on displaying emotions was let go for doing so, a few women were fired for daring to talk back to employers. Talking back contradicts the script of deference but also questions and threatens the authority of employers more directly.

To reduce the risk of being fired, other domestic workers, like Rowena Chavez, use a softer communication approach. They take advantage of employers' expectations for domestic workers to "entertain" them with conversation by sometimes inserting information that would elicit feelings of guilt:

I told my signora, "Signora, you think that this is the only kind of job that we know how to do." Then she asked me: "What kind of job did you used to have?" I told her: "I used to work in a bank." Then she asked: "Well, why did you come here then?" I told her: "The salary there is enough to support yourself, but it's not enough if you want to help your family. Even though I did not know that this is what I was going to experience here, it's fine as long as I can help my family."

Many educated domestic workers are like Rowena and often insist on letting their employers know of their educational qualifications. They tend to share this information when they are responding to an insult made by an employer against migrants or Filipinos.

If talking back or displays of emotional discontent do not transform working conditions for the better, migrant Filipina domestic workers—not unlike the domestic workers in Dill's 1994 study—rely on quitting as a last resort. Leaving a job, however, is not a very accessible option. Because their families rely on their earnings, they often cannot risk losing even a week's salary. Many of them do not always have the resources that they need to quit. This is true despite the social networks and sentiments of collectivism that have developed in the migrant communities in Rome and Los Angeles.

The individual acts of immediate struggles that I have enumerated here are in fact collective acts. They do not reside at the level of the individual but are rooted in the collective consciousness of a shared struggle among domestic workers. When domestic workers do complain, it is highly likely that they had heard or articulated those same complaints to another domestic worker before they did so to their employers. Domestic workers find the strength to incorporate tactics in the daily activities of domestic work from the "hidden transcript" that they maintain with other domestic workers, those with whom they share experiences in migration and at work. Coined by James Scott to explain the ability of the "weak" to develop a consciousness of collective struggle, the "hidden transcript" refers to the "discourse that takes place 'offstage,' beyond direct observation by powerholders" (1990: 5). In the case of domestic workers, the "hidden transcript" refers to the discourse that they maintain away from the employer's view. Together migrant Filipina domestic workers write their hidden script using the very limited resources available to them.

In addition to using the multinational space of magazines like *Tinig Filipino* and now social media, migrant Filipina domestic workers produce the hidden transcript in numerous local sites. These include churches, community centers, and buses, where they speak of the difficulties they encounter in the workplace and complain about the unreasonable demands and abusive behavior of employers. They reveal their true feelings. Consequently, this becomes an outlet for the built-up frustrations that domestics have accumulated in the workplace. Migrant Filipina domestic workers have access to information and resources they can use to decrease their dependence on employers and consider the option of quitting. As Mila Tizon of Los Angeles stated, "Most of the people whom I ride the bus with every morning are domestic workers. There are many of us [Filipinos]. There we compare our salaries to know the going rate. We also ask each other for possible job referrals. We often exchange phone numbers and contact each other." Providing domestic workers a consciousness of a collective struggle from their shared experiences, the "hidden transcript" enables them to establish wage standards, evaluate the fairness of their working conditions, validate suspicions, and finally garner the strength to disobey the script of the dominant order. Though not quite like the "hidden transcript," which is a discourse and not an institution, social networks can also be a resource for domestic workers to increase control over their labor (Hondagneu-Sotelo, 1994; Hunter, 1997). Like the "hidden transcript," social networks give domestic workers access to job referrals and knowledge about established labor standards. When the individual acts I have previously identified make their way into the hidden transcript and get dispersed through social networks, I argue that they are in fact not individual but collective.

Domestic workers neither passively acquiesce to the disciplining mechanisms of employers nor do they internalize the pain inflicted by contradictory class mobility. They contest them through the manipulation of the very same mechanisms of control used by employers, such as the script of deference and maternalism and the myth of being "like one of the family." Their use of established emblems of inequality suggests the fluid operation of power in society; that is, power is not simply imposed by "those on the top [over] those at the bottom" (Dreyfus and Rabinow, 1983: 186). This occurs for the simple reason that domestic workers, or generally anyone on whom power is exercised, are acting subjects (Foucault, 1980, 1983). At the same time, it points to the acquiescence of migrant Filipina domestic workers to the structural inequalities defining domestic work relations. Clearly, they do not attempt to subvert the structures that place them in a position of subservience. They only manipulate the direct results of these larger systems of inequality. However, the "immediate struggles" that they deploy have arguably brought concrete change, such as decreasing emotional adversities and increasing material rewards in the dislocation of contradictory class mobility. These struggles have also threatened the authority of employers, but not to the extent of questioning the subservience of domestic workers.

In light of their dislocated class position, how do they feel about domestic work? Neither group of women in my study developed "a highly critical perception of the host society," as Portes and Rumbaut (1996) speculated of Filipino migrants who experience downward mobility on migration. I found that the different "contexts of reception" that welcome them in Rome and Los Angeles have led to two very distinct feelings about domestic work. In Rome, they are resigned to domestic work and have settled with the job. In Los Angeles, however, they do not underplay their dissatisfaction with domestic work. They voice their definite dislike of it. Mila Tizon's sentiments reflected those of the women in Los Angeles: "Actually, I do not like the kind of work that I do. I am here, and I cannot do anything about it. So, I just have to do it and work. You cannot expect anything good with domestic work. You can never be content with yourself doing housekeeping work." Patricia Baclayon echoed this perspective, "When I worked in the home, I realized that this is the United Mistakes of America. I had never thought that this was what I was going to experience here."

Although women in Rome share the bitterness of their counterparts in Los Angeles, they are more resigned to accepting domestic work. Their resolution is probably influenced by the fact that almost all of them are domestic workers. In contrast, domestic workers in Los Angeles have to cope with the added pressures of seeing more "successful" Filipino migrants, such as the slew of health professionals immigrating since the late 1960s (Choy, 2003). I found only one woman in Los Angeles who holds an attitude that mirrors those of her counterparts in Rome. Dorothy Espiritu, once a domestic worker in Saudi Arabia, reminded me of the women in Rome when she stated, "Any kind of job would do, but at this point this is the only kind of job that I can find. I am not mad or angry about it. It's just the way it is."

Women's varying opinions raise the question of how men feel about domestic work. Although the number of male domestic workers remains fairly small, some men do find themselves funneled into or limited to domestic work. This is more so the case in Rome than in Los Angeles, as Filipino migrants in Italy still find themselves largely concentrated in domestic work. As we will see, more than struggling with the dislocation of contradictory class mobility, male domestic workers face the challenge of negotiating and reconciling their masculinity in a traditionally gendered occupation.

CHAPTER SIX

THE CRISIS OF
MASCULINITY

MOST MIGRANT DOMESTIC WORKERS ARE women. Still, a number of studies have observed the masculinization of migrant domestic work (Sarti and Scrinzi, 2010; Haile and Siegmann, 2014). Although the overall number of male domestic workers deployed from the Philippines remains small, they do comprise a larger proportion of newly deployed migrants to Italy—437 compared to 786 women in 2010[1]—which indicates a greater representation of men among domestic workers in this country than in other destinations. In Italy, government figures indicate that in 2002 approximately 18 percent of domestic workers who contributed to social security were men (Instituto Nazionale della Previdenza Sociale [INPS] and Caritas, 2004). In contrast, female domestic workers disproportionately overshadow their male counterparts in the few other destinations that host a sizeable number of male domestic workers: 141 men as compared to 21,143 women entered Kuwait as domestic workers in 2010; 448 men and 28,154 women entered Hong Kong in the same year, and 344 men as compared to

11,236 women entered Saudi Arabia then.[2] This chapter focuses exclusively on the case of Rome. Although men can be found doing domestic work in both Los Angeles and Rome, the racial segregation of Filipinos in domestic work in the latter makes it more compelling to examine how men in this community cope with having to do this labor.

Although Filipino men have been funneled into paid housework, the employer preference for female domestic workers has limited their employment opportunities (Scrinzi, 2010), resulting in high rates of unemployment or irregular employment. This, I found, is just one of a number of challenges to Filipino migrant masculinity, in addition to performing "feminine" work (Haile and Siegmann, 2014); depending financially on women; and being immersed in women-centered networks of migration, employment, and family (Scrinzi, 2010).[3] In this chapter, I examine how men negotiate their greater dependence on women and how they deal with the threats to their masculinity that this and the precariousness of their labor pose. More significantly, I ask if these socioeconomic conditions, which tend to be more beneficial to women, result in more egalitarian gender relations in the community.

In a small-scale study of Filipino male domestic workers in the Netherlands, Haile and Siegmann (2014) examine how men recuperate masculinity. They argue that male domestic workers are confronted by a diminished self-worth from their performance of "male femininities." By this they mean what Mimi Schippers describes as "the characteristics and practices that are culturally ascribed to women" (2007: 96), such as cleaning and cooking in the home. Further threatening their masculinity is the power that female employers wield over them. Male domestic workers supposedly counter their performance of "male femininities" by foregrounding their breadwinning responsibilities as fathers and underscoring the physical strength the job requires (Haile and Siegmann, 2014: 108). In her classic study of men in occupations traditionally held by women, sociologist Christine Williams (1995) similarly found that men's masculinity is not automatically assumed in their job. Consequently, this prompts them to deploy tactics to reestablish masculinity, including foregrounding the masculine aspects of the job, sex segregation, and disassociating from the work.[4] In contrast, my conversations with Filipino men in Rome indicate that they are less concerned with performing male femininity than they are with their diminished access to employment, one that is undoubtedly aggravated by the recession in Italy.[5] Additionally, they did not necessarily foreground breadwinning to counter the feminine aspects of their job. Instead, financially supporting the family embodies the larger purpose of their migration; this is a goal they share with women, and one that is notably threatened by their segregation in domestic work.

In questioning how the segregation of Filipinos into domestic work has shaped men's masculinity and gender relations in the community, I do not primarily seek to address how men negotiate their performance of a feminine occupation.[6] Unlike claims made in other studies (see Haile and Siegmann, 2014), male domestic workers I spoke to did not necessarily feel that the "feminine duties" they performed on the job threatened their masculinity. Perhaps this is because of the prevalence of male domestic workers in the Philippines (Medina, 1991). As historian Vicente Rafael describes:

Colonial households employed predominantly male servants, both Chinese and Filipino, usually obtained through the intercession of a relative already attached to the household or passed down, as it were, from one employer to another. . . . [I]n the Philippine colony over three-fourths of the live-in servants were males, with a smaller number of females working as day laborers, usually doing laundry. (2000: 69–70)

Rafael's observation suggests that domestic work is not inherently feminine. Likewise in Zambia, men historically did not consider domestic work as feminine but instead preferred this labor over the "grim work conditions on farms and mines" (Hansen, 1989: 33). As Hansen insightfully observes, "Gender roles are not given; they are made. Their construction depends on a complex interweaving of cultural factors and social practices with economic forces, and questions of power" (1989: 5). The male domestic workers I met in Rome insisted that their job is not *pang babae* or "for a woman," meaning feminine. I only met one who performed child care, a job definitively constructed as feminine (Medina, 1991; Ridgeway, 2011); the others cleaned houses, cooked, and looked after immobile individuals whose care required their physical strength.

Although not *pang babae*, domestic work does not necessarily evoke a dominant type of masculinity. Instead, it projects a demasculinized subject vis-à-vis other men. In Zambia, male servants regardless of age were considered "boys." As such, they were masculinized to be childlike, of simple mind, subordinate, and not decision makers. They were only secondarily male and thus were not considered sexually threatening, despite their close contact with white women (Hansen, 1989: 70). This suggests that the emasculation of male domestic workers does not necessarily occur in relation to female domestic workers but instead vis-à-vis the straw man of a traditionally masculine subject. In Rome, this could be a hegemonic masculine figure for the former engineer who now finds himself doing domestic work in Rome or a working-class masculine figure for the former security guard who now finds himself doing housework for a living.

Domestic work was not the first choice for male migrants in Rome; instead, it has resulted out of necessity due to labor-market segregation in the area. And although it is not at the top of their list, the job is still not easily accessible to men. Male unemployment is rampant in Rome's Filipino migrant community because employers continue to prefer female domestic workers. Accordingly, I illustrate that the segregation of Filipinos in domestic work has impeded the labor-market opportunities for men, resulting in them being less consistently employed than women; this, consequently, threatens their identity as a male breadwinner, which many scholars have established as the definitive marker of masculinity in the Philippines (Medina, 1991; Pingol, 2001; Parreñas, 2005). My examination of the plight of male domestic workers shows that women's greater income-earning power in Rome's Filipino migrant community has not reduced gender status hierarchies. Instead, gender inequality persists, as I illustrate in men's reconstitution of particular forms of domestic work as masculine, their avoidance of feminized forms of housework, and their embrace of leadership positions in the community.

PRECARIOUS WORK

In their introduction to a special issue on male domestic workers in the journal *Men and Masculinities*, Rafaella Sarti and Francesca Scrinzi (2010) claim that men constituted a significant proportion of domestic workers in Italy in the mid-1990s, reaching up to a third of all domestic workers in the country and at least 17 percent in 1996 (2010: 7). Despite their presence, employers still preferred to hire women (Haile and Siegmann, 2014). As Randy, a food vendor outside the Philippine Embassy, noted, "It is difficult here if you are a man. It is much easier to be a woman":

It is because our jobs are limited to domestic work, inside the home. If you have to hire a domestic worker, would you hire a man? Let us consider if you have a child. Isn't it true that most domestic workers are women? What they call a *badante*, an elder caregiver, they might need to hire men [due to the lifting of immobile wards]. But these days they even mostly hire women. It is because women know how to provide care. They are also seen as a safer group to hire.

The preference for hiring women raises the question of how the labor-market segregation of Filipinos in domestic work limits opportunities for men and, following Randy's observation, directs men away from jobs that entail care work.

Interviews I conducted in 2011 with twelve male domestic workers in Rome and informal conversations I had with dozens of men in parks and other known public gathering areas—such as the entrance to the Philippine Embassy—indicate that male domestic workers primarily do part-time work. This had also been the case among the ten male domestic workers I had interviewed in the mid-1990s. Unlike Polish men, Filipino men notably do not have opportunities to do the "masculinized domestic work" of handymen or gardeners that Majella Kilkey and her colleagues (2013) describe but remain limited to traditional forms of domestic work such as elder care and housekeeping. Notably, the housekeeping duties relegated to men often included masculine tasks such as cleaning outside windows and outdoor patios, which the male relatives of female domestic workers were hired to perform instead.

The Filipino men I met in Rome often painted a bleak picture of their labor-market options, pointing to their stunted integration into domestic work. A strong indication of the unemployment or irregular employment plaguing men is their visible presence in pockets of gathering in the community. On any given day, dozens of Filipino men can be seen gathered outside the entrance of the Philippine Embassy or in parks conveniently located near train stations like Eur Fermi and Piramide. These pockets are scattered throughout the city of Rome, representing the small-scale geographic sites (as opposed to one central site) that Filipinos occupy in the city. Men comprise approximately 90 percent of the Filipinos gathered in these spaces, which I had also encountered in the field in 1995 and 1996. And as they did in the mid-1990s, men continue to struggle to find regular employment now. In my interviews, I was repeatedly told, "It is very hard for men to find work." This was the case more recently as well as in the mid-1990s.

Moreover, their comments suggest that women still perform the bulk of domestic work in Italy, revealing that the men who do perform domestic work only do a fraction of this labor. Reflecting women's dominance in the occupation, it is even women who usually give men access to employment opportunities. As the hairdresser Gilbert explained, "It is very difficult. It's very hard here especially if there are no women to help you. Women can find jobs more easily than men. Employers prefer women. . . . What happens is that women have to be there to present you to the employer." Women's dominance in this aspect led me to wonder what type of niche men occupy in domestic work. In other words, how has the preference for and greater trust of women domestic workers shaped men's experiences in the labor market?

One of the biggest impacts of the segregation of Filipinos into domestic work is irregular employment for men. This means that men are often ineligible for a *permesso di soggiorno*, as qualifying for legal residency requires migrants complete a minimum of twenty-five hours of work per week. Instead, men often obtained their residency through the sponsorship of their wife.[7] This is the case with Valentina's husband, who by May 2014 still had not found a job since following her to Rome in 2009.[8] Prospective male domestic workers can secure only part-time cleaning jobs that usually entail no more than two to three hours per week. Working full time for them would require that they secure more than ten employers per week. In contrast, women have more opportunities to secure various regularized forms of domestic work, including those described as *lungo orario* (long hours), meaning live-out jobs with daily shifts, or live-in jobs. Men, in contrast, can often obtain a live-in job only if they are part of a *coppia*, working in tandem with their spouse or as an elder caregiver, usually of older men or of immobile individuals whose care requires physical strength. In rare cases, they might also be hired as a live-in nanny for a young boy. This was the case for Dennis, who has been caring for a young boy for the last ten years. However, his job is not ideal, as he only earns 700 euros [US$928] per month, less than the prevailing wage. In general, men secure forms of domestic work that require them to perform masculine tasks, whether it is lifting wards, providing male bonding activities for male children, or doing physically strenuous cleaning activities. Notably, the duties relegated to men are the arguably less-feminine tasks of domestic work. When asked what they do at work, many, as they are mostly part-time workers, responded, "*linis* and *plancha*," referring to cleaning and ironing clothes. Besides being mostly "nonnurturant" reproductive labor (Duffy, 2005), the nature of their job allows them to distance themselves from their mostly female employers, potentially minimizing the feminization men experience with female supervisors (Haile and Siegmann, 2014).

Yet, some would argue that nonnurturant reproductive labor is women's work. For example, Lorenzo, a domestic worker for more than ten years in Rome, did not initially feel comfortable doing "women's work." "In the beginning, I could not take it that I had to wash plates, cook, clean the house, do things that you would not normally do. You go grocery shopping. You iron clothes and even sew. Think about that," he explained. However, most of his counterparts, including those I initially interviewed in Rome in 1996, did not agree with Lorenzo's views; instead, they had more of a problem with the downward class mobility that doing domestic work signified for them. As Mark complained, "When at first I came here, I was embarrassed. It is true that you might clean your own house, but you were not a maid. Here we are the modern maids." Others dismissed the argument that they are performing women's work when cleaning, cooking, and doing the laundry, arguing instead that such work is not inherently feminine. As Jake defensively described,

They say that women can do what men do. Don't they say that? Well, men can do women's work better than women can do men's work. Isn't that true? We are more capable of doing what you women do than you can what men do. For example, lifting a sack of rice, you would not be able to do that, that is 50 kilos. I am just giving you an example. Of course, you are capable of doing some men's work, but we are more capable of what you do. What we just cannot do is wear a skirt.

For most men, the notion of domestic work as women's work did not faze them; instead they pointed to the aspects of the work that required physical stamina and other such masculine characteristics.

Another sizeable group of men one encounters in public pockets of gathering in the community are unemployed.[9] According to the listings in one job bank I visited, the most available job for domestic workers is live-in child care, which many employers do not want to give to men. The jobs that men would prefer, or employers would be open to hiring them for, are not available as frequently. Part-time cleaning and elder care jobs get filled quickly. At the job bank, I met a man in his twenties who asked me if I knew of any available jobs. He told me that he had been in Rome for six months, sleeping on the floor in his cousin's living room while he looked for work, which he had yet to find. He was not the only unemployed man I met. I ran into many of them in parks like Eur Fermi and, as I have already noted, at the entrance of the Philippine Embassy. Enrique, another unemployed man I met, had finally decided to follow his wife to Italy after spending ten years apart. He entered Italy with a residence permit that he had secured via *ricongiungimento familiare*, meaning family reunification. His wife, who petitioned for him, told him that he would be able to find part-time jobs easily, and he would not have to work as much because of her steady income. I could not ignore the sadness in his voice as he shared his story with me, expressing his deep regret for giving up his managerial job as an engineer in the Philippines. He had earned 30,000 pesos a month—approximately US$700—in the Philippines but had been unemployed since reaching Italy a little more than six months before I met him. Enrique told me that he no longer had the option of returning to his work in the Philippines because he had officially retired from his position. Thinking about his situation, he lamented, "I have no purpose anymore." Enrique is like many men who raised their children in the Philippines, not necessarily as househusbands but as working husbands while their wives also worked abroad. Their identities as fathers and income earners—joint breadwinners for the family—had given them purpose, both of which were lost when they relocated to Rome.

Another migrant struggling with his inability to provide for his family was Randy, a food vendor outside the Philippine Embassy. He told me that he and his wife would not be able to survive in Rome without the help of his wife's mother, who lets them stay in her apartment for free. Randy's mother-in-law has been in Rome for nearly thirty years, having raised her children, including Randy's wife, from a distance, and petitioning for most of her children before they turned eighteen years old. She also managed to get one of her employers to sponsor Randy's migration.[10]

Randy is currently looking for a live-in job as a *badante* (elder caregiver) that would allow him to provide housing for his wife and son. After shadowing his mother-in-law for his first five months in the country to learn housecleaning, he then landed a job in an agrotourism farmhouse where he worked alone as the "all-around." He was the "waiter, dishwasher, room boy, cleaner, and maintenance manager." He worked in isolation for two years. As he described, "At first, I thought I was going to go crazy. I did not hear a thing except the sound of cows. This is true. I did not have any neighbors." Randy would have had his wife and child join him there, but he worried that they would not survive the harsh winter conditions. Since quitting the farmhouse a year before we spoke, Randy had been struggling to find full-time employment. His wife had found more steady work doing part-time cleaning jobs throughout the city, and both were looking for a live-in job that would allow them to stay together as a couple.

The stories of Enrique and Randy suggest that what poses the primary threat to their masculinity is their struggle to find gainful employment in a labor market where they are racially segregated into domestic work; their unemployment or irregular employment not only takes away their breadwinner status but also heightens their dependence on women in the community. We see this in Randy's case, as he depends financially not only on his wife but also on her mother. It is usually women who migrate first in the family, initially hear of job opportunities in the labor market, and primarily sustain the family economically. Yet, a woman's capacity to sustain the family is also limited by her low wages as a domestic worker. Randy's wife's earnings, for instance, are not enough to afford them their own apartment. To attain a semblance of a nuclear family, that is a family that lives in an independent household and not in a bed-space arrangement with other Filipino migrants, both partners must contribute to the household.

What gives men greater flexibility in the labor market is their access to other types of jobs, though they are limited. On hearing that I live in California, one man I met in front of the Philippine Embassy remarked, "Lucky you. In California, you have plenty of job options." He continued, "Here we only have three options: house, restaurants, and hotels." An increasing number of Filipinos can now be found doing front-stage work as baristas, waiters, cashiers, bellhops, and front-desk clerks.[11] This had not been the case in the mid-1990s, when only domestic work was open to Filipinos. They have access to front-stage jobs not only because of their Italian language skills but also for their English language skills, which allow them to cater to the large number of tourists that descend on Rome and the Vatican every day. Front-stage workers tend to be the children of migrants who came to Italy during their teenage years and enrolled in high school. Because the Italian language skills of many older Filipino migrants are rudimentary at best, many never acquire access to front-stage employment.

Filipino men in Rome clearly have limited job options. To keep up with women, men construct a patchwork of employment in both the formal and informal sectors of the economy. Men commonly described performing a variety of "odd jobs." One young man in his twenties told me that before he secured a morning *lungo orario* job, which he offsets with an evening job as a bellhop in a three-star hotel in Rome, he worked full time "cleaning the ass of butchered pigs." Another man in his thirties told me that he adds to his earnings as a janitor at night by peddling cell phones in the Filipino community, allowing customers to pay in installments of 100 to 200 euros (US$133 to 266) per month. Men also turn to selling cooked foods. Unlike in the 1990s, when women dominated the informal food-vending market in the community, one now sees mostly men peddling prepared foods near the train stations and parks that Filipino part-time workers frequent. Men serve meals in prepackaged bags that are convenient for customers to take away or eat on the spot. Ironically, still it is women—the wives of the male vendors—who usually prepare these foods at night after returning home from a full day of domestic work. Some men also provide van tours to make a living, charging tourists 450 euros (US$597) for a day trip outside of Rome. As domestic work remains the primary job available to Filipinos in Rome, the preference for hiring women domestic workers has pushed men to creatively patch together a number of odd jobs to make a living.

MEN'S ASPIRATIONS AND REALITIES

Despite the difficulties men face in securing regular employment in Rome, a consistent flow of them still opt to migrate. Some former seafarers arrive by jumping ship; most enter not as tourists but as petitioned family members or directly hired workers. Randy is one of those who entered as a directly hired worker. But because his sponsor had never intended to provide him with regular employment, Randy faced the task of finding a new sponsor once he arrived in Rome. Although Randy has struggled to provide for his family, he has not given up. His aspiration, one he shares with many, is to secure full-time employment that would allow him to not only earn an income but also provide for his family.

Unlike other men I spoke with, Randy does not talk about going back to the Philippines. Various members of the community told me that men, particularly older ones, who follow their wives after years of separation are likely to return to the Philippines, coming to Rome only to annually renew their residency. Notably, many of these men had jobs in the Philippines that they had to quit to reunify their family. Randy, however, is intent on making it in Italy and establishing his position as an income provider. For this reason, he introduces himself every day to Filipinos coming in and out of the Philippine Embassy, asking them if they know of any jobs and sharing his phone number with them in case they hear of any. One reason he has not given up is the support of his mother-in-law, who frequently reminds him not to lose hope. This is bolstered by the trickle of men in the community who have successfully secured full-time work. Two such men are Raul and Danilo, whose full-time employment in Rome is the envy of many in the community.

A Filipino in his early thirties, Danilo works as a waiter in the city center, in a café on a side street off the Piazza Rotunda, location of the Pantheon. He works six days a week for up to eleven hours a day. His duties extend beyond serving. Describing himself as an "all-around" worker, he is a "sales lady," "cashier," "bartender," "waiter," "errand boy," and "car valet" for the owners. His employers own four businesses—a café, a hostel, a leather goods store, and an umbrella shop—that Danilo circulates among in the vicinity. Although he considers his work challenging, Danilo knows he is one of the more fortunate men in the community. Speaking of the plight of Filipino men in Rome, he describes their situation as "bad, bad, bad" and claims that up to 50 percent of them are unemployed.

Prior to working at the bar, Danilo moved from one live-in domestic job to another. His first was for a seventy-four-year-old single Italian man, a leather factory owner who lived in a large estate in the outskirts of Rome. Danilo worked as an "all-around" in the estate, mostly cleaning inside the house. A gardener took care of the grounds, which he described as one hectare in size, while a full-time cook handled the meals. Besides cleaning, he sometimes provided assistance at parties, "pouring champagne" for guests. Although the job gave Danilo some sort of security, his employer did not allow his partner to live with him. For this reason, he felt that he had no option but to quit, doing so once he secured a job as a *badante* for an older man in Rome.

His work as a *badante* was not ideal, but it gave him and his partner free housing. It did not pay well, and it was physically challenging:

[My employer] was eighty-four years old and diabetic. He was so fat. My live-in partner and the baby were stay-in at the house with me. We did not pay rent, but my salary was only 800 euros [US$1,060]. And my work was not normal. At 3 in the morning, the old man will call me over because he took a shit. When he took a shit, the smell would be everywhere in the entire house. And one time, when I woke up in the morning, he had shit, and it was scattered all over his back. It was because his diaper was filled and so it overflowed. . . . He had not taken a shit in three to four days. I sometimes had to give him a suppository. . . . When I saw it, I did not know what to clean. I did not know where to start.

The challenges of his work as a *badante* magnified feelings of contradictory class mobility for Danilo. As he described:

Sometimes I would think to myself, why am I subjecting myself to this kind of work? I told myself, in the Philippines, I did not do this. I have a college degree in Human Resources Management. I became a manager of a restaurant. My experience really was with managerial and supervisory positions. Then, when I got here, I did all the low-level jobs. I thought to myself, why not do it? I am now here after all. What else will I do? No turning back.

To negotiate his conflicting class mobility, Danilo took it upon himself to learn Italian. He wanted to secure a front-stage job, considered high status in the community, that he would not be embarrassed to share with family and friends in the Philippines. On working as a waiter, he stated,

It is like a middle-class kind of work. It is not professional, but it is not domestic work. So it looks good in a way. It is presentable. There is pride. . . . When you go back to the Philippines, someone will ask you what you do for a living. It is embarrassing to say you are a domestic worker, but you can say you are a waiter and bartender with pride. Then they are impressed. They are impressed you are a waiter and bartender. They think you are well versed in the language, you are skilled. But little do they know that it is really stressful.

When domestic workers approach him and say, "Wow, you are so lucky. Your job is so easy. You just stand around the whole day," he responds, "Because you work at home, your situation is this: When your employer is sleeping, you are also sleeping, and what your employers eat, you get to eat as well. Then after your work, you can go back to your room and rest. Us, in contrast, we have to stand around for ten hours, and we have to accommodate all these people." According to Danilo, his work as a waiter is much more strenuous than any form of domestic work he has performed in Italy.

Front-stage workers are also more likely to experience blatant discrimination. This occurs in their interactions with customers but also through unequal labor standards for migrant and nonmigrant workers, even though Italy has some of the more generous work benefits in Europe. Contractual employment in the formal sector secures the annual benefit of a thirteenth- and fourteenth-month pay, as well as liquidation pay at the end of the year— the equivalent of one month of salary per year of service. Such benefits help to secure retirement funds for workers, who also receive a "labor pension" from the government if they or their employer continuously contributed to their social security.[12] Yet, Filipinos complain that many employers circumvent the law and insist on paying them in cash. Employers are unlikely to do the same to Italian workers. This is the case with Danilo's partner, whose official salary on her paystub is only half of her monthly earning of 1,100 euros (US$1,458) per month. By declaring her income as less, her employers are not only evading taxes but compensate her with less benefits at the end of the year, less liquidation pay, and a smaller labor pension. Providing another example, Danilo also told me that he receives lower wages and works more hours than his Italian coworkers.

Many Filipino migrants envy Danilo's life. Not only is he a front-stage worker, but he also rents his own apartment, unlike many others who are forced to rent bed-spaces and share housing in crowded units with other Filipinos. Yet, Danilo does not see his situation as the most ideal. As he noted, his salary of 1,300 euros (US$1724) is less than that of his Italian coworkers, who put in fewer hours than he does. Moreover, while his Italian coworkers receive overtime pay, he does not. Due to the blatant wage disparities he sees in Italy, he would like to move somewhere else, possibly Canada, where he hopes wage disparities between migrants and nationals will not be as strikingly obvious.

Despite these challenges, Danilo prefers his current job to domestic work, as it not only eases his contradictory class mobility but also allows him and his partner to live independently of employers. Danilo now lives in a one-bedroom apartment that he rents with his partner in Rome. They split all the expenses evenly. "When we get our salary, we take the money—all cash—and we put it on the table. I get paid by check, and so I cash it at the bank first. But the next week, we lay out all the money on the table with my money on one side and hers on the other side. Then we start allocating the funds according to our expenses. So rent, we take 325 euros [US$431] from her pile and 325 [US$431] from my pile." Danilo earns 1,300 euros a month (US$1,724), while his partner earns 1,100. Each of them sends money to their respective families in the Philippines and also to their son, who resides with his maternal kin. Notably, the equitable split in expenses between Danilo and his partner has not translated to an equal division of labor in their family. When asked to describe his relationship, he told me, "She is very good to me. She takes care of me. She prepares everything. She irons my uniform. She makes dinner." The unequal division of labor in his family mirrors that of many others I met in the community.

For Danilo, avoiding domestic work does not necessarily recoup his masculinity. Instead, it is his full-time employment and income contributions to the family that secure his feelings of manhood. Further solidifying that is his partner's role of serving him, which without question establishes his higher status in the relationship. Notably, he and his partner's equal contribution to their household income has not translated to an equal partnership. Also reinforcing his masculinity is his ability to stray in their relationship. Danilo admitted to having had extramarital affairs in the past, behavior that he would never tolerate of his live-in partner. According to members of the community, extramarital affairs are apparently not uncommon among men in the Filipino migrant community, where the skewed gender ratio works to the advantage of heterosexual men. This is why I knew better than to take seriously one of the men I met at one of the common gathering place for the community. Not long after finding out that I was visiting from California, a man named Romelo started inviting me out to tour Rome, telling me, "My wife left me, which is probably why you and I met one another. If you are happy, then I am happy."[13] I later learned from the women around me that this behavior was typical among married men in the community, including Romelo, who, I was told, lives with his wife and child in Rome.

The dynamics between these two men and their partners illustrates the persistence of gender inequality, which Cecilia Ridgeway observes is continuously rewritten "into new social and economic arrangements" (2011: 28). This is clearly the case among Filipinos in Rome, where women's better labor-market opportunities have not necessarily led to an egalitarian distribution of housework. Danilo's perspective on his masculinity, or *pagkalalaki*, is not unique. Being a male provider—even if in a dual wage-earning household—is the primary marker that men in the community use to define their masculinity. For them, doing domestic work itself has not threatened their masculinity; for some, it has even been a way to achieve it. This is the case with Raul, one of the few Filipinos who managed to purchase a home in Italy as a domestic worker.

Raul and his wife came to Italy in 1990 with the help of her relatives, each paying US$4,000 to a travel agency that smuggled them to Italy via the former Yugoslavia. Since then, Raul has done nothing but domestic work. His first job was as a live-in worker for an Italian family. When I commented on how rare that seems, he clarified that he had been an "all-around who does everything—carpenter, gardener . . . everything." When I asked him about "care work," he responded, "I also cooked, cleaned the house, ironed, did the laundry." Raul's work has never included the nurturant reproductive labor usually assigned to women. Instead, he distinguished his work as "the hard work that women cannot do, for example, climbing up to reach the windows . . . if something is broken in the house, fixing it, anything electrical." However, Raul was not one to shy away from nurturing tasks, describing himself as "the gentle type" who was more than willing to look after his employers' grandchildren whenever they visited.

Raul lasted with his first employers for a few years, then transitioned to part-time employment. For the last sixteen years, he has had one steady employing family whose house he cleans for five hours a day, Monday through Friday. While his employers have only given him one raise in the last sixteen years, they have rewarded him in other ways. For one, they helped four of Raul's siblings come to Rome by recruiting friends to directly hire them. They also helped Raul and his wife Cynthia purchase an apartment in 2000, acting as a guarantor for the bank loan. As some of the few homeowners in the Filipino migrant community, Raul and Cynthia now pay a mortgage of 900 euros (US$1,193) a month for their three-bedroom apartment in a working-class neighborhood in the city's periphery. Both contribute to their monthly income. Finally, Raul's current employers—like all of his other employers—maintain a contract with him, which means they not only contribute to his INPS (social security) but also pay him for a thirteenth month at the end of each year.

Raul takes home approximately 2,300 euros (US$3,050) per month. He adds to the income he earns from his primary employer with a number of part-time jobs across the city. Working for an average of four families, sometimes up to a total of twelve hours per day, Raul travels by scooter from one job to the next. Earning only 8 to 10 euros (US$10.60 to 13.25) per hour, Raul works as much as fifty-two hours a week. Cynthia also works as a domestic, mostly a babysitter, from Monday through Friday. She works for two families for a total of nine hours per day, earning 1,800 euros (US$2,387) a month. Cynthia also works from their home on the weekends and during holidays as an unlicensed dentist. Trained in the Philippines, Cynthia had passed the dentistry board exams and worked for two years for a government hospital before she migrated to Rome. She avoids major procedures such as root canals but provides regular cleanings, fillings, and braces. When asked how much she charges, she told me "Philippine prices," 25 euros (US$33) for a cleaning, which is significantly less than the 80 euros (US$106) that a licensed dentist in Rome would charge. Braces cost significantly more, 600 to 700 euros (US$796 to $928) for the top and bottom teeth. Cynthia gets her supplies from a local dental-supply store, whose staff, upon learning of her training as a dentist in the Philippines, had actually encouraged her to provide dental services from her home. When I asked if she worried about getting in trouble, a friend of hers interrupted us and told me that working illicitly is the norm in Italy. As she said, "There are a lot of Italians that did not even graduate, and they even charge a lot."

Raul and Cynthia show signs of assimilation, for instance choosing to give their two children—Adriano and Martina—Italian names and insisting on serving me wine with our dinner. Yet, in response to my question of whether they feel Italian, Cynthia noted, "I don't feel that way." This is perhaps because they rarely spend time with Italians and mostly socialize with Filipinos. Raul and Cynthia's family is unusual, as they have chosen to raise

their two children in Rome. Cynthia had provided primary care for them until they started school, having sent their children back to the Philippines for
only two and a half years, when the oldest was two years old and the youngest
six months old. They decided to send them home because Cynthia struggled
to balance her work and child care responsibilities. They also had siblings in
the Philippines they needed to support. Only after they had "finished helping
those that [they] were assisting" did Raul and Cynthia decide to bring their
children back to Italy.

Raul and Cynthia's children will likely stay in Italy even after their parents
return to the Philippines, where they also own a home in a Manila suburb.
Both children were born in Italy, the oldest while Cynthia was undocumented.
This is now posing a problem for Martina, who wishes to apply for Italian
citizenship on the principle of *jus soli*, a right of birth given to those born to
documented mothers when they turn eighteen years old. In contrast, Adriano
will not have difficulty securing Italian citizenship when he applies in two years
time, as Cynthia had legal residency by the time he was born.

Gender inequalities persist in Cynthia and Raul's family, demonstrated
in Cynthia's role as primary caregiver and in the gendered distribution of
housework. Cynthia does most of the housework, but the couple attributes
this to Raul's longer work hours. During the weekends, Raul busies himself
with home-improvement projects such as painting, installing wallpaper, and
building shelves. Although proud of his cooking skills, especially of Italian
food, he spends more time grilling on their terrace than in the kitchen, where
Cynthia spends most of her time when she is not taking care of someone in the
dentist chair prominently stationed in their hallway. In their family there has
not been a dramatic reconstitution of the gendered division of labor, as most
of the housework remains Cynthia's responsibility. The resistance to change
in their household should not come as a surprise. After all, as Ridgeway notes,
"Changes in gender beliefs lag behind material changes" (2011: 160).

Danilo and Raul demonstrate that it is possible for Filipino men to secure
full-time work in Rome. Each has done a variety of full-time jobs since ar-
riving in Rome, and both initially pursuing live-in domestic work to legalize
their status. Yet the live-in work that they pursued allowed them to foreground
masculine skills such as lifting a heavy ward in Danilo's case, and household
maintenance skills in the case of Raul. Neither of them sees domestic work

as innately feminine. Instead, both men point out that certain types of domestic work require masculine skills; according to both of them, this is the bulk of the work they have had to perform in their jobs. This is perhaps why their employment as domestic workers has not translated to a more equitable division of labor in their homes; for the most part, each of them has mostly taken on "masculine" chores at home such as paying bills or handling repairs.

Although they have chosen to underscore the masculine attributes required in their jobs, Danilo and Raul have undeniably also taken on traditional female duties at home and at work, for instance cooking and ironing. These tasks remain primarily designated to women but are now acceptable for some men to perform. Yet, as such tasks constitute nonnurturant reproductive labor, men like Raul and Danilo can easily insist on their gender neutrality. Doing so suggests some form of potential gender transformation with the redefinition of certain women's work as doable for men. However, the marking of such work as low-status, racialized labor may hinder their transformative potential, as it could be seen as nothing but a racialized "male femininity" (Schippers, 2007) forced on men of color. Lastly, lest we forget that the majority of Filipino men in Rome struggle to secure employment, we should underscore that most men are irregularly employed or unemployed. In other words, most are denied the opportunity to perform any form of reproductive labor, whether the task is labeled masculine, feminine, or gender neutral.

By insisting that domestic work requires some masculine traits, men like Danilo and Raul possibly challenge the gender characterization of domestic work as feminine, suggesting that the presence of men and their performance of domestic work might lead to it being more highly regarded. However, this does not seem to be the case. The experiences of Raul and Danilo raise the question of whether the performance of domestic work by men diminishes its association as a feminine occupation. Although Francesca Scrinzi (2010) noticed the professionalization of the job when performed by men, it seems that this is not mirrored in their financial compensation. The prevailing wage for both men and women in Italy when I returned to the field in 2011 had been 8 to 10 euros (US$10.60 to 13.25) per hour. If we are to account for the greater likelihood that employers will contribute to the social security of female domestic workers, we could even argue that women are likely to be better compensated than their male counterparts. If we considered that only a marked increase in pay for domestic workers would indicate that involvement of men has indeed diminished the feminization of the job (Ridgeway, 2011), then we can argue that the performance of domestic work by Filipino men in Italy has not necessarily upgraded the profession.

PUBLIC DISPLAYS OF MASCULINITY

Filipino men's struggles in Rome's labor market resonate with the experiences of the Indian men that Sheba George (2005) focuses on in *When Women Come First*, a study on the gender division of labor in the households of female Indian nurses in the United States. Women earned a living in all of these households, whereas men did not always do so. In this context, George observed a variety of gender arrangements. In many of the families where men also earned a consistent living, couples usually retained a traditional division of labor in which women did child care and housework while men managed the family finances. In most households where men had uneven job histories, men assisted with child care, but women still retained primary responsibility for housework. Other households, in contrast, saw men retreat completely from housework, indicating their "gender revolt" (Parreñas, 2008b) against the greater income-earning power of women. Finally, a group of men and women formed "partnership households" in which neither the man nor the woman claimed to be the head of the household, negotiating women's higher income by sharing an equal distribution of housework, child care, and financial decision making. According to George, key to men's ability to accept women's greater income-earning power is their access to leadership activities in spheres outside the home. This is likewise the case among Filipino men in Rome. We see this most clearly in the growth of fraternal organizations.

In Rome, masculine displays are ubiquitous in the Filipino community, as men dressed in fatigues often roam community events. Groups of men donning matching tops emblazoned with acronyms seemingly indecipherable to the average person—"DGPI BRONZE WING," "UGBII SOLID BROTHERS, ROME CHAPTER" or "PDGII ROME, CHAPTER," and "GPII ANTI-CRIME"—are visible in any community gathering in Rome. Although I was able to learn what only a few of the many acronyms stood for—"PDGII ROME" refers to "Philippine Democratic Guardians International Inc.," for example—I did eventually learn that the groups of men I frequently saw gathered at community events, from fiestas sponsored by the Philippine Embassy to regular Sunday mass at Santa Prudenziana near Termini, belonged to the Guardians Brotherhood, a national organization in the Philippines that stands for "Gentlemen, United Associates of our Race, Dauntless, Ingenious, Advocators of Nation and Society." The organization's primary constituency is members of the Armed Forces of the Philippines and the Integrated National Police. This group is quite similar to the Guardian Angels in the United States, a volunteer-based group that works to safeguard inner-city streets.[14] The Guardian Angels likewise wear distinctive uniforms of red berets with white t-shirts emblazoned with their group's name.

The Guardians Brotherhood was started in the Philippines in 1976 by Sergeant Leborio M. Jangao Jr., who with other members in a remote area of Mindanao formed the "Dirty Dozen," which they later renamed to "Diablo Squad."[15] The organization initially formed to provide protection in areas threatened by the infiltration of separatist guerillas in Mindanao, in the southern Philippines. The original group eventually dissolved when its military members were reassigned to other areas in the region. In 1978, Sergeant Jangao revived the group as the "Diablo Squads, Crime Buster." By 1982, the group boasted 15,000 members throughout the region of Mindanao. Eventually the group spread throughout the Philippines, reaching 30,000 members by 1984. It was then that Sergeant Jangao, whom current members refer to as "Master Founder Godfather 'Abraham,'" or "GMFGF, the Father of All Guardians," registered the organization with the Security and Exchange Commission under the name the "Guardians Brotherhood, Inc." The purpose of Guardians Brotherhood is to provide "service through strong brotherhood." As described in a local community magazine, the organization's members "seek to fight for the aspiration of the people. Until death, until the last drop of blood. . . . Together they foster the promotion of peace and harmony" (Cruzat, 2010: 15). The organization follows six main principles: "Brotherhood, Justice, Peace, Discipline, Service, and Equality." Accordingly, members are expected to provide brotherly camaraderie and uphold law and order in their community. Although the group initially formed to protect civilians in areas of armed conflict in the Philippines, it now provides law and order in various areas of the Philippines. Due to the relatively low rate of crime in Rome, it was a surprise to meet a number of self-appointed male "guardians" at various community events. In Rome, members of the Guardians Brotherhood offer protection to dignitaries and celebrities in public events, ensure law and order in parties and other gatherings in the community, and provide financial support to the needy and relief goods to areas in the Philippines afflicted by natural disasters. In other words, they are self-appointed protectors of the community and providers for the country.

Although Master Founder Abraham is the credited founder of the organization in the Philippines, Master Founder Scorpion is said to have initiated the first chapter in Rome in 2000. Since then, fifteen chapters of Guardians Brotherhood have formed in Rome, all registered with the headquarters in the Philippines. Each member pays a fee of 5 euros (US$6.60) per month, 1 euro (US$1.33) of which is sent to the headquarters in the Philippines while the rest is spent on group activities. Women can join local chapters of the organization, but I was told by one interviewee they are excluded from positions of leadership.

Guardians Brotherhood not only provides men with moral support but also allows them to buttress their masculinity as leaders of the community. The roles of protector and provider that male "guardians" have assigned themselves in the community evoke feelings of masculinity. Intensifying those are the tattoos that represent the "Markings of GBI Guardian Brothers." The elaborate "marking" or tattoo system of Guardians establishes one's membership and place in the hierarchy of the organization. The tattoo is placed prominently in between the thumb and index finger. According to members I spoke to in Rome, the tattoo allows them to identify one another in public; for instance, they often approach fellow Guardians when they spot each other on the bus. These tattoos also indicate their presence as a protector to other members of the community.

As I have now become familiar with their tattoo system, I have recognized many Guardians across the diaspora including in Dubai and Singapore, meeting them usually on buses and trains. Their tattoos have given me a convenient entryway to meet potential male interviewees in the Filipino migrant community. On completion of a Basic Membership Course that instills the principles of Guardian Brothers, a member earns a color-coordinated tattoo (or a mark) on his right hand; civilian members get an "MG" tattooed in mint green for "Magic Group," and members of the Armed Forces are assigned different letters: R for members of the police force, B for members of the army, V for members of the air force, and so forth. Promotion to an officer, or good behavior, allows civilian members to add an R in front of the MG tattoo, while military personnel receive a G in front of their original tattooed letter to stand for "godmother" or "godfather." Women in the Philippines can become officers, but we can assume that their numbers are small. Notably, women don't usually get tattoos in the Philippines and perhaps it is for this reason that in my travels I have yet to encounter a woman with letter markings that denote Guardian Membership. In contrast, I have seen quite a number of men. A higher promotion allows military personnel to add an S in front of the inscribed G tattoo to stand for "supreme godfather" or "supreme godmother." Whereas the left hand shows the rank and membership of a guardian, the right-hand tattoo establishes the regional group membership: GL for Guardians Luzon, GV for Guardians Visayas, and GM for Guardians Mindanao.

Guardians Brotherhood represents the largest formal organization in the Filipino community of Rome. The largest community center in the city, Sentro Filipino, even sponsors two chapters of Guardians Brotherhood—Guardians Anti-Crime and Guardians Bronze Wings. The Sentro, or Center, also hosts a third fraternal group, Solid Brothers. Suggesting the higher rate of men's participation in migrant associations (Correa-Jones, 1998), the Sentro only hosts one women's organization—the Legion of Mary—even though women far outnumber men in the community.

The prominence of groups like the Guardians Brotherhood in Rome suggests that men have not accepted a subordinate or even equal position to women in the community. Participating in such groups allows men to not just recuperate masculinity by acting as protectors but also to establish their higher gender status (Ridgeway, 2011). Doing so helps counter threats to their masculinity—from their performance of domestic work to their immersion in women-centered networks to their greater financial dependence on women—by participating not only in fraternal associations but more precisely hypermasculine organizations. Without question, Guardians Brotherhood represents a symbolic gender display that counters the community's "gender deviance" (Ridgeway, 2011: 135).

UNEMPLOYMENT: THE REAL CRISIS OF MASCULINITY

A prevailing assumption in academic discussions on domestic work is that male migrants do this work. Although films such as *Paper Dolls* (2006), a documentary by Tomer Heymann that follows the lives of five Filipino transgender migrant workers in Israel, seem to suggest the increasing participation of diverse genders in migrant domestic work, the number of men doing domestic work remains disproportionately small in comparison to the number of women in the field. Looking at the case of Israel, newly deployed Filipino women careworkers, for instance, outnumbered their male counterparts from 2008 to 2010 at a ratio of 6.5 to 1.[16] However, one could still argue that 15 to 20 percent makes for a sizeable number of male domestic workers, suggesting their noteworthy presence in the Israeli labor market. Still, we should note that a visible presence of Filipino male domestic workers could be found only in countries where Filipinos are segregated into that particular type of labor. These countries would be limited to Israel, Italy, and Spain. In other destinations in the diaspora, Filipinos have access to a wider range of jobs, and men expectedly pursue other types of work if given the opportunity. Still, some may find themselves segregated into domestic work. This is the case, for instance, for older migrants in Los Angeles, whose prior labor-market experiences in the Philippines may not be recognized by prospective employers and whose networks may funnel them solely to the immigrant niche of elder care.

Paid domestic work arguably remains women's work. The incorporation of men into this work is limited to particular "token" jobs such as caring for elderly men, physically strenuous cleaning, and ironing. Although some men cook, the figure of the male nanny remains a rarity. Although men may have found a niche in domestic work, employers still prefer to hire women—including for the few jobs open to men. For instance, women are still far more likely to be hired to take care of elderly men, to do work that requires lifting wards, and to do part-time cleaning jobs. That women are doing masculinized domestic work arguably suggest the masculinization of women, or the downplaying of femininity in domestic work (Constable, 1997).

The performance of domestic work by men does signal gender transformations and the breaking down of traditional gendered divisions of labor in the family and at work. Men's participation in domestic work has, for instance, encouraged them to take on "feminine work" at home. Households I observed in Rome suggest that men perform cleaning and cooking, even if to a lesser extent than women do. However, men's performance of domestic work seems not to have diminished their higher status in the community. The prominence of hypermasculine displays of protection by members of groups such as the Guardians Brotherhood suggests that this is far from the case.

Many scholars have wondered about the challenges male domestic workers face when doing "women's work." This is also a question I pursued in the ten interviews I initially conducted with male domestic workers in the mid-1990s. However, I learned that it is not so much the act of doing domestic work that challenges men's masculinity, but the difficulty of securing full-time employment. We see this in Rome, where men's greater presence in the community has not necessarily led to their stable employment. As they did in the mid-1990s, Filipino men in Rome still struggle to find regular employment as domestic workers. The crisis of masculinity is not caused by the performance of domestic work but by the lack of work for men in a labor market where they face racial segregation. In other words, unemployment, which is arguably a result of the partial citizenship of migrant domestic workers, is what plagues men more than their performance of domestic work. And as addressed in the next chapter, the dislocation of unemployment aggravates the precariousness of retirement for men, leaving them more vulnerable than women as they age.

CHAPTER SEVEN

THE AGING OF
MIGRANT DOMESTIC
WORKERS

WHEN I FIRST VISITED ROME IN THE mid-1990s, the Filipino community was fairly homogeneous. Most Filipinos were working-age women, and most were domestic workers. Men were sparse, as were children and older adults. The median age of my interviewees was thirty-one years old. When I returned in 2011 and 2012, I found a larger group of men in various pockets of gathering, children skipping school were a frequent sight near the central train station of Termini, and large groups of elderly women sat around cafés in the Termini basement. Although elderly women constituted a larger constituency of migrants in Rome, they had always comprised the bulk of domestic workers in Los Angeles. In the mid-1990s, the median age of domestic workers I interviewed in Los Angeles was fifty-two years old.

Given this change in demographics, it is important to address the elusiveness of retirement for migrant domestic workers and examine the challenges that they face as they reach retirement age. Retirement is one other way we can illustrate the precariousness of low-wage workers (Kalleberg, 2011). The security or insecurity of retirement for domestic workers also provides an instructive lens to examine their citizenship rights, as it sheds light on whether host societies reward their reproductive labor contributions. In this chapter, I focus primarily on the situation of older-aged migrants in Los Angeles. My discussion is informed by interviews I conducted in Rome and Los Angeles, but the bulk of my analysis relies on a survey of 100 domestic workers and two focus-group discussions with thirty domestic workers in Los Angeles.[1]

The question of old age and retirement remains absent in the literature on migrant domestic work, or on domestic work in general. Most studies focus on the quotidian plight of domestic workers, describing employer-employee relations (Lan, 2006; Brown, 2011; McDonald, 2011), the organization of the work (Romero, 1992; Hondagneu-Sotelo, 2001), and the labor process (Glenn, 1986; Constable, 1997; Lan, 2006). Others focus on the political economy of domestic work, describing the privatization of the social welfare system (Estes and Zulman, 2003) and the subsequent reliance of families on the low-wage work of racial minorities and immigrants (Glenn, 1992; Bakan and Stasiulis, 1997a; Glenn, 2012). With the exception of Raka Ray and Seemin Qayum (2009), who poignantly describe the displacement of migrant domestic workers as they age in modern India, not much attention has been given to domestic worker retirement.

The absence of this discussion implies that migrant domestic workers would somehow fare well as they age. When it comes to retirement, studies on migrant domestic workers have left it for readers to assume that migrant domestic workers will somehow accrue enough savings to retire in the home country; that migrant domestic workers will invest in the future of their children, who in turn would secure jobs abroad and eventually support them on retirement in the home country—indeed, this is an assertion I made in the first edition of *Servants of Globalization*—and that migrant domestic workers would eventually assimilate, leave domestic work, and secure a better job, perhaps in the formal labor market. Underlying these assumptions is the neoliberal sentiment that retirement is the private responsibility of migrant domestic workers and not a citizenship right they have earned from their labor.

However, the presence of older migrant domestic workers in both Rome and Los Angeles shows us that not all are able to retire. Most of the older migrants I had interviewed in Rome in the mid-1990s had managed to retire, but a few have not. For instance, Sol used her savings to retire in the Philippines, whereas another worker, Judy, followed her daughter to the United States, where the daughter now works as a nurse. The few who have not managed to retire have turned to elder caregiving. One former interviewee in Rome, now sixty-five years old, cares for a couple, both eighty-eight years old. The elderly women I met in Rome's central train station were unemployed, and almost all of them were looking for live-in jobs as an elder care provider. Likewise, some of the migrants I had interviewed in Los Angeles are still working, specifically in elder care. Seventy-eight-year-old Letty, for instance, still works on the weekends caring for an elderly client. Another interviewee, Mimi, told me she is looking for an able-bodied elderly person in need of a caregiver. Of the thirty focus-group participants, many of the older ones did not foresee retiring anytime soon. As Paul noted, "I don't know. I'm not thinking about it. I can still do the job. I am sixty-nine years old." Another older-aged migrant chimed in that she would not stop working "until the right time."

The presence of domestic workers who continue to labor in old age tells us that some domestic workers struggle to retire. What does their continued labor signify? How does it reflect socioeconomic inequalities that allow some people to retire whereas others must continue working in their later years? What do we make of their concentration in elder care, and what does this concentration signify about relations among the elderly? Lastly, what does it reveal regarding the state's accountability to the plight of workers who labored their entire life in the informal labor market? This chapter not only illustrates the precariousness of retirement for migrant domestic workers but also shows inequalities among the elderly. The comfortable retirement of a group of elders increasingly relies on the care provided by another group of elders, including Filipino elder caregivers who are elderly themselves.

THE STORIES OF ERNESTO AND LETTY

I originally interviewed Ernesto and Letty in the 1990s in Rome and Los Angeles, respectively. When I spoke with them again twenty years later, both told me they would like to return to the Philippines "for good," but neither is able to, and both still participate in the labor force. I ran into Ernesto in the summer of 2011, at one of the sites I had frequented while doing fieldwork in Rome during the mid-1990s. Not long after seeing me, Ernesto let me know that he had not done so well as a migrant worker. As he told me, "*Natalo ako*," meaning "I lost." Ernesto explained to me that he had "invested in the wrong person." To secure his retirement, he had adopted a young woman in the Philippines and paid for her to complete nursing school. Sending a younger relative to college is a common retirement strategy among migrant Filipino domestic workers; they invest in the education of a younger relative who they hope will eventually secure a professional job outside of the Philippines. Then what would allow them to retire in the Philippines would be neither a pension nor social security benefits but the remittances of the person they had supported through school. A typical aspiration would be to fund the schooling of a nurse or seafarer. Following this retirement strategy, Ernesto chose to adopt a young woman and support her through nursing school. Unfortunately for Ernesto, his daughter failed the nursing board exam in the Philippines, which is the first hurdle for securing a work contract to become a nurse outside the country.

Ernesto told me that, although he wants to retire in the Philippines, he is now stuck in Italy because he would have no source of income in the Philippines. Besides not having a younger relative who could financially support him, Ernesto also lacks a retirement pension that he could receive while in the Philippines. Without that (referred to as a "labor pension" in the Filipino community), Ernesto survives on his social allowance of approximately 500 euros from the state. In Italy, a social allowance is given to poor individuals who are at least sixty-five years old and are Italian citizens or resident permit holders. Individuals qualify for a social allowance regardless of their contributions to social security. But there is one catch: One can qualify for this allowance only if one stays in Italy; in other words, returning to the Philippines would disqualify Ernesto from receiving a social allowance. Though he is no longer a domestic worker, he subsidizes his social allowance by working as an in-house janitor, receiving a free room instead of a salary for his work cleaning and maintaining the building.

Ernesto does not have a retirement pension because he never managed to secure consistent employment during his thirty years in Rome. That means he did not have employers consistently declaring his hours at the National Institute of Social Security or making retirement contributions for at least twenty-one hours of work per week. Had that been the case, he would have secured a retirement pension from the government, which someone who lives out of the country can collect.[2] Among the domestic workers I know, their retirement pension usually does not exceed 700 euros per month, which would be a sizeable amount in the Philippines.

Employer participation in this government retirement program is voluntary, and male domestic workers such as Ernesto often do not qualify for it because, as I discussed in the previous chapter, male domestic workers have a harder time finding more than twenty-one hours of work per week. Most only hold a string of part-time jobs cleaning homes for no more than four hours per week. In this kind of situation, employers are less likely to make retirement contributions. This means that, even if they work for more than twenty-one hours per week in a number of different households, they would still struggle to convince their various employers to each contribute to their retirement.

Ernesto's case suggests that male domestic workers are more likely to have a precarious retirement situation, whereas female domestic workers are more likely to secure a retirement income that could support them back in the Philippines; here we see yet another example of the erosion of the male breadwinner. To view his retirement as a gamble—one he lost—speaks of the precarious situation not just of Ernesto but of migrant domestic workers in general. Furthermore, and perhaps most significantly, Ernesto considers retirement a private, not a public, responsibility. He blames himself, not the system, for not planning wisely and investing in the "wrong" person. Finally, Ernesto's situation demonstrates how minimally the host society compensates him for his reproductive labor contributions as a migrant worker. With its two types of retirement—a pension earned by the productive retiree who has consistently worked and contributed to the system of the country and a social allowance allotted to the poor who are assumed to have been unproductive workers—Italian society distinguishes between workers. The productive ones get to retire in the Philippines, and the unproductive ones, like Ernesto, stay in Italy. This distinction between the deserving and undeserving elderly migrant domestic worker disregards their history of reproductive labor contributions, puts the onus on them to ensure their retirement, and downplays their low wages and just how difficult it is for underpaid workers in the shadow economy to contribute to retirement.

Likewise, seventy-eight-year-old Letty, who helps care for a ninety-six-year-old woman on the weekends, is struggling to retire. According to Letty, the elderly woman can "walk fast without a walker" and thus does not require ambulatory care. Letty receives $125 a day for her services, which is not her first elder caregiving job. She has been taking care of the elderly in Los Angeles for twenty years, and before that she worked as a live-in nanny in New York City. Letty would like to return to the Philippines "for good," but with neither savings nor social security she primarily relies on her Supplemental Security Income (SSI), which she must subsidize with her continued part-time weekend work.

Although well past sixty-five years old, Letty has no plans to retire, despite the fact that she broke her femur bone on the job. As she explained, "These patients that have dialysis, they are very weak and can hardly walk. When [my patient] stood up, I tried to catch her, but then we both fell. And then that is why I got my knee injury, broke my femur bone, and [now] do not work full-time anymore." This led her to reduce her hours to part-time at the age of sixty-eight. Even though Letty was injured while working, she did not receive any sort of disability compensation; this is normal, as employers rarely provide this or any other benefits to domestic workers. As one elder caregiver I met at the Pilipino Worker's Center in Los Angeles complained, "The caregivers don't have security of payment . . . through the agency, but also in the situation where employers hire directly. . . . [T]he reason that employers hire directly is because they want to save money. They don't like . . . the payment for the Social Security or medical insurance. They save money. They really want to save money on that."

After working for more than twenty years in Los Angeles, Letty cannot rely on any sort of pension, as none of her employers has ever contributed to her Social Security. This is despite the fact that she is now a U.S. citizen, a status she obtained via the sponsorship of her son—an accountant in Long Beach—and despite the fact that the U.S. government requires employers who pay household workers at least $1,900 in annual cash wages to deduct Social Security and Medicare taxes and report the wages once a year.[3] The informal nature of her employment has clearly worked against her. In fact, one employer even discouraged her from paying taxes and contributing money to Social Security. Not having done so is Letty's biggest regret. "I should have gone home with my pension now. I am OK with the pension, with $800 I can go home. . . . I was already paying my income tax for two years, and then Mona [her employer] said, 'Letty, don't pay [those] taxes, because you'll pay more than what you'll get.' That is what she told me. So that is why I stopped paying. What a waste, right? Really, what a waste."

To survive, Letty lives rent-free with her son and relies on $720 of SSI, which she subsidizes with her weekend income of $125 to $250 per week. She qualifies for SSI because she is over sixty-five years old, is a U.S. citizen, and has a limited income and resources. Although SSI allows her to partially retire, it keeps the option of retirement in the Philippines elusive; SSI recipients cannot leave the United States for more than thirty days. If they do, they lose their benefits until they reestablish thirty days of residency in the United States.[4] Also preventing her from retiring is the continued financial dependence of not just Letty's adult children but also her grandchildren in the Philippines. Letty still supports four adult children, three of whom are single parents, and nine grandchildren in the Philippines. None of her four adult children in the Philippines has a regular income; one owns a beauty parlor that is always losing money, and three dropped out of college and are unemployed. Despite her limited income, Letty still manages to send them US$1,000 on the first of each month and an additional US$800 on the fifteenth. Most of these funds cover the medications her disabled son needs. To provide this transnational support to her children and grandchildren in the Philippines, Letty also relies on her three children in the United States—two accountants and a nurse—each of whom contributes between $300 to $700 a month. Because of her continued reproductive responsibilities and the absence of state compensation for her labor, Letty sees no end in sight to her employment as a part-time elder caregiver. Still, she jokes that she will retire in the Philippines once she can no longer drive.

Without question, many domestic workers eventually retire, some with a nest egg to enjoy in their home country. Yet, the situation of domestic workers like Ernesto and Letty tells us that not everyone can manage to build sufficient retirement funds. This is due to a combination of factors, including working for low wages, the continued dependence of family members in the Philippines, and the inadequate government compensation that low-wage workers, particularly those employed in the informal economy, receive. Furthermore, even if Ernesto and Letty were to benefit from a state pension, it would not necessarily guarantee their retirement. Economist Teresa Ghilarducci (2010), in her research on Mexican migrants in the United States, shows how most Mexican workers rely on Social Security but find that it does not provide them with sufficient funds for retirement. The challenges of retirement for migrant domestic workers, as well as other low-wage workers, invites us to examine their plight in old age and ask if host societies should be accountable for the welfare and well-being of domestic workers and other low-wage workers as they age.

OLDER DOMESTIC WORKERS

In conjunction with the Pilipino Worker's Center, a graduate student, Jennifer Nazareno, and I conducted a survey of 100 Filipino elder care providers in Los Angeles that revealed the average age of respondents to be 57.5 years old. This finding suggests that elder caregivers tend to be older, near or past retirement age. This is not surprising. When doing domestic work, older migrants prefer elder caregiving. In my many conversations with migrants over fifty years old, they often told me, *"Ayaw ko ng bata,"* meaning "I do not want to take care of a child." As sixty-three-year-old Lilly told me, "At my age, I'd rather take care of old people, not kids. I could not run after them any more." In contrast, the younger domestic workers I met preferred to care for children instead of the elderly, describing elder care as "boring." Older domestic workers prefer to care for the elderly because the pace is slower, they do not have to be as alert as they would be looking after a child, and the work is less demanding. As Letty explained, "It's only you and the lady. If she sleeps, you sleep, too."

Elder care, however, is not without its challenges. Elderly patients who suffer from dementia, Parkinson's disease, Alzheimer's, and other such common ailments in the aging population are usually very stressful for domestic workers to care for. It is these patients who are sometimes younger than their elder caregiver. Letty, for instance, had cared for a sixty-five-year-old Alzheimer's patient when she was seventy-three years old. Recalling the stress of managing an Alzheimer's patient, Letty told me,

Oh my god, . . . in the morning, . . . when I would say, "Good morning," she would say "How did you come here?!" I would say, "I stay here with you." She would say, "No, no, no, you go out, you go out." Then you know what, I go to the bathroom. I stay there for a few minutes, and just pray there, and then I go out and say, "Good morning," and she would be nice already.

Additionally, elder care can bring physical challenges. Lifting nonambulatory patients can lead to injuries like the one Letty sustained years ago. Those who can walk also pose their own set of physical challenges. As Lilly complained about her Alzheimer's patient, "I took care of a lady, a big one. And when we go to the bathroom, the water goes everywhere. It is like a boxing match."

Although considered "easier" than other types of domestic work by research participants, one of the greatest challenges of elder care is the twenty-four-hour shift. The job requires most to wake up in the middle of the night to bring the elderly ward a glass of water, to respond to their crying and requests to sleep in the same bed as them, or to check on any noise they make. For instance, the majority of survey participants (60 percent) had to get up at least twice in the middle of the night. Add to this the other duties of elder care. Survey participants noted that their job duties are similar to other types of domestic work. The majority (70 percent) report their primary tasks to include cooking, laundry services, ambulation assistance, bathing, toileting, grooming, and feeding, while a slightly lesser percentage also had to perform housecleaning.

Despite its challenges, research participants in Los Angeles and the older domestic workers I met at the central train station in Rome prefer the job of elderly caregiving. First, as they explained, the job allows them more rest time than other types of domestic work. As Letty noted, "It is better than if there are family around with children. It is hard because you would have to keep on working. You don't have rest because you are ashamed also. But if you are only two, . . . if they say 'I want to rest,' then you can rest too." Second, elder care pays a higher daily rate than other types of domestic work. In contrast to the $80 that housecleaners make per day, elder caregivers usually earn $125 to $130. To keep wages high, elder caregivers avoid undercutting others. Letty and her neighbor Julie, for example, made an agreement to ask for the same wage to set their own standard. Letty explained,

My neighbor, the one who recommended me, she is from Iloilo. We are friends. [When the mother of her employer's neighbor] was hospitalized, she asked Julie if they knew somebody who can take care of the mom. So Julie called me, and I went for an interview. She told me, "If they ask you how much, don't ask for something lesser than this [$150 per day] because I am getting that much. So you have to get something like me or else they will think that I get more than what I should." That is what we usually do. When your friend recommends you, they want you to ask the same money as what they are getting.

Although Filipino elder caregivers try not to undercut each other's wages in the labor market, this is not always the case. Notably, some elder caregivers earn less. This happens when they have to pay an agency fee or commission to the person who had recommended them. Agencies, which receive anywhere from $150 to $200 from a patient, usually pay elder caregivers no more than $80 a day. For this reason, domestic workers prefer to be hired directly. Often that happens through an informal reference, but that can also result in a lower take-home pay once they give $20 to $30 per day to the person who referred them, usually another Filipino elder caregiver. In her last full-time job, Letty indeed earned $150 a day, as did her friend Julie, but Letty took home less than Julie because she gave her $20 per day of service for providing her with the job lead. Every Saturday Julie would come to Letty's house to collect $100. When asked why she paid Julie for so many years, Letty responded, "If I do not, then we will quarrel. They will get mad at you." Letty kept this arrangement for years. Many would frown at the lack of altruism among elder caregivers. However, charging commission for job leads opens up opportunities that would otherwise be inaccessible to elderly members of the Filipino community. The commission gives others the incentive to share job opportunities, which in turn provides Filipino elder caregivers access to prospective employers they otherwise would not have found. This system of commission thereby sustains an underground economy of Filipino elder caregivers in Los Angeles, providing a steady flow of job information to older workers who otherwise would not have access to the job market.

What does the old age of elder care providers tell us? In both Rome and Los Angeles, I found that it often means the elderly care for the elderly. It also reveals that age not only determines job preference but also is indicative of a distinct life cycle in domestic work. Whereas younger migrants prefer child care and housecleaning, their older counterparts do not. Older migrants prefer elder care for its slower pace and the lighter one-on-one workload. In contrast, younger workers prefer child care to avoid the slow, monotonous, and isolated routine of elder care. The presence of elderly migrants doing elder care is not particular to Los Angeles. This has also been documented in Vincent Horn's dissertation research on Peruvian caregivers in Spain, as well as Johanna Krawietz's on Polish caregivers in Germany.[5] The few remaining elderly migrants I spoke with in Rome likewise prefer elder care to other types of domestic work.

The increasing presence of elderly domestic workers doing elder care points to the emergence of a new form of social inequality among the elderly. One group of elderly people who cannot retire is enabling another group of elderly to do so. Benefiting from this arrangement are the "haves," who, as Lilly said, are "those with money. If the old people don't have money, they cannot afford an elderly caregiver." This new inequality among the elderly—an international division of elder care—is likely to characterize the aging population in many receiving countries.

THE INTERNATIONAL DIVISION OF ELDER CARE

The phenomenon of elderly caring for the elderly points to the emergence of a particular configuration of an international division of caring labor. In Los Angeles, some aging baby boomers—individuals born between 1946 and 1964—are paying elder care workers to care for their parents, who are in their eighties and nineties. For instance, focus-group discussions included a sixty-two-year-old who cares for a ninety-six-year-old, a sixty-year-old with an eighty-nine-year-old patient, and a seventy-one-year-old with a seventy-eight-year-old patient. The Filipino elder care workers I met give the baby-boomer children of their elderly patients the freedom to retire. This tells us that the inability of domestic workers to retire works to the advantage of aging baby boomers in their early years of retirement; to give themselves greater freedom on retirement, they hire a crop of workers who tend to be former nannies and housekeepers.

One such elder caregiver is sixty-three-year-old Lilly, who cares for an eighty-five-year-old woman in Tustin, a suburb in Orange County. The woman has mild symptoms of dementia and Parkinson's, and she had become increasingly forgetful in the recent months prior to my discussion with Lilly. Living close to Lilly's elderly patient is her sixty-five-year-old daughter Mary, who remains active in her mother's life. Mary handles the grocery shopping for her mother and Lilly. Because Lilly does not know how to drive, Mary also takes her mother to therapy. Mary leaves it to Lilly, however, to see to her mother's day-to-day needs and bear the brunt of her dementia. Lilly also provides emotional support for the mother, who confides in Lilly when she has problems with the daughter. As Lilly explained,

Because of her dementia and Parkinson's, she thinks she is still young and she could get better still. She doesn't want to leave the house and get a smaller house because she has a big, big house. . . . And she's always upset with her daughter because her daughter wants her to move and she doesn't want to. So you're caught in between.

Without question, Lilly relieves Mary, a retired schoolteacher, of the responsibility of caring for her mother. Despite the close relationship she has cultivated with the mother, Lilly knows better than to romanticize their relationship. As she told me, "You just care but [do] not emotionally get involved. . . . You care; you do your job. It is my job. If someone asks, 'Lilly, how can you do this?' It is my job." Lilly knows to keep her distance because she is aware that she lacks job security, or, as one caregiver put it, "security of tenure." If the mother passes, then her job will end. From experience, Lilly knows she is unlikely to receive any form of compensation for her long-term service to Mary and her mother.

Lilly's perspective suggests that studies on the interpersonal relations of elderly employees and caregivers need to better account for the inequality that underlies their relationship. In other words, employer–employee relations in elder care do not necessarily reflect a "deep alliance," as anthropologist Maria Luz de Ibarra (2010) notes, but instead may constitute a deeply unequal alliance. The loyalty of elder caregivers, such as their commitment to work until their elderly patient passes (Ibid.) or their strategy of caring for their patient as they would for their own mother, is not necessarily reciprocated by employers, suggesting a one-sided relationship.

The degree of generosity employers demonstrate is one way that domestic workers determine if their loyalty and alliance is reciprocated or not. One sign that it is not is the inconsistency with which most elder caregivers receive pay raises. As one focus group participant shared, "I made $80 when I started, and I asked for a raise after five years." Another indication that their loyalty is not recognized is the absence of compensation for caregivers on the death of their employer. In focus group discussions, only two participants received money as part of the will, but "not enough to retire." Most others complained that they were not materially compensated for their loyalty, "Nowadays, even if you work for someone for twenty years, because of economic pressures, Medicare, taxes and the children are there too. . . . So they don't really give." For instance, most received no more than a week's salary, not enough to cover living expenses while they transition from one employer to another. Elder caregivers in the focus group discussions also noted that they are less likely to receive gifts from employers, which for them would signify some form of alliance or loyalty from those they care for:

I took care of [a] 103-year-old, and she gave me earrings for Christmas, and she told me they were real, but they were fake.

I have patients in Beverly Hills. She gave me [a] present—it was $25. I bought her pajamas for $21 so I got just $4. She even lied to me; she said, "I bought you something, a pendant, but I lost it."

For domestic workers, receiving inexpensive presents for their birthdays and holidays indicates a lack of appreciation or recognition for their labor.

Claims of a "deep alliance" between employer and employee downplay the precariousness of elder care, described by workers as "waiting for nothing" and having "no security of tenure." Although domestic workers may feel an alliance, employers do not necessarily reciprocate the sacrifices domestic workers are compelled to make out of allegiance to their employers. One such sacrifice is working for minimal wages (Luz de Ibarra, 2010). We can argue that the deeply unequal structural inequality between employers and employees in elder care work—one that manifests in low wages, the insecurity of retirement, the lack of disability compensation, and in many countries its lack of recognition as labor—are not eased by close interpersonal ties. Instead, employers can maximize a worker's labor, for instance by paying her less—as Luz de Ibarra's (2010) research shows—or denying them retirement benefits, when workers feel a natural tie to their elderly employers. In other words, sentiments of a "deep alliance" allow employers to maximize a domestic worker's labor because such claims of allegiance play down the economics of their relationship. As others have argued, claims of family membership, although potentially providing dignity in the workplace, could downplay the employer–employee relation in domestic work and result in less material compensation for the worker

(Romero, 1992; Bakan and Stasiulis, 1997b). Notably, sentiments of a "deep alliance" may secure the moral rewards of a job, such as the humane treatment of the employing family, but at the likely cost of lesser extrinsic rewards, such as lower pay. This shows us that the dynamics of intimacy in domestic work, including the notion of domestic workers as "one of the family," do not always lead to greater material rewards, as I discussed in Chapter Five, but it may lessen the financial gains of domestic workers.

Further aggravating the disregard for the labor of elder caregivers, specifically Filipinos, are claims of their natural affinity for that kind of work, which downplay the challenges such labor entails. Yet, this assumption was prominent in my discussions with caregivers. For instance, Ann noted, "I think the role of Filipinos is as natural-born caregivers. And so in a country that needs assistance specifically for the aging population, first and foremost, we Filipinos are the ones in the front lines of it. . . . We are being the ambassadors of our own country to do this job, do this work." Likewise, Thelma attributed Filipinos' ability to become elder caregivers to a "sixth sense." And, as Lilly proudly shared, "I think Filipinos are like the most caring people. . . . Yeah, most nurses in the medical field are Filipinos. It is inherent in us, I think." What compels Filipino caregivers to claim a natural affinity for caregiving? If we situate these narratives of a "care gene" in their macrostructural context, we can see that they translate to claims of indispensability among domestic workers. They become a tactic workers use to counter their disposability in an informal occupation.

The notion of a deep alliance that compels older domestic workers to care for elderly patients not for the money but for the emotional fulfillment of such labor is rooted in an unequal relationship between employer and employee or between care receiver and caregiver. One could argue that this "deep alliance" is based on unequal loyalties. In focus group discussions and interviews, domestic workers frequently described their deep sense of loyalty to their elderly patients. Betty, for example, followed her complaint about her low wages with a narrative of her deep commitment to her elderly patients: "They didn't pay [me] based on the hours, it's part of the trials of being a caregiver. [Still] my heart and my life are dedicated to taking care of the elderly because, if you put it in your heart, you will do everything to take care of them. How many times I've experienced holding their hands up to their last breath." The sentiment of Betty is similar to those of nannies who "pour their love" into the children to rationalize the contradiction of being unable to care for their own. Betty—an undocumented worker who is fighting cancer and is in and out of the hospital—foregoes caring for herself for the care of others. But this type of deep commitment is rarely reciprocated with material rewards. This was a common complaint that emerged in focus group discussions. The failure to materially compensate this care, which domestic workers see as emerging from their natural affinity for such labor or the spiritual fulfillment they get out of caring for the dying, without question speaks to the minimal value put on their care work. In other words, their allegiance is not reciprocated by the allegiance of their employers.

As the data and these stories reveal, many domestic workers are forced to work past retirement age. We should see this as a disturbing trend that signals a return to premodern practices in neoliberal times and the reemergence of the figure of the loyal domestic worker who stays with their employer until the end of life. Yet it is not loyalty but desperation that ensures the devotion of domestic workers, who had arguably been better off and more likely would have been rewarded for their devotion in earlier years. As Ray and Qayum (2009) document, in India employers historically rewarded the loyalty of domestic workers by providing them with food, lodging, and security following their retirement, maintaining a deep commitment to them until death. In contrast, in the age of neoliberalism, employers have less of a sense of accountability to their domestic workers. Hence, domestic workers are more likely to receive abysmal compensation on the termination of their employment (Ray and Qayum, 2009). This is surely the case among the domestic workers I recently surveyed in Los Angeles and for those I met more than twenty years ago as well.

Ironically, this lack of loyalty among employers seems to elicit greater loyalty in domestic workers. To ensure their security, domestic workers downplay their disposability by constructing themselves as indispensable workers who not only have a natural aptitude for the job but also naturally carry a deep commitment to their employer. This unequal allegiance reflects how neoliberalism absolves employers of accountability and loyalty to their workers while demanding the loyalty of workers to their employers, many of whom are forced to work past retirement.

THE ELUSIVENESS OF RETIREMENT

The presence of older-aged migrant caregivers in various destinations demonstrates a problem that plagues migrant domestic workers—the elusiveness of retirement. This, however, remains an unrecognized issue in policy discussions. For instance, it is absent in the recently ratified International Labour Organization's Convention 189, the Domestic Workers Convention, which has been passed by at least five ILO member countries.[6] The adoption of Convention 189 in 2011 signals a significant advancement in the recognition of domestic work as actual labor. In an attempt to mitigate the risks posed by the informal nature of the occupation, the Convention calls for the use of written contracts in accordance with national laws, regulations, or collective agreements in domestic work; safe and humane working conditions; freedom of movement; and regular pay, among others. Missing from the Convention is the question of retirement and the particular insecurities faced by the aging population of informal laborers. Thus, compliance with the Convention does not mean that retirement is any less precarious for domestic workers in member countries.

In focus group discussions, most participants did not have concrete retirement plans. Many said they hoped to save money for retirement but were incurring daily expenses that impeded this goal. We should not be surprised. First, their wages are low, making it a challenge to accumulate enough savings for retirement. Along with job security and access to health care, survey participants identified the accumulation of retirement funds as their biggest concern. Furthermore, the informal arrangement of the job puts the onus on the domestic worker, not the employer, to participate in government pension plans. Of 100 survey participants, only fourteen have employers who cover their Social Security tax. Finally, many elder caregivers continue working because there is a demand for elder care—a job that younger domestic workers prefer not to take. According to the U.S. Department of Health and Human Services (2012), the 39.6 million individuals who comprise the older population—sixty-five years and over—make up 12.9 percent of the U.S. population, about one in every eight Americans. Their numbers are expected to double to 72.1 million by 2030 (Solis, 2011). Due to the rise in the aging population, elder care is one of the fastest growing occupations in the United States (Solis, 2011).[7] Job availability—funneled into the Filipino community not only by the informal referral and commission system but also by the marked presence of Filipino migrants in the health industry (Choy, 2003)—gives access to and accordingly helps maintain the continued participation of elderly Filipinos in this industry.

Most of the elder domestic workers I interviewed in the 1990s have since stopped working. For instance, most of Ernesto's friends are long gone, having returned to the Philippines. Yet, his continued presence in Rome, as well as Letty's continued part-time work as an elder caregiver in Los Angeles, indicates that not everyone can. What is the social significance of the elusiveness of retirement for migrant domestic workers? First, it illustrates how the informal nature of domestic work often results in the absence of its recognition. Consequently, many domestic workers do not qualify for a government pension, be it a retirement pension in Italy or Social Security in the United States. In Ernesto's case, if he had worked under regular contracts that would have mandated his employers to contribute to his pension funds, he would have eventually received a retirement pension that he could have used in the Philippines. Unfortunately, Ernesto's situation is not unique. Of the 500,000 estimated migrant domestic workers in Italy, many do not have legal contracts. A study in 2007 by ACLI, a religious advocacy group for migrant workers, found that 57 percent of domestic workers in Italy are employed without a contract (Lombardo and Sangiuliano, 2009). In the United States, the informal nature of domestic work has without question hindered access to social insurance. The problem for domestic workers seems starker in the United States than in Italy. The U.S. General Accounting Office notes that in 1993 nearly 96 percent of private household workers lacked pension coverage (Grillo-Chope and Ramos, 2006).

The elusiveness of retirement is also a result of the assumption that domestic workers are unproductive workers, which stems from the basic tenets of neoliberalism that amplify the notion of individual responsibility while degrading the notion of public good. As legal migrants, both Ernesto and Letty receive some form of supplementary income from the government, a 500 euro social allowance for Ernesto and a US$720 supplementary income for Letty. Yet, this kind of social benefit is considered charity, not something they earned from their many years of low-wage service. This is why the supplementary income binds them to Italy or the United States. By construing it as charity, however, we disregard the structural inequalities that deter low-wage migrant workers in the informal economy from receiving labor pensions, as we also place the onus on workers, not employers, to ensure their retirement. Finally, the elusiveness of retirement tells us that elder care is precarious labor; it puts people in a vulnerable state that is exacerbated by the moral economy of elder care in neoliberalism. For the most part, employers do not feel a sense of accountability for the well-being of elder caregivers. The survey and focus group discussions I conducted indicate that employers will, at most, give domestic workers separation pay for a week of wages when their employer dies.

THE MORAL ECONOMY OF DOMESTIC WORK

What is the moral economy that makes retirement elusive? The situations of Ernesto and Letty seem to signal a return to servitude among migrant domestic workers, as retirement is not an option for either one of them and labor security seems to be accessible only via their continued loyalty to an employer. Yet this loyalty does not seem to be reciprocated by employers, who maximize the benefits of their informal employment by avoiding paying taxes and thus disqualifying domestic workers from unemployment, Social Security, and Medicare benefits.

Domestic workers ensure the reproduction of societies. Recognizing their reproductive labor—the work of caring, feeding, bathing, and clothing the population—requires that we acknowledge their reproductive rights. This refers not just to their right to a family life, as I argued in my discussion of transnational families, but for their right to retire. Their inability to retire, their forced loyalty and continued labor in old age, signifies a return to servitude in economic globalization. The rise of servitude signals the globalization of a feudal order between employers from the Global North and domestic workers from the Global South. This is a quite ironic effect of neoliberalism, for the rise of the nonliberal relations of servitude emerge from liberal policies that tout self-sufficiency. This feudal order—an economic reality of globalization—benefits the aging population of various host societies at the cost of the aging population that cares for them in servitude.

The presence of older domestic workers—most of whom are elder caregivers—signals a new type of care chain in which we find the elderly caring for the elderly, with one group of elderly allowing another group to retire at the cost of their own retirement. The inability of domestic workers to retire, because they do not qualify for Social Security or have any savings, poses a challenge for those of us who wish to advocate for the recognition of domestic work.

Then how can we solve the problem of the "elusiveness of retirement"? The solutions could be simple if we recognized the contributions of migrant domestic workers to the reproduction of host societies. Perhaps we should not see someone like Ernesto, who failed to contribute to his labor pension, as an indigent relying on the state in his old age. Instead, we should recognize the value of his labor by seeing his social allowance as a reward for his labor contributions, allowing him to spend these funds—measly in Italy and abundant in the Philippines—in his country of origin. Another solution would be to penalize employers who do not contribute to domestic workers' Social Security funds. Surely this would provide Letty with the option of retirement. We need to recognize that domestic workers earn little, making it difficult for them to generate savings or to contribute to their Social Security, and that providing them with minimal subsidies in the home society as a reward for their contributions to the reproduction of host societies will turn their migration into a win-win situation.

CONCLUSION

MIGRANT FILIPINO DOMESTIC WORKERS are the global servants of late capitalism. They work in more than 165 destinations, including in the cities of Rome, Milan, Madrid, Paris, London, Toronto, New York, Los Angeles, Taipei, Singapore, Hong Kong, Dubai, Riyadh, Beirut, Amman, and Doha, among others. The flow of migrant domestic workers from poor to rich nations speaks of what Pierrette Hondagneu-Sotelo (2001) calls a "new world domestic order," referring to an unequal division of care labor between the Global South and Global North. This flow of labor raises our attention to new forms of inequalities among women, particularly those that result in the "international division of reproductive labor" or "global care chains," who pay others with fewer resources in the global economy to care for their own children. Freed of their family care responsibilities by migrant workers, female employers in turn can avoid the penalty of the "mommy tax" or, more generally, the "caregiver tax" that stalls their advancement in the labor market (Crittenden, 2000).

By comparing the lives of migrant domestic workers in two destinations, Los Angeles and Rome, this study foregrounds not just the existence of a domestic worker diaspora from the Philippines but also underscores the similarities in their experiences across destinations. I began with the assumption that the experiences of migrant domestic workers in these two cities would be remarkably different due to their distinct conditions of settlement. Yet my scrutiny of their positioning vis-à-vis the state, family, labor market, and migrant community yielded similarities in their experiences.

First, they share a quasi-citizenship in relation to the nation-state at both ends of the migration spectrum. The Philippines can do little to protect them against abuse and discrimination, whereas receiving countries do not necessarily accord them full rights of citizenship. For instance, most receiving countries do not guarantee migrant domestic workers the right to family reunification. Migrant domestic workers' rights to reproduce their own families can vary widely. At one extreme is Singapore, which does not allow unskilled migrants to marry, and at the other is Canada, which grants residency to domestic workers after two years of continuous live-in service for one sponsoring family. As landed migrants, they can then petition for family in the Philippines to join them in Canada (Pratt, 2012). Also indicative of their stunted integration into host societies, migrant domestic workers are often without employer flexibility. Across the diaspora, they are bound to work for a sponsoring employer with countries granting domestic workers varying degrees of flexibility to change their sponsor. In Italy, they can change their sponsor immediately, whereas in Singapore and the Gulf Cooperative Council countries, they can change jobs only with their sponsoring employer's permission. What explains the partial citizenship of migrant domestic workers? In general, the macro-processes of globalization result in their stunted integration. For instance, the "opposite turns of nationalism"—the renationalization of politics alongside the denationalization of economies—result in the contradictory incorporation of migrant domestic workers as desired workers but rejected persons (Sassen, 1996). Migrant domestic workers are nothing but workers to the receiving states, which causes problems when they act in excess of this limited constitution (Constable, 2014).

Another shared characteristic of migration in my two disparate field sites is the formation of transnational households and, consequently, the everyday experience of the pain of family separation. Varying conditions of settlement in the United States and Italy, as well as other nations in the diaspora, have not led to different outcomes in household structure. Although the right to family reunification was granted to migrant Filipinos in Rome in 1990, the massive deportation of undocumented migrant children signals the escalating war against the reproduction of racialized migrants in the United States today (Golash-Boza, 2012).

A third similarity relates directly to the experience of domestic work. Many migrant Filipino domestic workers in Rome and Los Angeles had achieved high levels of education prior to leaving the Philippines, which they often do not use when working in the host country. This results in contradictory class mobility when they migrate. For many migrant domestic workers, their labor involves a simultaneous increase and decrease in labor-market status. They gain by earning more than they had prior to migration, but at the same time they lose the social status they had as white-collar workers in their country of origin. Considering that migrant workers are hardly ever the poorest of the poor (Portes, 1989), it is likely that many more migrant groups other than Filipino domestic workers in Rome and Los Angeles also share the dislocation of contradictory class mobility. Experiences in the workplace further aggravate the affective sentiments of contradictory class mobility for Filipino migrant domestic workers, including the routinization of domestic work and the "culture of servitude," or deference, that employers expect of them (Rollins, 1985; Ray and Qayum, 2009). *Nakakabobo*, or stupid-making, is how many described their jobs to me.

I had addressed all these dislocations in the first edition of *Servants of Globalization*. In this version, I have added two others that Filipinos confront in the process of migration—the crisis of masculinity associated with the segregation of migrant men into domestic work and the insecurity of retirement for elderly workers. Contrary to what we may assume at first, I concluded that the performance of domestic work by men does not necessarily threaten their masculinity. Men are able to identify masculine traits in the type of domestic work they do, such as the heavy lifting of elderly wards or the physicality that intensive cleaning requires. Men rarely perform what would be considered undeniably feminine work such as infant care. More than the actual performance of domestic work, then, the crisis of masculinity is caused by the insecurity of their labor. Employers still prefer to hire women, resulting in men's

higher rate of unemployment or irregular employment among domestic workers. Losing their role as breadwinners—as it is women more so than men who
usually have consistent employment—is what prompts the crisis of masculinity. This was also the case for a gay domestic worker I had interviewed, as his
inconsistent employment prevented him from providing regular support to
his aging parents in the Philippines, a task that he says is his responsibility as
an unmarried child.

Since the publication of the first edition of *Servants of Globalization*, I had
wondered about the plight of elderly domestic workers. The median age of my
interviewees from the initial study in Los Angeles was high at fifty-two years
old. I did not keep in touch with most research participants I interviewed
twenty years ago, but, as I learned when I went back to the field, some interviewees still continued to work—including the nearly eighty-year-old woman
Letty. Many, if not all, aspired to retire in the Philippines, but some could
not because they would lose access to their Supplementary Security Income,
their primary source of retirement funds, which many subsidized with week-
end jobs as "reliever" elder caregivers. Likewise, in Italy some domestic workers are unable to retire—specifically those who did not accumulate savings or
continuously contribute to their INPS; this includes men who could not find
regular employment. Low wages coupled with their financial responsibility to
sustain their family in the Philippines means that domestic workers are less
likely to accrue savings and more likely to struggle to retire.

The precariousness of retirement affects a growing number of poor, elderly migrants and nonmigrants in advanced capitalist countries, including
men and women from a diversity of racial and ethnic groups. Journalist
Jessica Bruder (2014) documents the plight of a group she calls "elderly
migrant workers," referring to downwardly mobile Americans who survive
by traveling across country in RVs in search of temporary and seasonal
labor. What differentiates the experiences of aging caregivers from this
group is not only that they have even fewer resources[1] but also the irony of
their labor. Aging domestic workers are concentrated in elder caregiving,
which means they represent a group of elderly caring for the elderly. In
other words, their labor in old age is allowing a group of more privileged
elderly to retire and relieve some members of the baby-boomer generation
of the burden of caring for their parents. Their labor represents a different

type of international division of caregiving or "care chain," one based on inequalities among the elderly.

By foregrounding the shared experiences of migrant domestic workers across destinations, I may have inadvertently downplayed the differences in their experiences. As Anju Mary Paul (2011) notes, there is a hierarchy of destinations in the Filipino diaspora determined by the distinct quality of labor and migration across different countries. Italy and the United States are at the top of the hierarchy, not only for the higher wages domestic workers earn there—five times more than what their counterparts in the United Arab Emirates normally earn, for example—but also for their higher labor standards, including better labor protections for domestic workers, the possibility of permanent residency for unskilled foreign workers in both countries, and, most significantly, especially in the case of Italy, their ability to freely choose employers. In contrast, domestic workers in Singapore, Israel, the United Arab Emirates, and most other destinations in the diaspora are not likely to gain permanent residency. Furthermore, as mentioned earlier, these workers are "unfree"—bound to working only for their sponsoring employer in most destinations, including Denmark, Taiwan, and Hong Kong. In Singapore and Gulf Cooperative Council countries, including the United Arab Emirates, migrant domestic workers must secure their employer's permission to be released from their contract. Even so, whereas we could say that labor and migration standards are better in Italy and the United States, the experiences of migrant domestic workers there do still resonate with their counterparts in lower-tiered destinations. Partial citizenship, the pain of family separation, contradictory class mobility, and the precariousness of retirement are not unique to Italy and the United States but are dislocations that domestic workers in lower-tiered destinations face as well.

Experiences of migration shift according to local conditions and varying "contexts of reception" (Portes and Rumbaut, 1996). For this reason, differences could be found across destinations, even within coveted host countries. Greater restrictions against family reunification in Canada than the United States result in lower rates of migration among Filipinos to the former than the latter. The greater sexualization of Filipinos in the United States, one rooted in the racial construction of Asian women as hyperfeminine and hypersexual subjects (Shimizu, 2007), is not mirrored in the racial perceptions of Filipinos by Italians. As a result, Filipinos are less likely to intermarry in Italy than in the United States.

Despite these differences, the similarities in domestic workers' experiences across destinations are striking and beg explanation. What accounts for the similar dislocations of migrant domestic workers, and how do those similarities advance our understanding of labor migration processes? The parallels emphasize their shared positioning across different local contexts as racialized foreigners, gendered feminine laborers, Third World subjects from an under-resourced nation, and workers with a low social status. Their particular categorization allows receiving states to reduce these subjects to workers without full citizenship rights. They are desired as workers but not as citizens, which is ironic given that their work in the household assists with the reproduction of receiving societies. The existence of these similarities underscores the status of migrant Filipino domestic workers as servants of globalization.

It is important to understand and emphasize that similarities across destinations emerge out of processes, not from some inherent migrant characteristic. They arise from local systems impelled by globalization, including not just xenophobia and the racialization of foreigners but also the constitution of gender in the household and workplace. The xenophobia that stunts their incorporation is notably not a natural occurrence but is instead fueled by globalization; the circulation of labor, currency, and goods threatens national identities and consequently fortifies national boundaries. Examining domestic work also provides us with a window into how women's increasing labor-market participation affects gender relations. The preference for female over male domestic workers indicates the continued relegation of housework to women. Lastly, domestic work gives us perspective on larger economic inequalities and the unequal development of regions in globalization. Migrant domestic workers end up in diverse destinations that encompass a wide range of "wealthier" countries, including the emerging financial centers of the United Arab Emirates and Singapore as well as the declining postindustrial economies of Europe. Yet, migrant domestic workers in these varying locations still share the experience of contradictory class mobility. The lower value of an educational degree from a developing country such as the Philippines translates to it being a source of low-wage workers in the transnational workforce. This is not to say, however, that the Philippines is not a labor source for professional migrants. Instead, I point out that not all professionals use their professional training once outside the country. I also highlight the construction of an educational hierarchy across the globe, one that places the Philippines and other developing countries at the bottom.

In short, this study insists on situating our understanding of migrant domestic work in the macro context. Studies on domestic work have historically focused on the quotidian, including the daily work routine and employer–employee relations.[2] This study diverges from others by situating our discussion in the macrostructure that shapes the microprocesses of labor migration. The literature could benefit from more studies that link domestic work to larger processes in society. To conclude, I recommend possible future studies that bridge the macro and micro in our discussion of domestic work.

Another sorely needed line of inquiry could link domestic work to the discourse on human trafficking. Scholars of domestic work are largely absent in public discussions on trafficking, despite the prominence of migrant domestic workers among those identified as trafficking victims (Bales and Trodd, 2008; Bales, 2010; Brennan, 2014). Yet, government policies and programs are constantly being enacted on human trafficking across the globe, and migrant community organizations are increasingly focusing their efforts on the prevention of trafficking in response to the massive amount of U.S. government funds earmarked to address this issue (Parreñas, 2011). How antitrafficking campaigns shape the labor migration of domestic workers across the globe is a question that has yet to be examined in the literature.

Similar to the way Kimberly Hoang (2015) situates her discussion of sex work in Vietnam in larger political economic processes in Asia, we could also look at domestic work as a way of accounting for the shifting global economy. The migration of domestic workers represents a global movement of women that occurs in various spheres: global (South to North) or regional (East to West or South to South). The frequent routes of migration for domestic workers include their movement from Mexico and Central America into the households of working families in the United States (Hondagneu-Sotelo, 2001); Sri Lankan women to Greece and West Asia (Gamburd, 2000); Indonesians to East and West Asia (Silvey, 2004, 2006; Lan, 2006; Constable, 2007); Ethiopian women to West Asia (Mahdavi, 2011); Polish women to Germany and Italy (Lutz, 2011); Caribbean women to Canada and the United States (Bakan and Stasiulis, 1997a, 1997b); and Filipino care workers to more than 165 destinations across the globe (Parreñas, 2008a; Pratt, 2012). Flows are, however, not equal in size. The shrinking economy of the Global North—as we see in the case of traditional receiving countries in Europe, including Spain and Italy—and the diminishing of available jobs in the West after the 2008 global financial crisis point to a new global economic reconfiguration, one potentially mirrored in the transformation of labor standards as well as the density of migration flows across destinations. These changes are reflected, for instance, in the stagnation if not decline of salaries among domestic workers in Italy as compared to the upward surge in salaries among domestic workers in Singapore in the last four years.

In general, more studies on migrant domestic work outside the Global North are needed as the majority of such workers are located elsewhere on the globe. It is assumed that the Global North, including Italy and the United States, offers more substantial opportunities, including, for instance, the promise of intergenerational mobility, high wages, and permanent residency. However, the decrease in available jobs is making these countries less accessible for migrant domestic workers. Moreover, the economic ascension of other countries may lead to improved conditions for domestic workers elsewhere. Although atypical, it is not unheard of for domestic workers to earn more than US$1,000 a month in Singapore and the United Arab Emirates, as well as to hear of the children of domestic workers following their mothers to these destinations in search of professional jobs. In other words, mobility may also be achieved outside the Global North.

Finally, the efforts of intergovernmental organizations such as the International Labour Organization to formalize domestic work, for example, through the ratification of protocols like the Domestic Workers Convention (C189) in 2011, have commanded greater recognition of this occupation across the globe.[3] Countries considered the worst destinations for their refusal to recognize domestic work as labor have faced mounting pressure to recognize the human rights of domestic workers, and many have accordingly revisited their labor laws. Since 2013, Singapore, for instance, has required employers to grant domestic workers a mandatory weekly day off. Looking at how public discourse on the formalization of domestic work shapes the everyday experiences and consciousness of workers would not only address an important question but could bridge the study of labor processes and social movements, expanding the depth of our knowledge and understanding of domestic work.

Domestic work is an occupation that is unlikely to go away. The higher rate of women's labor-market participation and the aging of society have only increased the demand for domestic work. However, this has not resulted in workers' gaining a greater ability to negotiate for better working conditions. A convenient and simple explanation for this is the argument that the supply of domestic workers exceeds the demand (Lan, 2007). Still, we are seeing an increase in wage rates for domestic workers and the implementation of a mandatory day off, as well as heightened public pressure for recruitment agencies to lower the fees they charge to facilitate worker migration. At the same time, relations between employers and domestic workers are hardly becoming egalitarian. Servility and deference still reign across the globe. Domestic workers are never maternal experts, but puppets; they are not considered skilled, but unskilled (McDonald, 2011). The contradictory standards of the occupation, and the inconsistencies we find, invite more studies on domestic work. They encourage research to identify possible sources of negotiating power for domestic workers, the shifting dynamics of employer–employee relations with labor advocacy's turn toward human-rights discourse, and the everyday strategies domestic workers use to not just improve their working conditions but also to make their labor indispensable.

ACKNOWLEDGMENTS

IN A SPAN OF TWENTY YEARS, NUMEROUS individuals have helped me hone the arguments developed in this book. More recently, they include those who read a draft of this new edition, Yu Kang Fan, Maria Hwang, and Kimberly Hoang. Ideas developed in this new edition also benefited from conversations I had with research collaborators from recent years, including Jennifer Nazareno, Hung Thai, and Rachel Silvey, as well as friends and family including Celine Shimizu, Rheana (Juno) Parreñas, Dina Okamoto, and Nicole Fleetwood. One challenge of working on a second edition is developing a version that seamlessly ties old and new materials. For helping me do this, I thank the editor Anitra Grisales.

The initial funding for this project came from a National Science Foundation Graduate Research Fellowship. Allowing me to update my findings are the financial support provided by Brown University; the National Science Foundation (SES-1346750); an Advancing the Humanities and Social Sciences Award from the University of Southern California; Social Science and Humanities Research Council of Canada (File No: 895-2012-1021), "Gender, Migration and the Work of Care: Comparative Perspectives," with PI Ito Peng and co-PI ("Sending Country Perspectives") Rachel Silvey; and a small grant from Atlantic Philanthropies administered by USC's Center for the Study of Immigrant Integration. I thank Ito Peng, Rachel Silvey, Rhonda Ortiz and Manuel Pastor for their support of this project. I presented earlier versions of Chapter Seven at conferences in Germany and Switzerland and benefited from the comments shared by Cornelia Schweppe.

I managed to complete this book while in the middle of my three-year term as chair of the sociology department at USC. I could not have done so if not for the efficiency of the department's superb staff and the daily support they provide me and the other faculty. I thank Melissa Hernandez, Stachelle Overland, Amber Thomas, and most especially Lisa Losorelli.

The cooperation of many individuals enabled me to complete the research for this project, including Sabrina Marchetti, Charito Basa of the Filipino Women's Council in Rome and Aqui Soriano and Lolita Lledo of the Pilipino Worker's Center in Los Angeles. Making this book possible is my editor at Stanford University Press, Kate Wahl, who has given me her unwavering support for almost a decade. This book would also not have been possible if not for the domestic workers who willingly gave me their time to participate in this project in both Rome and Los Angeles, as well as in Copenhagen and Dubai. Lastly, I must thank Benjamin Rosenberg, my life partner and biggest supporter, for patiently engaging me as I rehashed my ideas for each new chapter and listened to me without complaint as I reworked one sentence after another in the rewriting of this book.

R.S.P.
Los Angeles, CA

NOTES

ENDNOTES TO PREFACE

1. The Italian Ministry of Interior reports 155,945 registered Filipinos with a valid permesso di soggiorno (permit to stay) or a carta di soggiorno (residence card). They remain concentrated in domestic work. See "Know Your Diaspora: Italy," Positively Filipino, January 1, 2013; retrieved on October 14, 2013, from http://positivelyfilipino.com/magazine/2013/1/1/know-your-diaspora-italy.

2. "The Chain of Love," VPRO TV, Netherlands (Episode 42 of the television program The New World, November 12, 2000).

3. Robert Frank, "Child Cares: To Be a U.S. Nanny, Ms. Bautista Must Hire A Nanny of Her Own," Wall Street Journal, December 18, 2001, A1.

4. UN-INSTRAW, "Global Care Chains: Toward a Rights-based Global Care Regime?" January 2013; available at https://unp.un.org/Details.aspx?pid=21307.

ENDNOTES TO CHAPTER ONE

1. For statistics on au pairs, see the Danish Immigration Service, 2012. The sizeable presence of former domestic workers in Denmark supports Cameron McDonald's (2011) categorization, which places au pairs in the realm of domestic work as opposed to seeing them as a distinct group that is merely participating in a cultural exchange program.

2. In June and July of 2012, I spent six weeks in Copenhagen, where I conducted preliminary research on Filipino au pairs. I interviewed seventeen, a handful of whom had worked in either Hong Kong or Singapore prior to entering Denmark. I located interviewees by visiting known gathering places in the community, including the Roman Catholic Church they frequented and the central train station. I also identified interviewees through the local migrant advocacy organization Babaylan-Denmark. Interviews were one to two hours in length, anonymous, and focused on the labor, migration, and family life of au pairs.

3. Nene relocated to Denmark from Singapore in 2011, not long before the Philippine government lifted its ban against the migration of au pairs to Europe on February 16, 2012. In 1988, the Philippine government banned Filipinos from leaving the country as au pairs due to a reported case of abuse in Sweden. By migrating directly from Singapore to Denmark, Nene managed to bypass the ban that would have been imposed on her as a Philippine national if she had traveled to Denmark directly from the Philippines. Migration to Denmark as an au pair does not require the facilitation of an agency, which helps keep the cost of migration low. Instead, the au pair or sponsoring family can post an advertisement on a number of websites, including www.newaupair.com/visas_copenhagen .aspx, and directly negotiate the terms of the au pair contract.

4. International Labour Organization, "Domestic Workers Convention (No. 189)," adopted on June 16, 2011, 100th ILC Session; retrieved on October 14, 2013, from www.ilo.org/dyn/normlex/ en/f?p=NORMLEXPUB:12100:0::NO::P12100_ILO_CODE:C189.

5. Philippine Overseas Employment Administration, "OFW Deployment by Occupation, Country, and Sex—New Hires, Full Year 2010"; retrieved on October 14, 2013, from www.poea.gov .ph/stats/2010%20Deployment%20by%20Occupation,%20Destination%20and%20Sex%202010% 20-%20New%20hires.pdf.

6. Philippine Overseas Employment Administration OFW Statistics, "Deployment Per Skill Per Sex, 2008–2010"; retrieved on October 14, 2013, from www.poea.gov.ph/stats/statistics.html.

7. My calculation includes those deployed as caregivers and domestic helpers. The migrant worker's entry visa usually determines the category of employment. For instance, those employed as domestic workers in Israel would enter as "caregivers," whereas those who work in the United Arab Emirates would enter with a "servant visa." The former would depart the Philippines with the employment category of "caregiver," and the latter would be categorized as a "domestic helper." See POEA Statistics, "2008 Deployment by Major, Sub-Major Occupation and Sex"; retrieved on October 23, 2013, from www.poea.gov.ph/stats/Skills/Skill_Sex/Deployment%20per%20Skill%20 and%20Sex%202008.pdf.

8. My calculation includes those deployed from the country as caregivers and domestic helpers. See POEA Statistics, "2009 Deployment by Major, Sub-Major Occupation and Sex"; retrieved on October 23, 2013, from www.poea.gov.ph/stats/Skills/Skill_Sex/Deployment%20per%20Skill%20 and%20Sex%202009.pdf.

9. My calculation includes those deployed from the country as caregivers (9,293) and domestic helpers (96,583). See POEA Statistics, "2010 Deployment by Major, Sub-Major Occupation and Sex"; retrieved on October 14, 2013, from www.poea.gov.ph/stats/2010%20Deployment%20by%20 Major,%20Sub-Major%20Occupation%20and%20Sex%202010%20-%20New%20hires.pdf.

10. The latest stock estimate of Filipinos residing overseas shows a total number of 10,455,788 individuals with 4,867,645 permanent residents, 4,513,171 temporary migrant workers, and an estimated 1,074,972 undocumented or irregular migrants. See Office of the President of Philippines Commission on Filipinos Overseas, "Global Mapping of Overseas Filipinos"; retrieved on October 15, 2013, from http://cfo.gov.ph/index.php?option=com_content&view=article&id=1340%3 Astock-estimate-of-overseas-filipinos&catid=134&Itemid=814. Of temporary migrant workers, most are women; figures from POEA indicate that women comprised 62.5 percent of all newly deployed temporary labor migrants from 1992 through 2007. See Philippine Migration and Development Statistical Almanac, "Total Deployment of New-Hire Temporary Contract Workers by Gender, 1992–2007"; retrieved on October 15, 2013, from http://almanac.ofwphilanthropy.org/index .php?option=com_docman&task=doc_view&gid=335&Itemid=5.

11. Although the Philippine government does not consider au pairs to be laborers, many scholars have argued that the category of au pair merely masks the employer–employee relationship inherent in this cultural exchange program. See Mitchell (1996), McDonald (2011), and Stenum (2011).

12. ILO, 2013: 24.

13. I base my estimation of 2,800,000 from a calculation of the percentage of female workers from the stock estimate of approximately 4.5 million temporary migrant workers in 2011. See Commission on Filipinos Overseas for the estimated figures on temporary migrant workers. This conservative estimate is based on the percentage of domestic workers among newly deployed female workers reported by POEA, comprising approximately 56 percent of deployed female workers in 2010; 45 percent in 2009; and 54 percent in 2008 (POEA, 2009, 2010, 2011; retrieved on October 15, 2013, from http://cfo.gov.ph/index.php?option=com_content&view=article&id=1340%3Astock-estimate-of-overseas-filipinos&catid=134&Itemid=814). For the estimated count of female workers, see POEA estimate. Of temporary migrant workers, most are women; figures from POEA indicate that women comprised 62.5 percent of all newly deployed temporary labor migrants from 1992 through 2007. See Philippine Migration and Development Statistical Almanac, "Total Deployment of New-Hire Temporary Contract Workers by Gender, 1992–2007"; retrieved on October 15, 2013, from http://almanac.ofwphilanthropy.org/index.php?option=com_docman&task=doc_view&gid=335&Itemid=5.

14. According to a migrant broker I met in Dubai in June 2013, this nominal fee is imposed on domestic workers only so they would feel invested on their jobs. In other words, the fee of US\$115 is supposed to deter them from quitting if faced with a difficult employer.

15. The term *migrant institutions* refers to the "sets of rules and resources which govern the actions and interactions of agents who operate within them" (Goss and Lindquist, 1995: 334).

16. I conducted sixty-seven interviews with migrant Filipina domestic workers in Singapore in July and August 2014.

17. Paul provides a fairly accurate tier system that represents the hierarchy of destinations. Most accurate in her assessment is the prevailing wage in different tiers. Yet her description of the tier system has many inaccurate claims, including the assertion that labor laws protect domestic workers in Taiwan and not in the lower-tier destination of Malaysia.

18. Further problematizing Paul's hierarchy, migrant domestic workers in the United Arab Emirates did not agree with the hierarchical distinction of West Asia as a fourth-tier destination and Southeast Asia as third tier. Many had previously worked in Malaysia and Singapore and did not see the United Arab Emirates as a worse place to work.

19. In Singapore, she had autonomy in the workplace. Still, her situation had not been ideal. One day off a month, long work hours, and a heavy workload nearly eliminated her discretionary time, thereby limiting her temporal autonomy and, some would say, her freedom.

20. Four others entered with immigrant visas they had obtained via the sponsorship of a family member, and five others entered as companions of a business investor from the Philippines. One initial interviewee entered the United States by clandestinely crossing the border from Canada.

21. UN Convention against Transnational Organized Crime, Resolution 55/25, "The Protocol to Prevent, Suppress, and Punish Trafficking in Persons, Especially Women and Children," December 12–16, 2000; retrieved from www.uncjin.org/Documents/Conventions/dcatoc/final_documents_2/convention_%20traff_eng.pdf.

22. In 2014, Canada changed its laws and gave domestic workers the option to live out of their employer's homes. Despite granting bound laborers a pathway to citizenship, this program is still criticized by domestic worker advocates such as the scholar Geraldine Pratt. A great number of Filipinas who enter Canada under the Live-in Caregivers Programme do not qualify for landed status because they could easily fail to meet the basic requirement of regular employment for two continuous years within a four-year period. Employers—not rarely—have let their domestic workers go before they meet the two-year requirement. Canada is restricted to those who have completed the equivalent of two years of post-secondary education (Pratt, 2012).

23. See Glenn (2012). Those restricted to live-in employment would be B-1, G-5, or A-3 visa holders. B-1 visa holders are domestic workers of ex-pats who have relocated back to the United States;

G-5 visa holders work for foreign government diplomats; and A-5 visa holders are domestic workers of employees of international organizations.

24. Arguably the most rigid and restrictive sponsored-migration program is the *kafala* program in Gulf Cooperative Council nations: Bahrain, Kuwait, Oman, Qatar, Saudi Arabia, and the United Arab Emirates. Under the *kafala* system, the residency of the foreigner is contingent on her or his sponsorship by a local citizen known as the *kafeel*. The *kafeel* grants the foreigner permission to enter and exit and holds responsibility for the foreigner's stay. In many cases, although not always, the *kafeel* must also consent to a change in employment or sponsor. In Kuwait, for example, one must have worked for a minimum of three years before qualifying to change jobs independent of her or his citizen-sponsor's consent, whereas domestic workers, regardless of years of employment, are always required to obtain the permission of their citizen-sponsor (Human Rights Watch, 2011: 554). A withdrawn sponsorship could result in the illegality of the foreigner, which is a crime that potentially results in imprisonment.

25. However, abused and illegally placed migrant workers can petition to change employers.

26. Bound labor also occurred in the United States via its Foreign Labor Certification Program.

27. In the United States, they do so via marriage. In the past, domestic workers had the opportunity to participate in the Labor Certification Program, which allowed them to transition to permanent residency. See Parreñas, 2005, for my previous discussion of this program.

28. The status of partial citizenship emerges from the contradictory forces of nationalism in economic globalization in which the denationalization of economies incites the renationalization of politics (Sassen, 1996). The increased demand for migrant labor usually goes hand in hand with heightened anti-immigrant sentiments, as immigrants are frequently used as scapegoats for the economic displacement of "native" workers in the deindustrialization of economies. Migrant workers are consequently included as laborers yet excluded as persons and imposed with limited citizenship rights.

ENDNOTES TO CHAPTER TWO

Ideas presented in this chapter draw from my essay, Parreñas (2012).

1. By definition, *patriarchy* refers to the systematic inequality between men and women in any given society. In a patriarchal society, men carry greater power and privilege over women.

2. The community first assumes the cause of separation to be a "deficiency" with the wife (for example, she nags or is lazy) for not being able to hold on to her partner.

3. In the Philippines, for example, "barrenness on the part of the wife may be a ground for separation or an excuse for the husband's infidelity" (Lopez-Rodriguez, 1990: 21).

4. Italy, though known to be "the traditional 'bambini' country," has the lowest birth rate in the world at only 9.6 per 1,000 inhabitants (Beck and Beck-Gernsheim, 1995: 102).

5. In making this assertion, I do not claim that Filipinas are defined racially as domestic workers. They are more so categorized and identified as nurses. Yet in the Filipino migrant community, it is known that a visible contingent of recent migrants has turned to domestic work. In a study of undocumented women in the San Francisco Bay area, Hogeland and Rosen found that 41 percent of fifty-seven survey participants from the Philippines were care providers, and an additional 23 percent were employed as housekeepers (1990: 43).

6. Reflecting Glenn's observations, Jacqueline Andall (1992) likewise finds a direct correlation between the entrance of migrant women into Italy and the entrance of native Italian women into the labor force.

ENDNOTES TO CHAPTER THREE

1. Although I use the terms *household* and *family* interchangeably in this chapter, I generally follow the definition of the *family* as a determinate group of people usually related by marriage,

partnerships, or blood and the *household* as a "a set of relationships that impose a mutual obligation to pool resources from a multiplicity of labor forms whether or not one of those resources is a common residence" (Friedman, 1984: 48). Moreover, I do not limit my view of a household to the modern conception of a residential unit inclusive of kin and nonkin (Mintz and Kellog, 1988).

2. The complexity of household maintenance is not completely captured in my typology. Extended kin are ever present and intrinsically woven in the migrant family. However, by placing individual subjects in a type of household, I limit my formulation of the family to the family of orientation for married domestic workers and the family of origin for single domestic workers. For married migrants, core family members include spouses and children. For single migrants, the core family refers to parents and siblings; however, the core families of single migrants do include married brothers and sisters and their children.

3. Although I could have placed single migrants in the category of "independent household," I found that strong family ties between single migrants and relatives in the Philippines would be nullified by classifying them as single householders. With the formulation of the category adult child(ren) abroad transnational households, I link single migrants to dependent relatives in the Philippines and emphasize the interdependent transnational ties that they sustain in migration.

4. A jeepney is a vehicle made from a U.S. military jeep left over from World War II and is a popular mode of transportation in the Philippines.

5. Although I have chosen not to profile any of the families in Los Angeles, the intergenerational relations in those families are reflected in the two that I featured here. What is different are the circumstances forcing the formation of split households, as the undocumented status of parents in Los Angeles has primarily prevented them from petitioning for the migration of their now-adult children[o].

6. A nipa hut has a bamboo structure and a roof made of nipa palm leaves.

7. According to French theorist Etienne Balibar, racism is based less on traditional biological constructs of race and more on the exclusion of immigrants as culturally unassimilable Others (Balibar and Wallerstein, 1988). He refers to this trend as "neoracism."

ENDNOTES TO CHAPTER FOUR

1. Although the state grants free public education until high school, it neither enforces nor mandates the education of children, nor does it strictly enforce children's legal protections from abuse.

2. Paz Cruz conducted a survey of 212 high school and college students with international migrant parents, as well as with ninety students with internal migrant parents living elsewhere in the Philippines.

3. Matthei and Smith (1998) also observe the tendency of parents in Belizean transnational households to commodify love.

4. Although my interviews include only a limited number of children—six in Rome—who had grown up without their mothers, my assessment of the children's perspectives also uses the survey conducted by Victoria Paz Cruz (1987), writings by children published in *Tinig Filipino*, and previous interviews that I had conducted with children who had followed their parents to the United States after a prolonged period of separation.

5. Constable (1999) also recognizes the greater priority children give to emotional bonds in the family than their transnational parents in Hong Kong do.

ENDNOTES TO CHAPTER FIVE

1. Due to the greater labor market opportunities for migrants in Los Angeles, it is surprising to see a number of my interviewees having chosen to stay in domestic work. I assume that there are many women who left domestic work for more skilled employment immediately after they obtained

legal residency. However, it is still surprising that some women have not used middle-class Filipino American community networks to gain access to other opportunities in the labor market.

2. See works by Cock (1980), Rollins (1985), Colen (1989), Romero (1992), Gregson and Lowe (1994), Bakan and Stasiulis (1997b), and Hondagneu-Sotelo (2001).

3. I thank Karen Brodkin for making this observation.

4. In Los Angeles, migrant Filipina domestic workers may avoid this type of work because of their vulnerability as undocumented workers and the competition from the larger pool of Latinas who also do day work.

5. Part-time workers include an equal representation of single and married women. Interestingly, the few lesbians in my sample are all part-time workers; their sexual orientation seems to restrict their employment options.

6. The take-home pay of those who secured their employment via a job placement agency is significantly less, averaging $80 after the agency deducts its percentage.

7. Two interviewees in Los Angeles had been trained midwives in the Philippines. This suggests that in the United States not all trained medical workers have been able to use their skills after migration.

8. Explaining her contention, Romero states, "As capitalists middle-class employers—like factory owners—own the means of production and the product of the labor; they constantly rationalize the work and control the labor process. . . . Domestic service must be analyzed as a sphere of capitalist production in which race and gender domination are played out" (1992: 93).

9. Filipina domestic workers tend to feel more comfortable eating with Filipino employers. For example, Marilou had felt more at ease eating with her former Filipino employers. This tendency could be due to their familiarity with these families' cultural practices, the more informal meal setting, or the absence of racial difference. However, this does not translate to a preference for Filipino employers, most likely because of the wide discrepancy between what white and Filipino employers pay. Those working for Filipino families received on average $500 a month.

10. See Colen (1989: 172–176) for discussion of the process of employment sponsorship in the United States.

11. See Rollins (1985: 157–173 and 173–203) for a more extensive discussion of "deference and maternalism."

12. See Cock (1980), Rollins (1985), Glenn (1986), Palmer (1989), and Romero (1992).

13. Based on Rollins's personal experiences, an employer was wary of hiring her because she seemed "too educated."

14. This information is based on field research.

15. Robert Smith has also noticed the use of racial bifurcation among Mexican migrants in New York City. Citing Smith, Goldring observes that Mexicans in New York "are doubly bounded by attempts to distance themselves from African Americans and Puerto Ricans, thereby defining themselves as *not black*, and by being defined by the dominant society as *not white*. Mexicans in California also distance themselves from the bottom of the racialized hierarchy" (1998: 170).

16. See the works of Cock (1980), Young (1987), Romero (1992), Gregson and Lowe (1994), Wrigley (1995), and Bakan and Stasiulis (1997a, 1997b).

ENDNOTES TO CHAPTER SIX

1. See POEA Statistics, 2010 Deployment by Major, Sub-Major Occupation and Sex; retrieved on October 14, 2013, from www.poea.gov.ph/stats/2010%20Deployment%20by%20Major,%20Sub-Major%20Occupation%20and%20Sex%202010%20-%20New%20hires.pdf.

2. Ibid.

3. In the Netherlands, likewise men's employment frequently depended on women domestic workers who would subcontract jobs to them (Haile and Siegmann, 2014) or bring them along as assistants (Van Walsum, 2011).

4. See Williams, 1995: 123–141.

5. Italy has confronted a series of recessions since 2008. See "Italy Slips Back into Recession," *Wall Street Journal*, August 6, 2014; retrieved on October 27, 2014, from http://online.wsj.com/articles/italy-slips-back-into-recession-in-second-quarter-1407318527.

6. Many other studies have focused on this aspect. See Sarti and Scrinzi (2010) and Scrinzi (2010).

7. Additionally, most men found themselves ineligible for thirteenth-month pay or separation pay as they worked for each employer for no more than two to three hours on any given week. In Italy, employers are required to pay domestic workers termination pay, which is one month of salary for every year of completed service.

8. Valentina is one of the many interviewees I maintain contact with through Facebook.

9. I also encountered unemployed women in Rome, though less frequently. According to volunteers at the job bank at Centro Filipino, women can find jobs more easily than men can, even during the recession, when women are expected to settle for a job they would not necessarily prefer. A noticeably growing number of unemployed women are elderly, meaning in their late fifties and older. I encountered small groups of them in the basement of Termini, where some approached me to ask if I knew of any job leads.

10. Randy's wife had opted not to join her mother as a teenager, a decision she later regretted after struggling to make ends meet with her husband Randy in the Philippines. Both she and Randy migrated as direct hires.

11. Women notably have a wider range of options, as they also have access to retail jobs.

12. Domestic workers likewise receive the same benefits, though they qualify only for a thirteenth-month pay per annum.

13. In Filipino, he had said "*Iniwanan ako ng asawa ko, kaya siguro nag tampuan tayo. Pag maligaya ka, maligaya ako.*"

14. See the website of the organization Guardian Angels at www.guardianangels.org/.

15. See "Guardians Brief History," available at http://gpi-i.tripod.com/id1.html, for an unofficial history of the organization.

16. See deployment per skill, country, and sex from 2008 through 2010 from the Republic of the Philippines, Department of Labor, "OFW Statistics," last update, July 22, 2014; available at www.poea.gov.ph/stats/statistics.html.

ENDNOTES TO CHAPTER SEVEN

1. Results of the survey, which I authored with Jennifer Nazareno and Yu-Kang Fan, will be made available on the website of the Pilipino Workers' Center. The survey findings were featured in one of the largest circulating newspapers in the Philippines, *Philippine Inquirer*. See Mico Letargo, "Most Aging Filipino Caregivers Can't Afford to Retire, Says Report," July 10, 2014; retrieved on July 14, 2014, from http://globalnation.inquirer.net/107752/most-aging-filipino-caregivers-cant-afford-to-retire-says-report.

2. For policies on retirement contributions, see INPS; retrieved on July 14, 2014, from www.inps.it/portale/default.aspx.

3. See Social Security Administration, "Household Workers," January 2014, which summarizes the policies on Social Security benefits for domestic workers; retrieved on July 9, 2014, from www.ssa.gov/pubs/EN-05-10021.pdf.

4. See Social Security Administration, "Social Security Payments Outside the United States"; retrieved on July 9, 2014, from www.socialsecurity.gov/international/payments.html.

5. Authors gave presentations at the conference on "Transnational Aging," September 27–28, 2012, Department of Education, University of Mainz, Germany. See Vincent Horn, "Material Disponible? Aged Peruvians as Multiple Resources in Transnational Families"; and Johanna Krawietz, "Organizing Care for the Elderly between Germany and Poland: The Case of Recruitment Agencies"; retrieved on October 27, 2014, from www.transnationalsupport.de/fileadmin/user_upload/Veranstaltungen/Transnational_Aging/transnational_aging_programme.pdf.

6. See International Labour Organization, "C189-Domestic Workers Convention, 2011," June 16, 2011; retrieved on July 14, 2014, from www.ilo.org/dyn/normlex/en/f?p=NORMLEXPUB:121 00:0::NO::P12100_ILO_CODE:C189.

7. Currently there are approximately 2.5 million paid domestic workers in the United States and 1.8 million workers who provide care for elderly and disabled populations (Poo, 2009; Solis, 2011).

ENDNOTES TO CONCLUSION

1. This group of elderly includes those who could rely on their children and other family but are choosing to remain independent. In contrast, the aging domestic workers I have met do not have this option. Many still provide financial support to their own children. See Nazareno et al. (2014).

2. See Rollins (1985), Romero (1992), Hondagneu-Sotelo (2001), and Lan (2006).

3. See International Labour Organization, "C189-Domestic Workers Convention, 2011," June 16, 2011; retrieved on August 31, 2014, from www.ilo.org/dyn/normlex/en/f?p=NORMLEXPUB:12100:0::NO::P12100_ILO_CODE:C189.

REFERENCES CITED

Abel, Emily K. 1990. "Family Care of the Frail Elderly." In *Circles of Care*, edited by Emily K. Abel and Margaret K. Nelson, pp. 65–91. Albany: SUNY Press.

Abel, Emily K., and Margaret K. Nelson. 1990. "Circles of Care: An Introductory Essay." In *Circles of Care*, edited by Emily K. Abel and Margaret K. Nelson, pp. 4–34. Albany: SUNY Press.

———, eds. 1990. *Circles of Care: Work and Identity in Women's Lives*. Albany: SUNY Press.

Abrego, Leisy. 2014. *Sacrificing Families: Navigating Laws, Labor, and Love across Borders*. Stanford, CA: Stanford University Press.

Acgaoili, Gloria. 1995. "Mother Behold Your Child." *Tinig Filipino* (May): 14.

Agence France-Presse. 2011, June 30. "Saudi Arabia Bans Filipino and Indonesian Maids." *The National*. Retrieved on October 20, 2013, from www.thenational.ae/news/world/asia-pacific/saudi-arabia-bans-filipino-and-indonesian-maids.

Andall, Jacqueline. 1992. "Women Migrant Workers in Italy." *Women's Studies International Forum* 15 (1): 41–48.

Aratan, Clarita U. 1994. "Money or Family." *Tinig Filipino* (December): 34.

Arevalo, Nina Rea. 1994. "Inay, Pasko Na Naman." *Tinig Filipino* (December): 28.

Asia Pacific Forum on Women, Law and Development. 2010. *The Right to Unite: A Handbook on Domestic Worker Rights across Asia*. Changmai, Thailand: Asia Pacific Forum on Women, Law and Development.

Bakan, Abigail, and Daiva Stasiulis. 1997a. "Foreign Domestic Worker Policy in Canada and the Social Boundaries of Modern Citizenship." In *Not One of the Family: Foreign Domestic Workers in Canada*, edited by Abigail Bakan and Daiva Stasiulis, pp. 29–52. Toronto: University of Toronto Press.

———. 1997b. "Introduction." In *Not One of the Family: Foreign Domestic Workers in Canada*, edited by Abigail Bakan and Daiva Stasiulis, pp. 3–7. Toronto: University of Toronto Press.

Balangatan, Dolores. 1994. "The Two Sides of Migration." *Tinig Filipino* (October): 10.

Bales, Kevin. 2010. *The Slave Next Door: Human Trafficking and Slavery in America Today*. Berkeley: University of California Press.

Bales, Kevin, and Zoe Trodd, eds. 2008. *To Plead Our Own Cause: Personal Stories by Today's Slaves*. Ithaca, NY: Cornell University Press.

Balibar, Etienne, and Immanuel Wallerstein. 1988. *Race, Nation and Class*. London and New York: Verso.

Basch, Linda, Nina Glick-Schiller, and Christina Szanton Blanc. 1994. *Nations Unbound: Transnational Projects, Postcolonial Predicaments, and Deterritorialized Nation-States*. Langhorne, PA: Gordon and Breach Science.

Beck, Ulrich, and Elisabeth Beck-Gernsheim. 1995. *The Normal Chaos of Love*. Cambridge, UK: Polity Press.

Bianchi, Suzanne, John Robinson, and Melissa Milkie. 2006. *Changing Rythms of American Family Life*. New York: Russell Sage Foundation.

Brennan, Denise. 2014. *Life Interrupted*. Durham, NC: Duke University Press.

Brenner, Johanna, and Barbara Laslett. 1991. "Gender, Social Reproduction and Women's Self-Organization: Considering the U.S. Welfare State." *Gender and Society* 5 (3): 311–333.

Brown, Tamara. 2011. *Raising Brooklyn: Nannies, Childcare, and Caribbeans Creating Community*. New York: New York University Press.

Bruder, Jessica. 2014. "The End of Retirement: When You Can't Afford to Stop Working." *Harper's Magazine* (August). Retrieved on August 30, 2014, from http://harpers.org/archive/2014/08/the-end-of-retirement/.

Bryceson, Deborah, and Ulla Vuorela, eds. 2002. *The Transnational Family: New European Frontiers and Global Networks*. Oxford, UK: Berg Press.

Castles, Stephen, and Alastair Davidson. 2000. *Citizenship and Migration: Globalization and the Politics of Belonging*. New York: Routledge.

Castles, Stephen, and Mark J. Miller. 1998. *The Age of Migration: International Population Movements in the Modern World*, 2nd ed. New York and London: Guilford Press.

Catorce, Rodney. 1995. "Dad Is Away, So What?" *Tinig Filipino* (June): 9.

Chant, Sylvia. 1997. *Women-Headed Households: Diversity and Dynamics in the Developing World*. New York: St. Martin's Press.

Chant, Sylvia, and Cathy McIlwaine. 1995. *Women of a Lesser Cost: Female Labour, Foreign Exchange and Philippine Development*. London and East Haven, CT: Pluto Press.

Chin, Christine. 2013. *Cosmopolitan Sex Workers: Women and Migration in a Global City*. New York: Oxford University Press.

———. 1998. *In Service and Servitude: Foreign Female Domestic Workers and the Malaysian "Modernity" Project*. New York: Columbia University Press.

Choy, Catherine. 2003. *Empire of Care: Nursing and Migration in Filipino American History*. Durham, NC: Duke University Press.

Cock, Jacklyn. 1980. *Maids and Madams: Domestic Workers under Apartheid*. London: The Women's Press.

Codini, Ennio. 2010. "Developments in Law and Regulations." In *The Fifteenth Italian Reports on Migration 2009*, edited by Vincenzo Cesareo, pp. 58–72. Milan: Polimetrica.

Colen, Shellee. 1995. "'Like a Mother to Them': Stratified Reproduction and West Indian Childcare Workers and Employers in New York." In *Conceiving the New World Order: The Global Politics of Reproduction*, edited by Faye D. Ginsburg and Rayna Rapp, pp. 78–102. Berkeley and Los Angeles: University of California Press.

———. 1989. "'Just a Little Respect': West Indian Domestic Workers in New York City." In *Muchachas No More: Household Workers in Latin America and the Caribbean*, edited by Elsa Chaney and Mary Garcia Castro, pp. 171–194. Philadelphia, PA: Temple University Press.

Constable, Nicole. 2014. *Born Out of Place*. Berkeley: University of California Press.

———. 2007. *Maid to Order in Hong Kong: Stories of Filipina Workers*, 2nd ed. Ithaca, NY, and London: Cornell University Press.

———. 1999. "At Home but Not at Home: Filipina Narratives of Ambivalent Returns." *Cultural Anthropology* 14 (2): 203–228.

———. 1997. *Maid to Order in Hong Kong: Stories of Migrant Workers*. Ithaca, NY, and London: Cornell University Press.

Correa-Jones, Michael. 1998. "Different Paths: Immigration, Gender, and Political Participation." *International Migration Review* 32 (2): 326–349.

Covert, Bryce. 2013, September 17. "Why It Matters that Home Care Workers Just Got New Labor Rights." *Think Progress*. Available at http://thinkprogress.org/economy/2013/09/17/2634411/home-care-workers-rule-change/.

Crittenden, Ann. 2000. *The Price of Motherhood: Why the Most Important Job in the World Is Still the Least Valued*. New York: Metropolitan Books.

Cruzat, Maryjane. 2010. "Guardians, *magkakaisa nga ba?*" *Akit Magazine* 2: 14–15.

Daguio, Liza C. 1995. "Family Still Number One." *Tinig Filipino* (February): 40.

Danish Immigration Service. 2012. *Statistical Overview: Migration and Asylum*. Copenhagen: Author.

De Certeau, Michel. 1984. *The Practice of Everyday Life*. Berkeley and Los Angeles: University of California Press.

Dill, Bonnie Thornton. 1994. *Across the Boundaries of Race and Class: An Exploration of Work and Family Among Black Domestic Servants*. New York and London: Garland.

———. 1988. "'Making Your Job Good Yourself': Domestic Service and the Construction of Personal Dignity." In *Women and the Politics of Empowerment*, edited by Ann Bookman and Sandra Morgen, pp. 33–52. Philadelphia, PA: Temple University Press.

Dreby, Joanna. 2010. *Divided by Borders: Mexican Migrants and their Children*. Berkeley: University of California Press.

Dreyfus, Hubert, and Paul Rabinow. 1983. *Michel Foucault: Beyond Structuralism and Hermeneutics*. Chicago, IL: University of Chicago Press.

Duffy, Mignon. 2007. "Doing the Dirty Work: Gender, Race, and Reproductive Labor in Historical Perspective." *Gender & Society* 21 (3): 313–336.

———. 2005. "Reproducing Labor Inequalities: Challenges for Feminists Conceptualizing Care at the Intersections of Gender, Race, and Class." *Gender & Society* 19 (1): 66–82.

England, Paula, Michelle Budig, and Nancy Folbre. 2002. "Wages of Virtue: The Relative Pay of Care Work," *Social Problems* 49: 455–473.

Espiritu, Yen Le. 1997. *Asian American Women and Men*. Thousand Oaks, CA: Sage Publications.

Estes, Carroll L., and Donna M. Zulman. 2003. *Informalization of Long Term Caregiving: A Gender Lens*. San Francisco, CA: Institute for Health & Aging.

Eviota, Elizabeth Uy. 1992. *The Political Economy of Gender: Women and the Sexual Division of Labour in the Philippines*. London: Zed Books.

Feagin, Joe. 1997. "Old Poison in New Bottles: The Deep Roots of Modern Nativism." In *Immigrants Out!: The New Nativism and the Anti-Immigrant Impulse in the United States*, edited by Juan Perea, pp 13–43. New York: New York University Press.

Fondazione Giacomo Brodolini. 2009. *Women and Unpaid Family Care Work in the EU*. Brussels: European Parliament.

Foner, Nancy. 1997. "The Immigrant Family: Cultural Legacies and Cultural Changes." *International Migration Review* 31 (4): 961–974.

Foucault, Michel. 1983. "The Subject and Power." Pp. 208–26 In *Michel Foucault: Beyond Structuralism and Hermeneutics*, edited by Hubert L. Dreyfus, pp. 208–226. Chicago, IL: University of Chicago Press.

———. 1980. *Power/Knowledge: Selected Interviews and Other Writings, 1972–1977.* New York: Pantheon.

Friedman, Kathie. 1984. "Households as Income-Pooling Units." In *Households and the World Economy*, edited by Joan Smith, Immanuel Wallerstein, and Hans-Dieter Evers, pp. 37–55. Beverly Hills, CA: Sage.

Gamburd, Michelle. 2000. *The Kitchen Spoon's Handle.* Ithaca, NY: Cornell University Press.

George, Sheba. 2005. *When Women Come First: Gender and Class in Transnational Migration.* Berkeley: University of California Press.

Ghilarducci, Teresa. 2010. "How to Supplement Social Security Fairly and Effectively," *Journal of Aging and Social Policy* 22: 222–235.

Glazer, Nona. 1993. *Women's Paid and Unpaid Labor: The Work Transfer in Health Care and Retailing.* Philadelphia: Temple University Press.

Glenn, Evelyn Nakano. 2012. *Forced to Care: Coercion and Caregiving in America.* Cambridge, MA: Harvard University Press.

———. 1992. "From Servitude to Service Work: The Historical Continuities of Women's Paid and Unpaid Reproductive Labor." *Signs* 18 (1): 1–44.

———. 1986. *Issei, Nisei, Warbride.* Philadelphia: Temple University Press.

———. 1983. "Split Household, Small Producer and Dual Wage Earner: An Analysis of Chinese-American Family Strategies." *Journal of Marriage and the Family* (February): 35–46.

Glenn, Evelyn, Grace Chang, and Linda Forcey, eds. 1994. *Mothering: Ideology, Experience and Agency.* New York: Routledge.

Glick-Schiller, Nina, Linda Basch, and Cristina Szanton-Blanc. 1995. "From Immigrant to Transmigrant: Theorizing Transnational Migration." *Anthropological Quarterly* 68 (1): 48–63.

Goddard, V. A. 1996. *Gender, Family and Work in Naples.* Oxford, UK, and Washington, DC: Berg.

Golash-Boza, Tanya. 2012. *Due Process Denied: Detentions and Deportations in the United States.* New York: Routledge.

Goldring, Luin. 1998. "The Power of Status in Transnational Social Fields." In *Transnationalism from Below*, edited by Michael Smith and Luis Guarnizo, pp. 165–195. New Brunswick, NJ: Transaction Publisher.

Gonzaga, Junelyn. 1995. "Listen to Our Small Voices." *Tinig Filipino* (December): 13.

Goss, Jon, and Bruce Lindquist. 1995. "Conceptualizing International Labor Migration: A Structuration Perspective." *International Migration Review* 26 (2): 317–351.

Grasmuck, Sherri, and Patricia Pessar. 1991. *Between Two Islands: Dominican International Migration.* Berkeley and Los Angeles: University of California Press.

Gregson, Nicky, and Michelle Lowe. 1994. *Servicing the Middle Classes: Class, Gender and Waged Domestic Labour in Contemporary Britain.* New York: Routledge.

Grillo-Chope, Luisa, and Carlos Ramos. 2006. "Domestic Workers Working Hard to Sustain American Families, Compromising their Social Security." Washington, DC: National Council of La Raza.

Haile, Aster George, and Karin Astrid Siegmann. 2014. "Masculinity at Work: Intersectionality and Identity Constructions of Migrant Domestic Workers in the Netherlands." In *Migration, Gender and Social Justice: Perspectives on Human Insecurity*, edited by Thanh-Dam Truong, Des Gasper, Jeff Handmaker, and Sylvia Bergh, pp. 105–119. New York: Springer.

Hansen, Karen. 1989. *Distant Companions.* Ithaca, NY: Cornell University Press.

Harvey, David. 1989. *The Condition of Postmodernity.* New York: Basil Blackwell.

Heyzer, Noeleen, Geertje Lycklama á Nijeholt, and Nedra Weerakoon, eds.1994. *The Trade in Domestic Workers: Causes, Mechanisms, and Consequences of International Labor Migration*. London: Zed Books.

Hoang, Kimberly. 2015. *Dealing in Desire: Asian Ascendency, Western Decline and the Hidden Currencies of Global Sex Work*. Berkeley: University of California Press.

Hochschild, Arlie. 2000. "Global Care Chains and Emotional Surplus Value." In *On the Edge: Globalization and the New Millennium*, edited by Anthony Giddens and Will Hutton, pp. 130–146. London: Sage Publishers.

———. 1989. *The Second Shift*. New York: Avon Books.

———. 1983. *The Managed Heart: Commercialization of Human Feeling*. Berkeley and Los Angeles: University of California Press.

Hogeland, Chris, and Karen Rosen. 1990. *Dreams Lost Dreams Found: Undocumented Women in the Land of Opportunity*. San Francisco: San Francisco Coalition for Immigrant Rights and Services.

Hondagneu-Sotelo, Pierrette. 2001. *Doméstica*. Berkeley: University of California Press.

———. 1994. *Gendered Transitions: Mexican Experiences of Migration*. Berkeley and Los Angeles: University of California Press.

Hondagneu-Sotelo, Pierrette, and Ernestine Avila. 1997. "'I'm Here, but I'm There': The Meanings of Latina Transnational Motherhood." *Gender and Society* 11 (5): 548–571.

Huang, Shirlena, Brenda Yeoh, and Mika Toyota. 2012. "Caring for the Elderly: The Embodied Labor of Migrant Care Workers in Singapore." *Global Networks* 12 (2): 195–215.

Human Development Network. 2010. *In Search of a Human Face: 15 Years of Knowledge Building for Human Development in the Philippines*. Manila: Author.

Human Rights Watch. 2011. *World Report 2011*. New York: Author.

Hunter, Tera. 1997. *To 'Joy My Freedom: Southern Black Women's Lives and Labors after the Civil War*. Cambridge, MA, and London: Harvard University Press.

Illo, Jeanne. 2010. "Gender Concerns and Human Development." HDN Discussion Paper Series No. 2. Manila: Human Development Network.

ILO (International Labour Organization). 2013. *Domestic Workers across the World: Global and Regional Statistics and the Extent of Legal Protection*. Geneva: Author.

———. 2012. *ILO Global Estimates of Forced Labour: Results and Methodology*. Geneva: Author.

———. 2010. *Decent Work for Domestic Workers*. Geneva: Author.

Instituto Nazionale della Previdenza Sociale and Caritas. 2004. *Il Mondo Della Collaborazione Domestica: I Dati Del Cambiamento*. Rome: Caritas.

International Organization of Migration. 2008. *World Migration 2008: Managing Labour Mobility in the Evolving Global Economy*. Geneva: International Organization of Migration.

Israel-Sobritchea, Carolyn. 1990. "The Ideology of Female Domesticity: Its Impact on the Status of Filipino Women." *Review of Women's Studies* 1 (1): 26–41.

Jones, Jacqueline. 1985. *Labor of Love, Labor of Sorrow: Black Women, Work and the Family, from Slavery to the Present*. New York: Vintage Books.

Kalleberg, Arne. 2011. *Good Jobs, Bad Jobs: The Rise of Polarized and Precarious Employment Systems in the United States, 1970s to 2000s*. New York: Russell Sage Foundation.

Kav LaOved. 2010. "Kav La Oved's (Worker's Hotline) Shadow Report on the Situation of Female Migrant Workers in Israel." Tel Aviv: Kav LaOved.

Kessler Harris, Alice. 1981. *Out to Work*. New York and London: Oxford University Press.

Kilkey, Majella, Diane Perrons, and Ania Plomien with Pierrette Hondagneu-Sotelo and Hernan Ramirez. 2013. *Gender, Migration and Domestic Work: Masculinities, Male Labour and Fathering in the UK and USA*. Hampshire, UK: Palgrave Macmillan.

Kimura, Masataka. 2003. "The Emergence of the Middle Classes and Political Change in the Philippines." *The Developing Economies* XLI-2 (June): 264–284.

Kuptsch, Christiane, and Eng Fong Pang. 2006. *Competing for Global Talent*. Geneva, Switzerland: International Labour Office.

Laguerre, Michel. 1994. "Headquarters and Subsidiaries: Haitian Immigrant Family Households in New York City." In *Minority Families in the United States: A Multicultural Perspective*, edited by Ronald Taylor, pp. 47–61. Englewood Cliffs, NJ: Prentice Hall.

Lan, Pei-Chia. 2007. "Legal Servitude, Free Illegality: Migrant 'Guest' Workers in Taiwan." In *Asian Diasporas: New Formations, New Conceptions*, edited by Rhacel Parreñas and Lok Siu, pp. 253–278. Stanford, CA: Stanford University Press.

———. 2006. *Global Cinderellas: Migrant Domestics and Newly Rich Employers in Taiwan*. Durham, NC: Duke University Press.

Layosa, Linda. 1995a. "Economy Menders." *Tinig Filipino* (June): 7.

———. 1995b. "A Salute to Filipino Women." *Tinig Filipino* (March): 6–7.

———. 1994. "Families Are Forever." *Tinig Filipino* (December): 12–13.

Licuanan, Patricia. 1994. "The Socio-Economic Impact of Domestic Worker Migration: Individual, Family, Community, Country." In *The Trade in Domestic Workers: Causes, Mechanisms, and Consequences of International Labor Migration*, edited by Noeleen Heyzer, Geertje Lycklama á Nijeholt, and Nedra Weerakoon, pp. 103–116. London: Zed Books.

Liebelt, Claudia. 2011. *Caring for the "Holy Land": Filipina Domestic Workers in Israel*. New York and Oxford, UK: Berghahn Books.

———. 2008. "'We are the Jews of Today': Filipino Domestic Workers in Israel and the Language of Diaspora." *HAGAR Studies in Culture, Polity, and Identities* 8 (1): 105–128.

Lombardo, Emanuela, and Maria Sangiuliano. 2009. "Gender and Employment in the Italian Policy Debates 1995–2007: The Construction of 'Non-Employed' Gendered Subjects." *Women's Studies International Forum* 32 (6): 445–452.

Lopez-Rodriguez, Luz. 1990. "Patriarchy and Women's Subordination in the Philippines." *Review of Women's Studies* 1 (1): 15 –25.

Lutz, Helma. 2011. *The New Maids: Transnational Women and the Care Economy*. London: Zed Books.

Luz de Ibarra, Maria. 2010. "My Reward Is Not Money: Deep Alliances and End of Life Care among Mexican Workers and Their Wards." In *Intimate Labors: Technologies, Cultures and Politics of Care*, edited by Eileen Boris and Rhacel Parreñas, pp. 117–131. Stanford, CA: Stanford University Press.

Madianou, Mirca, and Daniel Miller. 2012. *Migration and New Media: Transnational Families and Polymedia*. New York: Routledge.

Mahdavi, Pardis. 2011. *Gridlock: Labor, Migration and Human Trafficking in Dubai*. Stanford, CA: Stanford University Press.

Mariano, Jocelyn. 1995. "Child Abuse and OCWs." *Tinig Filipino* (October): 26–27.

Martin, Philip. 1993. "Migration and Trade: The Case of the Philippines." *International Migration Review* 27 (3): 639–645.

Massey, Doreen. 1994. *Space, Place and Gender*. Minneapolis: University of Minnesota Press.

Matthei, Linda Miller, and David A. Smith. 1998. "Belizean 'Boyz 'n the Hood.'" In *Transnationalism from Below*, edited by Michael Smith and Luis Guarnizo, pp. 270–290. New Brunswick, NJ: Transaction Publisher.

McDonald, Cameron. 2011. *Shadow Mothers: Nannies, Au Pairs, and the Micropolitics of Mothering*. Berkeley: University of California Press.

Medick, Hans, and David Warren Sabean. 1984. "Interest and Emotion in Family Kinship Studies: A Critique of Social History and Anthropology." In *Interest and Emotion: Essays on the Study of*

Family and Kinship, edited by Hans Medick and David Warren Sabean, pp 9–27. Cambridge, UK: Cambridge University Press.

Medina, Belinda. 1991. *The Filipino Family: A Text with Selected Readings*. Quezon City: University of the Philippines Press.

Meerman, Marije. 2000. *The Chain of Love*. Amsterdam: VPRO-TV.

Meyer, Donald. 1987. *The Rise of Women in America, Russia, Sweden, and Italy*. Middletown, CT: Wesleyan University Press.

Mintz, Steven, and Susan Kellog. 1988. *Domestic Revolutions: A Social History of American Family Life*. New York: Free Press.

Mitchell, Julia. 1996. *Other People's Children*. New York: Basic Books.

National Statistical Coordination Board. 2013. *NCSB Fact Sheet: Updates on Women and Men in the Philippines*. Makati, Philippines: Author.

Nazareno, Jennifer Pabelonia, Rhacel Salazar Parreñas, and Yu-Kang Fan. 2014. *Can I Ever Retire? The Plight of Migrant Filipino Elderly Caregivers in Los Angeles*. Los Angeles, CA: Pilipino Workers' Center.

Nelson, Margaret K. 1990. "Mothering Other's Children: The Experiences of Family Day Care Providers." In Abel and Nelson, *Circles of Care*, pp. 210–232. Albany: SUNY Press.

O'Connor, Julia S. 1996. "From Women in the Welfare State to Gendering Welfare State Regimes." *Current Sociology* 44 (2): 1– 130.

Ong, Aihwa. 1996. "Cultural Citizenship as Subject-Making: Immigrants Negotiate Racial and Cultural Boundaries in the United States." *Contemporary Anthropology* 37 (5): 737–762.

Padavic, Irene, and Barbara Reskin. 2002. *Women and Men at Work*, second edition. Thousand Oaks, CA: Pine Forge Press.

Palmer, Phyllis. 1989. *Domesticity and Dirt: Housewives and Domestic Servants in the United States, 1920–1945*. Philadelphia, PA: Temple University Press.

Parreñas, Rhacel. 2014. "Migrant Domestic Workers as 'One of the Family.'" In *Care and Migrant Labor: Theory, Policy and Politics*, edited by Bridget Anderson and Isabel Shutes, pp. 49–64. Hampshire, UK: Palgrave Macmillan.

———. 2012. "The Reproductive Labor of Migrant Workers." *Global Networks* 12 (2): 269–275.

———. 2011. *Illicit Flirtations: Labor, Migration and Sex Trafficking in Tokyo*. Stanford, CA: Stanford University Press.

———. 2008a. *The Force of Domesticity: Filipina Migrants and Globalization*. New York: New York University Press.

———. 2008b. "Perpetually Foreign: Filipina Migrant Domestic Workers in Rome." In *Migration and Domestic Work: A European Perspective on a Global Theme*, edited by Helma Lutz, pp. 99–112. Hampshire, UK: Ashgate.

———. 2005. *Children of Global Migration: Transnational Families and Gendered Woes*. Stanford, CA: Stanford University Press.

———. 2000. "Migrant Filipina Domestic Workers and the International Division of Reproductive Labor," *Gender & Society* 14 (4): 560–580.

———. 1998. "The Global Servants: (Im)Migrant Domestic Workers in Rome and Los Angeles." PhD dissertation, Department of Ethnic Studies, UC Berkeley.

Paul, Anju Mary. 2011. "Stepwise International Migration: A Multistage Migration Pattern for the Aspiring Migrant." *American Journal of Sociology* 116 (6): 1842–1886.

Paz Cruz, Victoria. 1987. *Seasonal Orphans and Solo Parents: The Impacts of Overseas Migration*. Quezon City, Philippines: Scalabrini Migration Center.

Paz Cruz, Victoria, and Anthony Paganoni. 1989. *Filipinas in Migration: Big Bills and Small Change*. Quezon City, Philippines: Scalabrini Migration Center.

Peterson, Jean Treloggen. 1993. "Generalized Extended Family Exchange: A Case from the Philippines." *Journal of Marriage and the Family* 55 (August): 570–584.

Pingol, Alicia. 2001. *Remaking Masculinities: Identity, Power, and Gender Dynamics in Families with Migrant Wives and Househusbands.* Quezon City: University of the Philippines Press.

POEA (Philippines Overseas Employment Administration). 2013. "2008–2012 Overseas Employment Statistics." Manila: Author.

———. 2011. POEA Statistics, "OFW Deployment per Skill and Country—New Hires for the Year 2010." Manila: Author.

———. 2010. POEA Statistics, "OFW Deployment per Skill and Country—New Hires for the Year 2009." Manila: Author.

———. 2009. POEA Statistics, "OFW Deployment per Skill and Country—New Hires for the Year 2008." Manila: Author.

———. 2007. "Governing Board Resolution No. 13." Manila: POEA. Available at www.poea.gov.ph/hsw/GB%2013.pdf.

Poo, Ai-jen. 2009. "Domestic Workers Bill of Rights: A Feminist Approach for a New Economy." *The Scholar and Feminist Online* 8 (1). Available at http://barnard.edu/sfonline/work/poo_01.htm.

Portes, Alejandro. 1997. "Immigration Theory for a New Century: Some Problems and Opportunities." *International Migration Review* 31 (4): 799–825.

———. 1989. "Contemporary Immigration: Theoretical Perspectives on Its Determinants and Modes of Incorporation." *International Migration Review* 23 (3): 606–630.

Portes, Alejandro, and Rubén Rumbaut. 1996. *Immigrant America: A Portrait*, 2nd ed. Berkeley and Los Angeles: University of California Press.

Pratt, Geraldine. 2012. *Families Apart: Migrant Mothers and the Conflicts of Labor and Love.* Minneapolis: University of Minnesota Press.

Rafael, Vicente. 2000. *White Love and Other Events in Filipino History.* Durham, NC: Duke University Press.

Ray, Raka, and Seemin Qayum. 2009. *Cultures of Servitude: Modernity, Domesticity, and Class in India.* Stanford, CA: Stanford University Press.

Reich, Robert. 1991. *The Work of Nations.* New York: Viking.

Reskin, Barbara, and Irene Padavic. 1994. *Women and Men at Work.* Thousand Oaks, CA: Pine Forge Press.

Ridgeway, Cecilia. 2011. *Framed by Gender: How Gender Inequality Persists in the Modern World.* New York: Oxford University Press.

Rinolfi, Vilma. 2007. "New Collective Agreement for Domestic Workers." *European Industrial Relations Observatory.* Available at www.eurofound.europa.eu/eiro/2007/02/articles/it0702079i.htm.

Roberts, Dorothy. 1997. *Killing the Black Body: Race, Reproduction and the Meaning of Liberty.* New York: Pantheon Books.

Rollins, Judith. 1985. *Between Women: Domestics and Their Employers.* Philadelphia, PA: Temple University Press.

Romero, Mary. 1992. *Maid in the U.S.A.* New York and London: Routledge.

Rothman, Barbara Katz. 1989a. *Recreating Motherhood: Ideology and Technology in a Patriarchal Society.* New York and London: W. W. Norton.

———. 1989b. "Women as Fathers: Motherhood and Child Care under a Modified Patriarchy." *Gender and Society* 3 (1): 89–104.

Rubin, Lillian. 1976. *Worlds of Pain: Life in the Working-Class Family.* New York: Basic Books.

Ruiz, Ramona. 2012, October 9. "Minimum Wage for Filipino Maids in Saudi a Model for Gulf Countries." *The National.* Retrieved on October 30, 2013, from www.thenational.ae/news/uae-news/minimum-wage-for-filipino-maids-in-saudi-a-model-for-gulf-countries.

Sabban, Rima. 2012. *Maids Crossing: Domestic Workers in the UAE*. Saarbruken, Germany: LAP Lambert Press.

Sarti, Rafaella, and Francesca Scrinzi. 2010. "Introduction to the Special Issue: Men in a Woman's Job, Male Domestic Workers, International Migration and the Globalization of Care." *Men and Masculinities* 13 (1): 4–15.

Sassen, Saskia. 1996. *Losing Control? Sovereignty in an Age of Globalization*. New York: Columbia University Press.

———. 1988. *The Mobility of Labor and Capital: A Study in International Investment and Labor*. New York: Cambridge University Press.

———. 1984. "Notes on the Incorporation of Third World Women into Wage Labor through Immigration and Offshore Production." *International Migration Review* 18 (4): 1144–1167.

Schippers, Mimi. 2007. "Recovering the Feminine Other: Masculinity, Femininity, and Gender Hegemony." *Theory and Society* 36 (1): 85–102.

Schmalzbauer, Leah. 2004. "Searching for Wages and Mothering from Afar: The Case of Honduran Transnational Families." *Journal of Marriage and Family* 66: 1317–1331.

Scott, James. 1990. *Domination and the Arts of Resistance*. New Haven, CT: Yale University Press.

Scrinzi, Francesa. 2010. "Masculinities and the International Division of Care: Migrant Male Domestic Workers in Italy and France." *Men and Masculinities* 13 (1): 44–64.

Shimizu, Celine Parreñas. 2007. *The Hypersexuality of Race*. Durham, NC: Duke University Press.

Silvey, Rachel. 2006. "Consuming the Transnational Family: Indonesian Migrant Domestic Workers to Saudi Arabia." *Global Networks* 6 (1): 23–40.

———. 2004. "Transnational Migration and the Gender Politics of Scale: Indonesian Domestic Workers in Saudi Arabia, 1997–2000." *Singapore Journal of Tropical Geography* 25 (2): 141–155.

———. 2000. "Stigmatized Spaces: Moral Geographies under Crisis in South Sulawesi, Indonesia." *Gender, Place and Culture* 7 (2): 143–161.

Singapore Ministry of Manpower. 2013. "Work Permit (Foreign Domestic Worker)—Before You Apply." Available at www.mom.gov.sg/foreign-manpower/passes-visas/work-permit-fdw/before-you-apply/Pages/default.aspx#elac.

Siu, Lok. 2007. *Memories of a Future Home: Diasporic Citizenship of Chinese in Panama*. Stanford, CA: Stanford University Press.

Smith, Robert C. 1998. "Transnational Localities: Community, Technology and the Politics of Membership within the Context of Mexico and U.S. Migration." In *Transnationalism from Below*, edited by Michael Smith and Luis Guarnizo, pp. 196–238. New Brunswick, NJ: Transaction Publisher.

Solis, Hilda. 2011. "Providing Protections for In-Home Care Workers." *The Official Blog of the U.S. Department of Labor*. December 15. Retrieved on May 21, 2012, from http://social.dol.gov/blog/providing-protections-for-in-home-care-workers/.

Soysal, Yasemin Nuhoglu. 1994. *Limits of Citizenship: Migrants and Post-National Membership in Europe*. Chicago and London: University of Chicago Press.

Specter, Michael. 1998. "The Baby Bust." *New York Times*, July 10.

Stacey, Judith. 1991. *Brave New Families: Stories of Domestic Upheaval in Late Twentieth Century America*. New York: Basic Books.

Stack, Carol, and Linda Burton. 1994. "Kinscripts: Reflections on Family, Generation, and Culture." In *Mothering: Ideology, Experience, and Agency*, edited by Evelyn Nakano Glenn, _Grace Chang, and Linda Rennie Forcey, pp 33–44. New York: Routledge.

Stenum, Helle. 2011. *Abused Domestic Workers in Europe: The Case of Au Pairs*. Brussels, Belgium: European Commission.

Taiwan National Immigration Agency. 2012. *Foreign Labor Work Permit*. Retrieved from http://iff.immigration.gov.tw/ct.asp?xItem=1086938&ctNode+29928&mp=T002.

Thorne, Barrie. 1992. "Feminism and the Family: Two Decades of Thought." In *Rethinking the Family: Some Feminist Questions*, edited by Barrie Thorne and _Marilyn Yalom, pp. 3–30. Boston: Northeastern University Press

Van Walsum, Sarah. 2011. "Regulating Migrant Domestic Work in the Netherlands: Opportunities and Pitfalls," *Canadian Journal of Women and the Law* 23 (1): 141–165.

Williams, Christine. 1995. *Still a Man's World*. Berkeley: University of California Press.

———. 1992. "The Glass Escalator: Hidden Advantages for Men in the 'Female' Professions." *Social Problems* 39 (3): 253–267.

Wong, Sau-ling. 1994. "Diverted Mothering: Representations of Caregivers of Color in the Age of 'Multiculturalism.'" In *Mothering: Ideology, Experience and Agency*, edited by Evelyn Glenn, Grace Chang, and Linda Forcey, pp. 67–91. New York: Routledge.

Wrigley, Julia. 1995. *Other People's Children: An Intimate Account of the Dilemmas Facing Middle-Class Parents and the Women They Hire to Raise Their Children*. New York: Basic Books.

Yeates, Nicola. 2012. "Global Care Chains: A State-of-the-art Review and Future Directions in Transnationalization Research." *Global Networks* 12 (2): 135–154.

Young, Grace Esther. 1987. "The Myth of Being 'Like a Daughter.'" *Latin American Perspectives* 14 (3): 365–380.

INDEX

CPSIA information can be obtained
at www.ICGtesting.com
Printed in the USA
LVOW11s1014150917
548860LV00002B/121/P